'An authentic snapshot of the profound effect national service had on those who served their country, rightly or wrongly; of the camaraderie and crap; idealism and idiocy; professionalism and bungling that's part of any military organisation or operation.

Thompson has captured every facet ... and succeeded in letting the different voices be heard, without bias or judgment. And in doing so, she has not only provided all South Africans with a critically important account of a forgotten time, but also lifted the lid on something that needs to be out in the open to finally be allowed to heal.'   – Kevin Ritchie, *Saturday Star*

'Revealed at last: ex-national service soldiers' shocking experiences.'   – *You* magazine

'The first book of its kind in South Africa to unmask the private lives behind South African Defence Force soldiers.'   – *People* magazine

'A riveting, personal look at recent South African history, and a poignant reminder of the multi-faceted effects of war on innocent youngsters.'

– Kate Turkington, joburg.co.za

AN UNPOPULAR WAR

From afkak
to bosbefok

WAR

Voices of South African
National Servicemen

JH THOMPSON

ZEBRA

Published by Zebra Press
an imprint of Struik Publishers
(a division of New Holland Publishing (South Africa) (Pty) Ltd)
PO Box 1144, Cape Town, 8000
New Holland Publishing is a member of Johnnic Communications Ltd

www.zebrapress.co.za

First published 2006
Reprinted in 2006 (seven times) and 2007 (three times)

11 13 15 17 19 20 18 16 14 12

Publication © Zebra Press 2006
Text © JH Thompson 2006

Cover photograph © Christo Crous

Back cover photographs: © James Dekker (top row 1, 2 and 3);
© Christo Crous (top 4, bottom 1 and 3); © Simon Hare (bottom 2 and 4)

Photographs reproduced with kind permission of the copyright holders
and of sa-soldier.com

PUBLISHING MANAGER: Marlene Fryer
EDITOR: Robert Plummer
PROOFREADER: Ronel Richter-Herbert
COVER AND TEXT DESIGNER: Natascha Adendorff-Olivier
TYPESETTER: Monique van den Berg
PRODUCTION MANAGER: Valerie Kömmer

Set in 11.5 pt on 16 pt Adobe Garamond

Reproduction by Hirt & Carter (Cape) (Pty) Ltd
Printed and bound by Paarl Print, Oosterland Street, Paarl, South Africa

ISBN 978 1 77007 301 2

www.imagesofafrica.co.za

IMAGES OF AFRICA
PHOTO LIBRARY

Over 40 000 unique African images available to purchase
from our image bank at www.imagesofafrica.co.za

Contents

Preface

History is not another name for the past, as many people imply.
It is the name for stories about the past.
AJP TAYLOR (1906–1990)

Until 1994, all white male South Africans were called up for National Service in the year they turned 18. This could be deferred for a few years if the person was studying, but to avoid it meant a jail term. In the 1970s, 1980s and early 1990s, hundreds of thousands of young men served in the military, most going through intense physical training and many of them being sent to fight the war in northern Namibia and Angola.

I interviewed over 40 men who were required to do National Service, in order to record their personal memories of this military era. This book is a collection of mental snapshots from their time as SADF conscripts: an inspection, the routine of camp life, the monotony and dread of patrols, the terror of a battle. Whatever the experience, it came with an intensity absent in civilian life. The men I interviewed spoke honestly of fear, boredom, loss, crying, drinking, fighting, of deep friendships and a yearning for the camaraderie they had then. Their stories also give an anecdotal record of the idiosyncrasies and slang from that period, and the way that these varied in different regions and units.

The interviews covered a wide range of experiences. The men spoke of life in the army, the navy and the air force. Some were chefs and medics, others were Recces and Parabats. One was a conscientious objector serving time in a military prison. A few of them stayed on for longer than their two years' National Service, such as the helicopter pilots. Most are identified by their first name and their age at the time, although some preferred to remain anonymous. There are a few duplicate names but no false ones.

Even though most National Servicemen called up for military service did not experience combat, their time with the military had a profound and lasting impact on them. The war, fought primarily in South Africa's protectorate South West Africa (Namibia) and in Angola, was an unpopular one on many fronts. Many young men, straight out of school or university, were not staunchly patriotic and did not want to give two years of their lives to the military, mothers didn't want to lose sons, and South Africa's apartheid government was condemned internationally for fighting an unjust war.

It was a radically different political climate – one that now, from the perspective of a non-racial and democratic South Africa, is almost impossible to comprehend. Today, it is not socially acceptable for these men to talk about their experiences. But even if the politics were abhorrent, this doesn't make the soldiers so.

These stories are their experiences as remembered by them. I wrote them as they were told, with no embellishment or editing to make them seem better men, or worse.

JH THOMPSON

Acknowledgements

It is not clichéd at all to say that without certain people this book would not exist. Most obviously and most importantly are the men whom I interviewed. Thank you for trusting me with your stories and memories, without which I could not have written this book. This is not my book, it is yours.

I hope there will be many more books on the experiences of South African soldiers, for there are thousands of stories that should be told, in print, not just among close friends. For those of you who kept diaries or notes of your time as a National Serviceman … get them to a publisher!

Whether it was a concern about reprisals, privacy or a more personal reason, some men requested to remain anonymous, while the rest agreed to the use of their first names in the main body of the book. I wish to thank every one of them. Some of the men whom I can list are Andy Thomas, Anthony Hansen, Christian Bowker, Christoph Hummel, Clint van Haght, Dave Keegan, David O'Sullivan, Ferdinand Taljaard, Jeremy Mansfield, John Scholes, John Walland, Martin Blignaut, Paul Redman, Paul Rotherham, Rick Venter. Thank you for the telling.

Thank you too to Kate Rogan for valuable insider information on the publishing industry, her guidance and encouragement. Lieutenant Colonel Taljaard for his invaluable information and checking of facts concerning the South African Air Force as well as military terminology – geen toffies vir jou! Richard Henry, Curator Armoured Fighting Vehicles at the SA National Museum of Military History, who saved me hours and hours of trawling through reference books to check obscure Angolan towns or military hardware facts, thank you for your sharp eye and for sharing your vast knowledge on all things military. Baie dankie Zelda en Anton le Grange vir julle humor en ondersteuning met al die vertalings vir wanneer my feeble en verkrampte hoërskool Afrikaans my in die steek gelaat het! Dan Moyane for his cross-border phone calls to ensure that every single diacritical mark was accurate and in its correct place regarding the Portuguese translations.

Marlene Fryer, thank you for your record-breaking response and giving me feedback only hours after I sent through the proposal. An unforgettable phone call. Robert Plummer, my managing editor, who managed my doubts and my unstructured manuscript so well. Thank you, Robert. Riveting? Marvellous? Your words meant the world. Thank you for always being patient with my ignorance of the publishing world and for your kindness and humour, and for being gentle!

Although this resembles one of those Oscar acceptance speeches, I must thank my mom. Thank you for instilling in me a love, appreciation and awe for books, as well as for creative thoughts and words. Thank you for the subbing, the left-field questions and being the first person to read the interviews and confirm my belief that the stories were worth telling.

Jem, you are so aptly named. You are my rock and my lighthouse. Thank you for pushing me to put pen to paper after a year of mulling over the idea, considering the possibility that, perhaps, this book could and should be written when I considered it only a firm definite maybe. Thank you for recognising my fears and procrastination and blitzing them. You shine.

Every person I have mentioned, and the many men I couldn't mention personally here, as well as friends and family, inspired me, motivated me, and most importantly believed in the book and the absolute importance and necessity of talking about personal experiences in a time of shadows in our country's history. I humbly thank you.

JH THOMPSON

Dedicated to Guy Sajer
and the forgotten soldiers

You're in the Army Now

It was the worst day of my life. I arrived on the troop train at Voortrekkerhoogte. The train went from Port Elizabeth and picked up conscripts all the way up. At every little siding there were guys waiting with their parents and a battered little suitcase. You knew because of the list you got with your conscription papers that every person with a battered suitcase had a two-metre length of chain, two padlocks, a list of addresses, a pack of envelopes, a sheet of stamps and one of those big Croxley writing pads with two pens. Also a small steam iron, and a picture of your girlfriend. The train stopped at every single siding. All I remember from that whole trip was parents crying. I don't think it was really because they were saying goodbye to their sons, but more because they didn't know where their sons were ultimately going. They knew their sons were initially heading to Voortrekkerhoogte, but they didn't know from there what would happen to their lives, and neither did we. The whole comic bravado story about the troop train is an absolute load of shit. They talk about how everyone gets pissed and throws the cushions out of the windows and fucks around all the way to Voortrekkerhoogte. It is absolute crap. It's a comic's way of trying to make the journey all right, but it was not. You're surrounded by corporals and Military Police who aren't being horrible in any way, but you know already that they are a sign of authority. You sit in your pre-assigned cabin, with your pre-assigned passengers, going to a pre-assigned destination with a supposed purpose, and you don't understand any of it.

We arrived at the shunting area at WSK at Voortrekkerhoogte, and that's when all the chaos broke out. You had troops from one railway line destination being shepherded into Personnel Services, Finance Services, Medics, Tiffies, MPs and a whole host of other regiments, and that's when the screaming began. I remember roll-call and Staff

Sergeant Marx. It was so ironic. There I was, prepared to fight Communists, and the first person I meet is called Marx. He's calling out the names and everyone answers differently: 'Yes', 'Present', 'Here.' Eventually he turned around and said, 'As ek jou naam uitroep, sê net ja Staff of ja poes. Maar net nie yes, present, en al dié kak nie' [If I call out your name, only say yes Staff or yes poes. But just not yes, present, and all that shit]. Three names later, this one guy is called out and he answers, 'Ja poes.' I don't know what happened to him. That night we got to the camp. I found I was in a tented section. We had a Highveld summer storm, the tent leaked, half my mattress was wet, I curled up into the dry upper half and even though I was 18, I cried.

– Jeremy, age 18

I remember us all showing our call-up papers to one another at school. I was called up for the July intake. That would have wasted a whole year: the six months from when I finished school at the end of the year until I went in, and the six months from when I came out until the beginning of the next year. So my dad pushed to get me called up for the January intake. We had this friend in the Medical Corps and she organised for me to get into SAGDOS in Voortrekkerhoogte. I was excited because it was January now and it was so close to home, much better than the July call-up to Phalaborwa. We got this little list of things I had to take. Some of the things I remember were soap, padlocks, one set of clothes, starch, a length of chain, a spray bottle, toiletries, towel, two boot brushes, a tin of Kiwi polish and an iron. No ironing board. I remember that, because on the first pass, that's the one thing everybody came back with – an ironing board. They did have an ironing facility in the dorm, but it was this horrible metal table against the wall. Because that was all everybody had to use, the queues were horrendous. We all had to meet at Nasrec and were taken through to Pretoria in a convoy of 20 or 30 buses. Once on the highway, I looked back and it was just buses. It's not an overly long journey, but, boy, it

AN UNPOPULAR WAR

took forever. I didn't know anybody. Nobody knew anybody. I was afraid of the unknown. Yes, I was supposed to go to Voortrekkerhoogte, but I didn't know for sure that that would happen. The buses were packed with guys from all walks of life. Some were wealthy, with the attitude of: okay, we've got to take it on the chin and have to go to the military, but we're going to handle it. Then there were those who were down and out, and this was actually saving them. Going to the army would provide them with a roof over their heads and three meals every day. We look at it now and think it was the non-whites who appreciated that, but it wasn't. It was the whites from down-and-out areas.

– Paul, age 18

We had to catch the train to Cape Town from the station near Milpark. I told my mom she couldn't come if she was going to cry like all those mothers on TV. The guys were very friendly and told us to make sure we left alcohol, drugs, knives or guns with our parents! I wasn't sure if they were joking or not. I remember thinking: this isn't so bad, I don't know what the fuss is about. It was quite pleasant. But the minute you stepped through the gate – what a rude awakening! They screamed and shouted and called us all sorts of names. Some of the things that stood out for me that day were: the stale sandwiches – which you had to eat – vrot bananas and coffee so sweet you could die from insulin overload, having to close the windows at Joburg station so that the enemy could not see in to count the number of troops, and that my mom didn't cry.

– Dave, age 19

I've always had a love of weapons and combat uniforms. I didn't get called up; I volunteered. It was the only way I could eventually get a job. No one would hire you unless you had completed military service. I managed to get an appointment with this bloke in Pretoria. I walked into this commandant's office and told him I wanted to sign up. He vloeked, 'Fok it! Niemand … nobody volunteers for this armies!' We talked and then he asked me, 'Where do you want to goes?' I didn't even know there were different divisions or anything. So I said I wanted to have a weapon and I didn't want to sit behind a desk. He said he would sort out something nice for me. Three days later I was at this huge field in Johannesburg with my parents and all the stuff I was told to bring. There must have been about 2 000 guys on the field. It was very exciting, busloads of people coming and going all the time, all these guys with rank and rifles. I couldn't believe it – I was now in the army! They took us to the train station late at night, and all the okes were friendly. We said goodbye to our parents and then everything changed. The guys started shouting and screaming, but all in Afrikaans. The swearing I understood, 'cause we used to swear in Afrikaans at school as it was more colourful. But even the basic commands were difficult to understand. The inflection they gave the commands made them difficult to understand. It wasn't *links, regs, links, regs*; it's more of a grunting shout. I didn't find it scary; it was more like anger. I was extremely mad at these guys for not speaking my language and screaming in my face. It wasn't one oke standing there, it was a few of them, backing one another up, and they were armed and I wasn't. I'm not easily intimidated, but I didn't like that. It made me want to take them out.

We left on the train with all the shutters closed. There was no indication where we were going or in which direction. The worst thing was just not knowing what was going on. The officers were patrolling the corridors, flicking the lights off and on at all hours of the night, shining torches in our faces so we couldn't sleep properly. They'd wake everybody up and make us line up outside our compartments. It was three or four days of chaos, total chaos. Bad chaos. Everything I knew and the way I was used to handling things wasn't possible. I was not a very disciplined kid at school. I got into a lot of fights. I was not a big guy, and yet I thought I could take on anybody, and now I was in a situation I couldn't control by fighting. This was all about taking you out of your routine. Already on the train some guys were cracking. They were crying and breaking down. I saw a lot of fear in guys' eyes, but I thought, I'm not gonna show these guys fear. Anything they ask me to do, I'm gonna wait two seconds before I do it; you know, start getting to them. But what happened was they all started taking turns in nailing me. Other guys in another compartment might get woken up two or three times, I'd be woken up nine times. Of course I was just making it harder for myself. We finally arrived at Rooikop Air Force Base, Walvis Bay, home of the infamous Dune 7 – the seventh-largest free-standing sand dune in the world. It was night and there was all the running, screaming, swearing and chaos as they sorted us into colour groups. I couldn't believe they had sent me to the furthest bloomin' training ground from South Africa. You couldn't get any further away for Basics. I volunteer and they send me to another country!

– **Brett, age 18**

I had been in boarding school for five years. I figured going to the army straight after school was a good idea. I was used to the routine and the discipline, all the bells ringing, inspections, eating meals at a certain time – all that shit. Even though I had dual citizenship, British and South African, I volunteered. I did so because I heard they were going to make it compulsory for immigrants. So I thought, rather get in now. And, ja, they did a year later. I was fucking glad I'd gone in earlier, 'cause they gave those new guys such a hard time. They really kakked off. I was the only Englishman among 13 Afrikaners. That's where I learnt to speak Afrikaans so well. I had to. – **Andy, age 18**

My father had pulled strings to get me a comfy clerical job in Pretoria for my two years' National Service. I remember just reading a paper-back on the way there. Arriving was a shock. I come from a home where there is no shouting, and I was even looking for porters to help me with my bags when we arrived at Pretoria station. The comfy job lasted only a week before they decided they needed more infantry. I tried everything to get out. I claimed to have a drug dependency. I said my girlfriend was pregnant. Nothing worked, and a whole lot of us were sent to 6 SAI in Grahamstown. I had no idea what to expect. Food was always an issue. I had a friend who was a Catholic. He attended Mass off base, which in itself was great, because the bigger churches like the NG Church were on the base. But the best thing was that they served lunch at his church. So, for that duration I became a Catholic and remained one for about a year after my National Service.

– Werner, age 21

Rooibaard was the devil incarnate as far as I was concerned. He was also one of my first memories of Ladysmith. We had originally congregated at Milpark in Joburg and then sat on the trains for nearly an hour, just looking at the Joburg skyline before we finally left. We were all so apprehensive, wondering where the hell we were going. We arrived at Ladysmith around 4 a.m. on the 2nd of July. It was pitch dark and freezing. The Bedfords were waiting to take us to the actual camp, and so were all these *ou manne* and sergeants. I heard this voice scream, 'Julle fokkin' bliksems! Klim uit!' [You fuckin' bastards! Climb out!], and saw this guy, Rooibaard, this madman with blazing eyes and a red beard. Later on, I heard rumours that he had drilled his nephew to death. The carriage doors on both sides were open, and on one side was this screaming loony with steely blue eyes. Out the other side, through the carriage doorway, were just empty railway tracks. I looked at these and thought, should I make a run for it and just go? But I didn't, and we got out of the train and were herded like sheep. Life as we knew it came to an end. We went to total zero. Less than zero. You were total dirt. You didn't count for anything. We were kitted out in the only two sizes the army has: too big or too small. You had to exchange with one another afterwards to try and get stuff to fit you. We were given a trommel, blanket, a grootjas and stuff, and sent to tents. I went to sleep with my grootjas and one blanket, and in the morning I had my grootjas on and five blankets, it was so cold. That same night this commandant came and spoke to us and he said if we wanna leave before we register tomorrow morning we must do so now. This would save him the time of coming to look for us if we went AWOL, because once we were registered we became his problem. He said, 'Are there any of you that object to holding a rifle?' And this I'll never forget, out of 2 500 guys this one lone guy stood up. We were all sitting down and he stood up and raised his hand and said, 'I do.' The guy was taken away. I'm sure he wasn't sent home.

– Nick, age 20

When we got the call-up forms at school, we had to complete them and fill in where we would like to go and what we would prefer to do. I chose Engineers, thinking I might as well learn something new. I also put something like 'Intend to study further in this direction'. Obviously someone read this and assumed I was an engineer. So I ended up with the graduate intake. It was great, because they abuse you that little bit less, probably because they realise that after four years of varsity, you know they can't kill you. None of that 'Val langs hom,' which means if a guy drops his rifle he has to fall next to it. This one guy was told not to bend his knees 'cause his rifle didn't do that, and he smashed up his face. Grads wouldn't do that. We klaared in at a place called Vegkop; we Engelsmanne called it Vegetable Head. There were only about 120 of us, and it was good because we had hot food and hot showers. It's much easier to feed 120 than 3 000 troops. Once we got onto Officer's Course, we even had waiters! Guys from the local prison. Bandita was the con that served us food and washed our plates. So it was not a very tough time for me! – Paul, age 17

I cried my first night in Voortrekkerhoogte. I just thought: I'm here, I'm really here, and I didn't know what lay ahead. It was the early hours of the morning, and we were still in our civvies, no browns. The loneliness of being with all these people, but not knowing anybody and no one knowing me, was hard. I still wonder if it was intentional, that no one was sent away with anyone they knew. No one from the same school or same class was together that I knew of. If you did end up at the same army base, you sure weren't in the same company or group.

Hurry up and wait. That's what it was all about. We stood in the streets separating the barracks and waited outside the barber for three days to get our hair cut for the first time. It was a very small room with two barbers in it and a corporal reading a newspaper. Even though the guy was a real barber contracted by the military, he wasn't gentle. It was a Number One all over. I watched guys with long, long hair just getting it all shorn off. Shoop! There were mountains of hair on the floor. I'll never forget that. I think it was part of taking away your identity to break you down. To avoid the queue, and because it was so easy to do, some guys went and bought clippers and charged five bucks a haircut. The guys who'd shaved their heads got into trouble 'cause you weren't supposed to be bald.   – **Paul**, age 18

It was the first time I had ever met other gay guys and realised I wasn't alone. Coming out was another story. There were two platoons in a bungalow that slept about 80 men. Running down the centre was a lowish wall. This one guy stood up on the wall and shouted out, 'For those who want to know, I am gay!' I couldn't believe it! That broke the ice, and later that week, when we were sitting in the bungalow, some of the other guys also 'came out'. I felt on top of the world. I'm rescued! I'm saved! I'm not alone! In that state of happiness and joy, I looked them all in the eyes and said, 'I'm gay too.' There was this heartbeat of silence, and the guys looked at me and said they were only pretending. For an instant I thought, oh my God, this is a trap. The army has set a trap and they've caught me out. It was only seconds later that they started laughing and said they were only joking, but I died in that time. It was the shittest coming out I've ever heard of. — **Rick, age 18**

I was 17 years old, so horribly young, when my dad and I drove up to Potch from Welkom. When we got there, we handed in my call-up papers and said I wouldn't be doing my military service. We were told to go to Voortrekkerhoogte. My dad drove me to the Law Offices there. The MPs collected me and took me to prison. It was a cell eight by six feet and held three of us. It was very daunting and I was very nervous, even though I had been preparing for this for years. I was charged with 'Refusing to Perform Military Service', and a date was set for my court martial – I think it was about two weeks after I arrived. Let me tell you, it's nothing like *JAG* or any of that stuff you see on TV. You stand facing this bank of brass, about five or six colonels, as they read out the charges. I was impressed by the colonel, or whoever it was in charge. When he read the sentence, he said something like, 'I don't really have a choice in this matter, and as much as I would like to do otherwise, by law I am bound to give you the maximum sentence for what you are charged with.' He very clearly conveyed to me that he didn't really believe in what he had to do. It was uplifting to hear that from him. I was sentenced to three years without parole. — **Alan, age 17**

Soutpiele and Dutchmen

We were taken to this large hall, surrounded by guys holding rifles, standing against the walls. I felt more like a prisoner. This RSM asks anybody who is English to put up his hand. So I put up my hand and I looked around, and in the entire hall, out of hundreds of guys, I was the only one who'd raised his hand. That was the thing, although we were in the same army, fighting for the same cause, they created this division between English and Afrikaans. It was huge, a huge division. This one soldier walked over to me with this red doibie which fits inside a helmet. Everyone else's was green. Although I didn't know at the time what the RSM's words – 'Engelsman, jy gaan bloed pis' [Englishman, you are going to piss blood] – meant, it didn't sound good. I also knew I was the only oke with a red helmet, which couldn't have been a good sign. We all had to wear our doibies all the time. It meant that I really stood out, and anybody with any rank could order me to do anything: dig a hole at midnight, do push-ups, roll in the dirt, iron clothes or dish up food. They could make you spray your bed and your clothes at night with water, fill your bed with sand, anything. The guys sorted me out, but without breaking me. But I have to say, it taught me discipline and – for the first time in my life – responsibility and endurance. It was the most significant contributing factor to me being selected for an elite unit. **– Brett, age 18**

There was quite a difference between the English and Afrikaans guys. A lot of the Afrikaans guys had bought into this 'volk en vaderland' lock, stock and barrel. The English guys thought it was a crock of shit. The English guys were more thinkers. And they were thinking that this was bullshit. The 'I don't want to be here' kind of thing. I fell into the latter category by a long way. English guys were given a hard time. Everything was set up to keep the Afrikaners in power. You would never find an Englishman as a bevelvoerder at any of these camps. It was all part of a massive set-up, and the army exploited the differences between us. The English guys were NAAFI and keen to gyppo. The Afrikaans guys were more paraat. I remember standing guard duty with this Afrikaans guy. I asked him why he asked to be selected for State President's Guard. He turned to me and said, 'Van kleins af was dit my droom om 'n Staatspresidentswag te wees' [Since I was a child it was my dream to become a State President's Guard]. That threw me. Nearly knocked my socks off. I just looked at him and said I chose it because 'dit was naby die huis' [it was close to home]. The Afrikaners called us soutpiele – one foot in England, one foot in South Africa, and with your dick hanging in the sea.

– Nick, age 20

We were told, 'Die weermag is vyftig vyftig. Vyftig persent Engels en vyftig persent Afrikaans. Die eerste vyftig jaar was Engels en die volgende vyftig jaar sal Afrikaans wees' [The army is fifty fifty. Fifty percent English and fifty percent Afrikaans. The first fifty years were English and the next fifty years will be Afrikaans].

– Paul, age 18

The corporal shouted at us to 'Pak tekkies uit!' This was usually bellowed at us before inspection. I'd got the hang of many things, like not sleeping in my bed when I knew there was an inspection, and using two dixies to make sure the bed was perfectly squared off at the corners. Being an Englishman, I was at a language disadvantage. The first time I heard 'Pak tekkies uit,' I quickly ran and placed my takkies neatly at the foot of the bed! Everyone had a good old laugh at the Engelsman. It meant the same thing as 'roer jou gat', which basically means hurry up and get sorted out as quickly as possible. Nothing to do with placing your takkies anywhere!   – John, age 18

Although I got a C+ for Afrikaans at school, I couldn't read it or write it very well. And the Afrikaans I learnt in the army often wasn't suitable elsewhere. I went on pass with an Afrikaans friend of mine, back to his folks' place for dinner. His mother was shocked by my language, as I said things were 'moerse goed'. He explained to me that you didn't talk that way at home. But, having said that, I met this girl in Amanzimtoti, and by then my Afrikaans was so good I could pick up from what she said and how she said it that one of her parents was English. That's how fluent I became.

Mixing with people from other backgrounds and classes was a real eye-opener for me. In my platoon of about 36 guys, I had a guy who couldn't even read! He had a Standard 4. He had to bring me his letters to read to him. Unbelievable. I was from a white middle-class family in a good middle-class suburb, and I knew if you weren't bright you got to Standard 8, and then went off to technical school. The girls would do a secretarial course or something. I didn't know anyone who just had a Standard 8 or had left school early. Guys from Joburg's John Orr Tech had the lowest academic level that I was aware of. The one guy had gone to 'Special School' and was a Code Seven. That meant he was not qualified to handle a rifle and was sent to Marievale. The Marievale troops did things like construction. One of the other guys' life's ambition was to be a tipper truck driver.

– Paul, age 17

G1K1, G4K-Fucked Up

The physical inspection to determine your classification was held outdoors. We all had to line up dressed only in our army issue underpants. There were these trestle tables in an L-shape and a long row of doctors, about 10 or 15, sitting at them. They were checking in our mouths, looking at our teeth and handling our goolies. For this they used a spoon. They'd shove it at you, hold them and say 'cough'. They had their fun, but at the same time they took the classifying very seriously. If there was something wrong with you and something happened to you, they could be sued. They'd also check your body for scars and whatnot. Then they would write on your back with a permanent Koki – a big 'G1K1' or whatever. This determined what duties you could perform. G1K1 was perfectly fit and capable, while G4K4 would make you a pen-pusher. G5 would exempt you. Then someone would slap you on the back and say, 'Go there.' The whole time this was going on, we were communicating. We weren't supposed to, but we were. Even if it was whispering, communication was going on all the time about what was happening and what would happen to those separated out. I saw this programme on TV about Robben Island and how the prisoners communicated in the jail, and it was just like that – illicit communication going on all the time. Some guys were trying to limp or saying they had problems with their kidneys, as they wanted to be kicked out of the army. Not me – I was very patriotic and I knew I had to be in the bush. I had to have a rifle. I wanted to kill gooks, terrs, guerrillas, whatever, but because of a motorcycle accident in which I had injured my neck and broken one leg so badly that it was shorter than the other, I had a big black G4K4 written on my back. I said to them, 'Stuff you guys, I'm here, I want to fight!' so the guys scrubbed the G4K4 off my back and I signed an indemnity form allowing me to perform G1K1 duties.   – **Brett, age 18**

I had a heart murmur and was classified as a G4K4, or 'G4K-fucked up', as we called them. It meant you couldn't do any physical training or opfok. That's when they discipline you for failing inspection and make you run. They make you run to a distant tree, pick leaves, and then run even more because you were destroying nature, ha ha. We G4K4s had to stay in the bungalow and drink water. Lots of it. About 13 litres in ten minutes or so. Then, when you puked it up, they made you leopard-crawl through it in your uniform. I lasted one week before I realised I'd rather be running. I got myself re-tested and was found to be okay, so I became a G1K1 – fit for active duty.

– Andy, age 18

It was mid-winter and we were in our grootjasse and army underjocks. This female medic is standing there, perving. When we had to take off our coats, she's just standing there *lagging* and looking at our crotches. It was so humiliating. Then, when we had to get our injections, there were two medics who came at you from either side and dug the needles into your arms at the same time, and she watched you squirm. It hurt like hell. The whole experience was undignified and degrading.

– Nick, age 20

During Basic Training we had a meningitis scare and a whole bunch of us had to see the doctor. We were lined up outside his room, all wearing our black gym shorts, brown army T-shirts and lekker brown army takkies, same colour as the shirt. It was my turn next, and I was peeking through the crack of the door and I saw them giving a guy a lumbar puncture. I turned around and I told the guys behind me what I'd seen and ten guys just disappeared. The doc came out and there was no one there! They dragged us back kicking and screaming, but it was just as well, because my headache wasn't from the physical training as I thought – I actually had meningitis. – Ric, age 18

Parades were awful. The parade ground was enormous, about the size of four rugby fields, and we had to march on last, in front of all the other troops who had assembled there already. When we marched on, we had to make the sound of an ambulance siren and, with hands at chest height, palms forward, flick our fingers to imitate flashing lights. We were G4K3s and they called us the LSD troops. Die Lam, Siek en Dooies. — **Rick, age 18**

Drill and Weapons

Part of your daily routine was learning how to march and drill on the parade ground. Every day around nine or ten in the morning we would break for tea. To get out of the sun and off that hot sandy gravel parade ground for tea was what kept me going. Sometimes people would pass out and be carried off. Teatime was 20 minutes. We were marched off the parade ground to have tea in these dreadful polystyrene cups. I had about three, four, five cups and about 30 or 40 biscuits! Psychologically I think it reminded me of home. It was heaven in a cup.   — **Paul, age 18**

It always amazed me how the different divisions of the army called time when marching their troops. I think the only people who did it according to the textbook were Infantry School in Oudtshoorn. The tradition must have been passed on to each intake from instructor to instructor where the two-liners and lieuties all used the same sort of calls to march their troops. Their instructors called time as '*Links, regs, links regs.*' In an area where there were a lot of different corps you could close your eyes and know who was being marched past. Stand outside SAWI on a Sunday morning at about eight o'clock, and without seeing them, you could tell which corps was being marched past Northern Transvaal Command HQ to the different churches. The Tiffies you would recognise by their call of 'Lux hearse, lux hearse', the 'hearse' always being a higher note than the 'lux'. PD School was always the best: 'Brie, ya-ya-ya-ya-ya, hearse!' The 'yas' were always sharp, like a little yapping dog, and the last 'hearse' was quite a high note. I'm sure corporals used to practise these in their spare time and also see, while drilling their troops, how many commands they could get into a sentence. The best ever was Staff Sergeant Marx at PD School, who was drilling JLs at double time towards an approaching lieutenant. His command to his platoon went something like this: 'Brie ya-ya-ya-ya-ya, hearse. Brie ya hearse kom mense trek af die duim elmboog reguit swaai jou arm saam met jou maatjie voor en langs jou nek teen die kraag maag in bors uit kyk op peloton oëëëëë regs, môre luitenant, oëëëëë front brie ya hearse!' [Come people thumb down, elbow straight, swing your arm with your buddy in front of and next to you, neck against the collar, stomach in, chest out, look up, platoon eyes right, morning lieutenant, eyes front!] The biggest fuck-up I ever saw on a parade ground was when the same Staff Sergeant Marx changed the commands on a Wednesday morning *bataljon aantreeparade* to English. He knew every single command perfectly, but the troops didn't have a fucking clue! You are supposed to do parades in both languages, but in three months we had only ever heard commands in Afrikaans. Most people understood 'attention', but anything from then onwards was just like cows shitting on a tarmac road. That was what they said when the drill was bad: 'Mense, julle klink soos koeie wat op 'n teerpad kak!' [People, you sound like cows shitting on a tar road!]   – Jeremy, age 18

In the summer, Phalaborwa was unbelievably hot. That's why the intake was always mid-year: July was much cooler. On parade or while training, guys would just drop from heat exhaustion, and we were not allowed to step out and go and help. We were army property and it was the responsibility of the medic to run over and try to revive the guy. If he was in a bad way, he'd be loaded into an ambulance, which was always on standby next to the parade ground. Otherwise the medic just got him back to his feet and he rejoined the parade. They were very good about you drinking lots of water, but some guys were not as fit or just didn't have a body mass that could cope with the heat as efficiently as others. The Infantry really had it rough. There were two hills, and we sat on top of one sipping colddrinks and firing the occasional mortar at the poor skiet piet guys running around doing fire and movement exercises below. A Red Cross flag hung from the flagpole at the top of the camp, and if the temperature reached 36 degrees Celsius, it was dropped to half-mast and an air raid siren went off. This meant there could be no more physical training and we had to return to our bungalows and lie on the floor under our bunks. Everyone was relieved when that happened.   – Clint, age 18

They've changed it back now, but in 1980 the legislation was that you had to have a licence for an air gun, a pellet gun. I went down to Parkview Police Station with my father to get one and was told I was too young. I was 17. My father had to apply for it. When I got to the army and they were issuing rifles, I said I wasn't yet 18 and was not allowed to have one. The corporal gave me a slap on the ear and said, 'Troep, vat die fokkin' geweer!' [Troop, take the fuckin' rifle!]

– Paul, age 17

They had this little saying when you got issued your rifle: 'This is my rifle' (shaking the rifle) – 'this is my gun' (and they'd point at their crotch) – 'this is for shooting' (shaking the rifle) – 'and this is for fun' (pointing at their crotch again). We were told our rifles were our mothers, fathers, girlfriend, wife, everything. It goes wherever you go, if you go to eat, it goes. When you take a dump, it goes with you. When you go to bed, you sleep with your rifle. That rifle goes everywhere with you. I gave one guy 45 minutes of rifle PT for leaving his rifle outside the bungalow. I fucked him up solid. For rifle PT you have to hold the rifle in one position with your arm locked straight for an extended amount of time without letting it drop. If it drops, you are in even more kak. Let me tell you, after holding a rifle with one hand right out in front of you or to the side, you want to die. Needless to say, he never left his rifle lying around again.

– Paul, age 18

I so badly wanted to hold a rifle that I cleaned other guys' rifles, and the only way I could get to hold a loaded weapon was to volunteer for guard duty. I was the only one who ever volunteered for guard duty. I did it just to be able to hold a loaded weapon. I used to run my arse off during the day and then pull duty at night just to hold a loaded weapon. I usually guarded the main gate of the base. This was war, and you were protecting your own area, your territory. To me it was just so amazing. Nothing ever happened when I was on guard duty, but I used to almost pray that something would happen and that I could take guys out. When I think of it now, I think: what a dick!

— **Brett, age 18**

The restrictions and controls regarding weapons in the military then were indescribable. You went onto the shooting range and you had to account for every single round. You'd have to go around and collect every single doppie after you'd finished shooting, as each round had to be accounted for. If you couldn't find one, the entire platoon scrounged around trying to locate it. That's how strict they were. We'd been issued with our weapons and I was off on a Sports Pass. I snuck my R5 and ammo into my balsak and took it home. I wanted to show my mates my gun. I have to say I was pretty stressed over the weekend 'cause I still had to smuggle it back into camp. When I think about it, I must have been mad! Now you could probably buy a gun on the side of the road, but then … If I had been caught, the consequences would have been so bad. Opfok from here to Christmas.   — **Paul, age 18**

Because we G4K3s were not allowed to shoot our R4 rifles, our responsibility was to be in the ditch at the far end of the shooting range and raise and lower the targets, on these big steel contraptions, for the regular troops who were doing target practice. When the troops came to the ditch to check their targets, I would inspect them from head to toe and always choose the really sexy ones, swopping places if need be to make sure I managed the sexy guy's target. After the sexy guy had fired his rounds – and for some reason they were often not very good – I would punch holes in the target with a pencil to make him look good. My assisting the 'gods in browns' ended the day they discovered more holes in the target than the guy had bullets. I got the uitkak of my life. **– Rick, age 18**

Near the end of my Basic Training I had to do guard duty around Voortrekkerhoogte. One evening I landed up being the guard duty commander, which meant I drew up lists, allocated shifts, checked rifles in and out, and made sure whoever was supposed to be on duty was, and that they were where they were meant to be. We had road-blocks around Voortrekkerhoogte and guards around the perimeter of Personnel Services School. The guys were transported from PSS by truck. Before they got onto the trucks, it was standard procedure to clear their rifles by removing the magazine and cocking the rifle a few times to make sure there were no rounds in the chamber. It obviously wasn't wise to travel in the back of a truck, in close proximity to other troops, with a loaded rifle. One guy cocked his rifle but forgot to remove the magazine, so he had, in fact, loaded his rifle. Not only that, but he had it on automatic. All I heard was *dddrrrrrrrrrrr* … as he accidentally emptied his magazine. Luckily, he didn't hit anyone 'cause the rifle was aimed at the ground, but he missed this one guy's foot by centimetres and the tarmac was full of holes. Naturally he was punished. PT with a rucksack full of bricks. **– Michael, age 21**

Washing, Ironing, Inspection

The guys had a fat laugh at me. When we first arrived at the army, they searched our bags. We'd been told to bring washing powder, and my mom had packed me Skip. Skip is for automatics, and the guys were, 'Hah! You think there are washing machines?' Fat chance. I knew to expect the worst. We washed everything by hand. I also learnt to iron using Robin starch, which helped iron the crease down the front of your browns and was excellent for ironing our shirtsleeves. What we also used to do was to go to a tailor and have that crease stitched in, which was called a gyppo naat.   **– Nick, age 20**

On my first pass I bought an iron – not one of those steam irons, just a good old-fashioned plain one. It took flippin' ages to iron overalls, but it was great for other things. This one night we stole bread – well, actually we were on guard duty, so we could pretty much go where we wanted, as we were the ones with the rifles. We took the bread to our room and used the iron to make toast. We craved the simple things.   **– Paul, age 17**

In the army you had to chain your washing to the line, and if you didn't, you soon learnt why it was necessary. I'd hang up my socks, shirts and our horrible old women's broekies, Santa Marias, and come back to find one sock and some shirts had been swiped. I didn't take a length of chain with me to the army, but I quickly bought one. It was a vicious circle: people just took what they were short of. Even if it was labelled, it didn't mean much; it was still stolen.   **– John, age 18**

Inspection involved so much. Your pikstel clipped into one another had to be spotless. Some okes started cleaning them with Brasso, not realising what it did to you. Do you know what Brasso does to your guts? You have no idea how horribly sick they got – such gippo guts. The knife had a bevelled edge, and they would hold it up to the window and check down the length of the blade. Any mark, water stain, anything, and you got opfokked. Your trommel at the foot of your bed also had to be polished.

We had to stryk our clothes and our bed. In Basics you got your overalls and a big floppy gardener's hat, your web belt, your water bottle, socks, boots, takkies for PT, so there wasn't too much to iron, but God help you if there were railway tracks; one line only. We did iron our clothes a lot too, because you wanted them to have houding. Browns that looked new weren't fashionable in a military way. You ironed your clothes until they were almost worn out. But that damn bed! You had to iron your bed so it looked like a matchbox. To do this you used your clean boot brushes, spray bottle, starch and shaving foam. They taught us how to fold the bedclothes, and God help you if you stood inspection in the morning en daar was 'n slang in die bed [and there was a snake in the bed]. It had to be level and flat. In order to get it that way, you had to climb underneath the bed and clip a clothes peg onto the mesh and the mattress. The beds were those horrible hospital metal mesh beds with a thin flat mattress used by hundreds of fat okes before you. You had to clip it in such a way that it didn't sag in the middle and look like a canoe. If there were any wrinkles or unevenness, you had to jump on your bed and 'maak dood daardie slange' [kill those snakes]. You stood inspection in your boots, and of course if you had to jump all over it, you got boot polish on your sheets and somehow you had to find the time to wash the sheets. It was better to sleep on the floor after you had made your bed for inspection; that way you could get a little extra sleep in. But they got wise to that and would come and check during the night.

– Paul, age 18

We had this one guy who was not very bright. Our platoon was made up of guys who were supposed to be physically and mentally challenged. Shame, he was very dumb. He would be sitting polishing his boots and we would shout his name and distract him. We then quickly removed his spotless boots and replaced them with a pair that needed cleaning and polishing. You could do the same thing with ironing. He didn't seem to notice that his ironing pile included a whole lot of our stuff. We really used him. I guess that was one advantage of having a person like that in our platoon.

– **Rick, age 18**

Some bungalows had stone floors, others had wood. All had to be polished like a mirror, otherwise you would fail inspection. Remember Cobra wax, in the big green tin? We used that. The floor was so slippery from being so highly polished that even your bed used to slide on the floor. For inspection they would look at the shimmer on the floor, and if they saw the slightest mark, they would empty the sand from the fire bucket, take the hose, and spray the floor down. This was after eight of you had spent hours on your knees polishing the floor. Even clean boots left a mark, so I made these slippers so that we didn't have to take off our boots when we came into the bungalow. They were square pieces of industrial polish cloth that looked like a carpet tile, and we cut them into giant feet and Mickey Mouse head shapes. I wrote Nike Air and put big ticks on mine. Imagine all these guys with shaved heads, in their browns, skating around the floor. It was brilliant. We kept the floor clean and polished it at the same time. If you demanded troeps to clean to that degree now, they'd lock you up in a loony bin. – **Paul, age 18**

I only remember one time that we actually got driven back from Schurweberg, the combined unit's shooting range, to Voortrekker-hoogte. Every other time they found some or other reason to make us run back to camp. I remember one time we must have really fucked up. According to them we had been 'shooting like women', so a Samil arrived and dropped off poles and tyres. We were told to get them back to camp by six that evening, when we were to stand inspection. I still remember running back and we were all singing, among other chants, the old 'Why are we run-ning? SWAPO! SWAPO! Why are we sweat-ing? SWAPO! SWAPO!' It's amazing how they got the indoctrination in, in everything we did. We got back in time, but of course we were sweaty and dirty and failed the inspection. We were told to stand again at nine that night. Shrapnel, our corporal – so named 'cause he had really bad acne scars – walked in and did the usual old hackneyed pickupapillowcaseandthrowitdownthelengthofthebungalow shit. Of course it's going to pick up something. And of course he's going to do the usual Dutchman corporal thing and say, 'You is pigs.' He then proceeded to throw two fire buckets of sand and two fire buckets of water onto the bungalow floor and make us do Bungalow PT – over a bed, under a bed, over a bed, under a bed – fucking up an entire inspection. We were told we would be standing inspection the next morning at seven. It's the first time I ever knew the whole bungalow to pull together. We decided en masse, after moving all of the trommels, beds and kaste out of the bungalow, and washing down and polishing the floor, that we wouldn't have time to wash and iron dry all the sheets and pillow cases, so we broke into teams. One team was responsible for washing and ironing dry the top third of the sheets and the whole pillowcase, while the rest were setting full uitpak inspection bed by bed. I'll never forget sliding around the polished floor on 'taxis' while I matched up everyone's numbered moving parts with their stripped-down rifles. We got our inspection done in time. Shrapnel never pulled back one sheet. If he had, he would've found the dirtiest beds in the entire Defence Force. So we took a usual standard opfok and smiled. JLs one. Poes corporal zero.   – Clayton, age 17

Sometimes we were at sea for long periods, and fresh water was precious on a small boat. There was no fresh water to wash our clothes in, so on wash day we used to thread the clothing onto ropes and stream it out behind the boat. It would churn along behind the boat, and sea water was the best way to get uniforms faded and soft.

– **Louis, age 17**

Your browns are all shiny and new, and only after nine months could you iron your first line across your back. That meant you were a *roof*. In our unit, after one year you could iron a second line, which meant you were a *blougat*. The third line ironed across your shirt back was when you had done 18 months. When you only had six months left in the army, you were then one of the *ou manne*.

– **Anthony, age 18**

Chefs and Blue Eggs

They taught me to cook, but it's different when you are cooking for over 1 000 guys. Everything's boil or oil. Catering in the army was about good quality food fucked up. We used to get the best quality food, fucked up by the chefs in the kitchen. Two thousand four hundred eggs? They were blue, whether boiled, scrambled or whatever. By the time the guys ate them, they were blue because they had stood for so long. We used to crack them, two at a time, into these huge varkpanne filled with about three inches of oil. You had to do it in such a way so that as you finished cracking in your last eggs, you started spooning out the first ones you had dropped in. You then put them on top of layers of bread in another varkpan. The bread absorbed the oil and the guys used to fight for that bread. Karoo lamb? Beef? Awesome quality. We would brown it a little, then chop up onions and unpeeled carrots – not nicely diced or chopped finely, you know, just hacked up – then we'd take the hosepipe and fill these huge pots with water, throw in the beef, onions and carrots, and walk outside to have a smoke and just leave it to cook. We left it until it was so completely cooked that it was brown in the middle. *Tentklappe* – tent flaps – that's what their 'roast' beef was called. There was fuck-all roasting involved! **– Anthony, age 18**

It was quite prestigious to be in the army in the early eighties. They looked after you and we had good equipment and really good food. By about the second month of Basics, we knew the importance of eating well, because of all the physical training we had to do. Once we went in for breakfast and the chefs had messed up our food. There were blue-green eggs and the bacon was this congealed mass. Our RSM used to eat with us, and when he came in and saw that we were refusing to eat, he took one look at the food and understood why. He said that it was unacceptable and pulled out all the chefs, every one of them that was currently on duty in the kitchen and all the others that were off duty and resting in their bungalows. Now we used to call the chefs tippy-toes 'cause many of them were of the more 'softer' persuasion. The RSM made them all do pole PT. A tar road ran through the camp for about a kilometre, and our entire battalion lined the road to watch. We didn't cheer – we wouldn't take away a man's dignity like that – but our presence was enough to show our displeasure at these guys in their white uniforms and brown boots, who were not used to physical exercise, running up and down the road. It was very funny to watch. One pair was trying to carry the pole, but one was very tall and the other very short, so they just didn't get it right. The RSM drilled them hard for three hours, and then they had to make our lunch. We never had another bad meal. — **Clint, age 18**

I was on watch on board SAS *Fleur* in Simonstown harbour when the new chef arrived. He presented himself, and then the petty officer took him off to show him his bunk and where everything was. Shortly after lunch the bell sounded and shouts went up that there was a man overboard. I rushed to the edge and looked down – there was this youngster, the new chef. The lunch he had prepared was kak, so the guys had thrown him overboard! It was amusing, but there is so much protocol and paperwork and so many procedures involved when a man goes overboard, and as it happened on my watch, I had to deal with all that. Dinner was no better, so that evening the chef ended up overboard again. The next morning he made everyone breakfast in bed. — **Louis, age 17**

Being a chef in the army was a very powerful position. We ran the bars and handled all the food. I had the keys to the fridges, so I could trade or sell anything. A box of meat could be traded for anything, especially to the troops who had been out on patrol for six weeks; they craved meat after living on rat packs. Anything I wanted. Anything. I could get it from them. I traded a case of meat to the loadies for a legitimate ticket on a Flossie from the Border to Pretoria and back. This saved me ten days' travelling pass, and I could spend more time on pass at home. For a one-litre sachet of milk I got a new pair of those flat-soled takkie boots, the ones that real soldiers, the Recces or 32 Battalion, wear. None of those normal army boots with a heel for me. I sold so much stuff too. I'd sell the old oil to the Ovambos for … I can't remember exactly, about R20 a drum. I never had to touch my army pay and I made a fortune on the Border. I made a lot of money. I was able to buy my first car when I klaared out. The army taught me how to wheel and deal. — **Anthony, age 18**

Basic Training in '93 was bad. We lived in tents and the food was shocking. The first day would be some sort of meat, the next day green kidneys, the third day black liver, and the fourth day mincemeat from all the leftover meat from the previous days. After a week, everyone started getting sick and lost weight. I complained about it, and because of that we had to clean up the kitchen. I was very unpopular. When we cleaned the kitchen, we found worms in the mincing machine. I was so happy when my folks drove down to see me in Ladysmith for an Open Day. I asked them to bring food. It was the only thing I asked for. They even brought me some KFC, which was like a dream! They brought tons of tinned food, which I used mainly to swop out for favours and duties. The condensed milk and bully beef were the most valuable. Condensed milk was like gold. We had to bite our bed to get the edges of the blanket sharp and neat. I swopped a tin of condensed milk out for a guy to bite my bed for me for inspections. I wasn't going to ruin my teeth on that crap! — **Martin, age 23**

We were up at 4 a.m. this one time for breakfast. Thousands of us were standing in line to eat our blue eggs, two slices of brown toast and the lumpiest mieliepap I've ever eaten in my life. I remember looking up at the stars and seeing the Three Kings. That's one good thing I remember from there: the stars there were unbelievably bright. It's like those three stars were shining down on me like some sort of protection. They were a comfort to me. To this day, I still think of that time when I looked up and saw those Three Kings.   – **Nick, age 20**

Afkak, Opfok, Rondfok, Vasbyt

We called the Parabats 'Vleisbomme', the State President's Guard 'Trompoppies', Gunners 'Kanondonkies'. Personeeldiens was called 'The PD Sun', and Valhalla was 'Valhalla Beach', 'cause we, being Infantry, thought we had the toughest time and the guys there had it easy. We had to deal with opfok. 'You see that leaf over there? Go and fetch me that leaf.' And you run miles to that bloody tree – that's opfok. And when you come back, he tells you it's the wrong leaf – that's rondfok. Opfok is more physical: all that running up and down. The fact that you've got to go again 'cause he says you have the wrong leaf is the rondfok. Physically it won't really harm you. It's more psychological. Another example was this one particular lieutenant, who hated my guts. He would take water and pour it all over my bed during inspection. This was a full inspection: all your stuff was laid out on the bed, your rifle was stripped, and everything in your kas and trommel had to be just so. All your shirts had to be ironed and hung up with the sleeves all pointing the same way. Your pakkie of folded clothing had to be perfectly squared off. What a lot of guys didn't cotton on to was the fact that it didn't matter how perfect everything was, 'cause the first time they came around they were going to say, 'Wat se kak is dié!' [What shit is this!], and pull stuff out and drag it around. Physically it won't kill you to put it all back together, and when he comes around again, the things will probably look worse than the first time, but he'll say, 'Nee, dis baie beter' [No, that's much better]. That's rondfok. — **Nick, age 20**

There was rondfok, opfok and vasbyt. The first is just stuffing you around. If the corporals were bored, they'd tell us to do things like take our beds to the parade ground and sleep there, but they had to be back in the bungalow for inspection the next morning. Opfok is more

a punishment, but it can be constructive, like a very heavy physical session, but the outcome is still geared towards improving the situation or your fitness. We had a vasbyt at Golden Gate in the middle of winter once. Up and down the hills, swimming through freezing rivers so all our kit was wet, and the white mist blowing towards us wasn't mist but tear gas. At the end of the day they'd say, 'There's a lekker braai down at the bottom; all you have to do is walk down there. Yes, we'll take you off the course, but, shame man, aren't your blisters hurting? Just take your boots off and walk down with us for some food. C'mon, the guys are having a lekker time down there, come and join us.' If it's done properly, the purpose of vasbyt is to show how quickly things can break down; morale can be broken very easily, and as potential leaders you need to deliver on your promises. If you tell your troops they don't need to take much food 'cause more will be delivered, and then for two nights it isn't and when the truck does come all it has are beetroot slices, the guys are going to start bitching and negativity sets in.
                                                                — Paul, age 17

The word *vasbyt* originated with 1 Parachute Battalion. It was a form of initiation started by the Parabats. New recruits arrived at the battalion and had to undergo this form of physical initiation by tensing their stomach muscles as a big guy hit them in the gut as hard as he could. The word is now used all over the place, on the rugby field, the rest of the SADF, but that's where it came from – 1 Parachute Battalion.
                                                                — John, age 18

I was extremely fit, so I didn't battle with the physical side of opfok. I could do 132 push-ups in two minutes. Running with a heavy backpack and carrying a Samil tyre and a tree trunk wasn't quite what I was used to, but the only thing I really battled with was running in boots. There was no cure for blisters; you just had to work your way through them. I still have scars on the top of my foot and on my heel. The only thing they seemed worried about was sunburn. You were in so much shit if you got sunburnt. You were never allowed to walk around without a shirt on, because if you got burnt on your shoulders, you couldn't carry a pack.   – Paul, age 18

We had the Olympics in State President's Guard. For three days you would get messed around horribly. Rondfok, opfok – everything. It was like an initiation. You knew it was starting when they did roll-call at 2 a.m. We'd do a 10-kay route march, 10-kay run, pole PT and fluitjie – whistle – PT. Fluitjie op, fluitjie af. They'd blow the whistle and you'd fall on your stomach, then they'd blow the whistle and you'd jump up, blow the whistle, back down. Then we'd have to drink water, roll on the ground in this fine powdery red dust, stand up, drink more water, roll, drink, roll, until you hurled. Then you still had to continue, so you were rolling in vomit and you and your uniform were filthy. Then they'd tell us to get back to our rooms. And they'd been in there. They had emptied the sand buckets and sprayed water over everything, and we were told we were standing major inspection at 6 a.m. Tempers frayed as everyone rushed to get everything done. But somehow we did it – in half an hour. During Olympics it was the only time the guys would go to the clerks and beg them to put them on guard duty.   – Nick, age 20

During COIN – counter-insurgency – training at Tempe, we were trained in map reading, orientation, standing guard duty and stuff like that. We were given our map and had to travel from one point to another carrying poles and ammo boxes. We were supposed to dig a trench when we reached the point where we were supposed to be for the night. But we got lucky and found an old trench dug by the guys who had been there before us. We were also supposed to set potjiefakkels, which we didn't, as we felt quite safe. We tied ourselves together, wrist to wrist, and there were two guys on either side of the trench, supposedly on guard. If they heard something they just pulled on the utility rope, this small green rope you got in Basics, and woke up the next man, and so it went down the line, everyone waking the next person by tugging on the rope. The first thing that happened was we heard these other guys approaching. We cocked our rifles – with live ammo – and instructed these guys to get down, identify themselves, the whole thing. We thought we had stopped our corporals, who were probably sneaking up to check on us. Meantime it was another, completely separate group that had accidentally, due to a communication error, stumbled across our trenches. We could have shot them.

A few nights after that, we're at another point where we had scraped out trenches for the night. The guards fell asleep and the instructors woke us by chucking thunderflashes at us. One landed inside my trench and blew a huge hole in my sleeping bag. It gave us a real wake-up call. Because the guards were asleep, we got the opfok of our lives. I think it was about three o'clock in the morning and the instructors went crazy. We had to do pole PT and fluitjie PT. They'd blow the whistle and we had to drop and crawl. The whistle blew and we had to get up and run, down again, leopard-crawl, up again – this was over rough terrain, mind you, not a smooth parade ground or anything, and if the guy in front of you vomited, you just crawled through it. If he stopped, you just crawled over him. It went on like that all the way back to base. When I saw the base, I thought it would be over and we could drop the poles and ammo boxes. But no, we then had to march with our rifles held out horizontally with stiff arms. It went on until mid-morning. It was a good lesson. As they said: 'In the war you won't get a second chance, they'll just kill you,' so ja, it was a good lesson.   **– Tallies, age 17**

In Berede – Mounted Infantry – in Potch, we did all the usual nonsense like everyone else – wake up at the crack of dawn, go and do your 2,4-kilometre run like everybody else, have inspection like everybody else – then early breakfast and straight to the horses. We'd muck out the stables; yes, we did all that ourselves, as we didn't have stable hands. In the early days of learning to ride, you ran with all your kit and your horse's kit. I hated it, 'cause we had these McLellan saddles which were supposed to be light, but let me tell you, they got pretty heavy, especially when you had to carry them on top of your head and carry your rifle. The idea behind it was that if your horse was shot or injured, you had to be able to carry all the kit out. You also had to do this while leading your horse, and if you had a horse that didn't like being led or was full of nonsense … wow … you had a rough time. We did horse training until 11, and then it would be 'too hot for the horses but not for the men'. We ran or whatever, and then did classes like learning how to set up roadblocks or take apart landmines. Once a week we would have *perdeparade* in the afternoon. All other days it was just the usual parade at five in the afternoon. Then, when we got back to base, we would have to clean up, shower, change, get allocated duties like guard duty, then have supper. We had to march everywhere; we could not just walk. If there were two of you, you had to march in step, and if there were more than two, one had to take control and call cadence for the others to march to. After dinner you went back to the bungalow and had about an hour to polish and clean your equipment – that's the usual inventory plus saddle, reins and all the additional equipment. You had to buy all your own stuff too: boot polish, dubbin and such. Then you prepared for inspection the next morning. Then it was Bible time. You had 15 minutes to read, and they checked up on you to make sure you were reading your Bible. After Bible time, we slept under our beds so that we didn't have to make them in the morning.   – **Martin, age 23**

There was this very shit place called Lohatla. I worked in the pay office, and at the end of every month a busload of us would head off to Lohatla. All the gay guys going off to pay the straight guys. It was like, *la la la la la*, because it was an outing, a road trip. It was exciting; we talked about the guys we would meet, all those Rambo types who were living in the bush there, surviving without food as they trained hard before being sent up to the Border to go and fight in the war. When we got there, we were given a tent far out in the middle of nowhere. It was so isolated, we thought it was a tent they used as a target for bombs and things. I mean it was completely by itself, far out in the veld. Of course, being gay, we decorated it and made it look nice with flowers and whatnot. We had to make it as pleasant as possible. You could feel the pain in the air. Lohatla was a hard place, and there were guys who were really messed up. Things like no food for days, all in preparation for going to the Border. I don't know why it worked out like this, but we always got tea and sandwiches served to us as the guys were queuing for their pay. These guys were a mess, exhausted, filthy, tired and hungry, and there we sat behind tables draped with white tablecloths, drinking tea and eating sarmies! Maybe they wanted to mess with the guys' heads, but we were only 18 and it was a game. We would send the tea back, declaring it was cold, or say we didn't eat cheese and we would send the food back while we called out, 'Next! *Magsnommer*?' It was also a way to get back at them. These were the guys who had judged me, victimised me and belittled me at school and had given me the hardest time of my life.   – **Rick, age 18**

Making and Breaking

You were a troep, you were fokall. Jy's niks. Corporal used to say to us, 'Jy's nie my donnerse ma nie, jy's nie my donnerse pa nie, jy's net 'n fokkin' troep' [You're not my bloody mother, you're not my bloody father, you're nothing but a fuckin' troop]. The first two weeks is just a constant breakdown. You're nothing. You're nobody. You're useless. Even if it was just water for shaving. Warm water? No ways. Ha! Try no water! Everyone had to shave dry, and if there was the slightest bit of stubble – opfok. I understood why they did it, but it didn't make it any easier. Sleep deprivation was one of the quickest ways to get to you. They would send us to bed around 10 p.m., saying we'd done a good day's work and to get a good night's sleep. Next thing we'd be woken at 11 p.m. and be up for the rest of the night. We had no normal sleep patterns; they broke those completely. Also, the waking up was never a gentle 'Wakey wakey, it's the corporal here, it's time to get up.' It was always abrupt, some loud noise or banging. We were constantly sleep deprived, and I'm sure medical opinion now would say what they did then was illegal. The military was a law unto itself.   **– Paul, age 18**

During training we had class competition between platoons. Things like bridge- or obstacle-building. We had this 20-kilometre run with a gum pole tree. It wasn't just a pole, it was an entire tree. Our platoon was the last one to reach the place where we had to pick it up and it was the only tree left, so of course it was the largest one. Even our platoon commander joined in and helped us stagger back with this thing, but we still came in about four hours after the others. It took us an entire bloody day. There was a braai afterwards, but it was pretty much finished by the time we got back. That night, one of the big Afrikaans guys broke down and cried, and then attacked that pole with an axe.   **– Paul, age 17**

I have never seen such dramatic weight loss. These two strapping guys from Charlie Company were on Corporal's Course, and each was given a rooi doibie and they went from being big guys to skin and bone in less than two weeks. Their major was an English guy, but a complete dick. The two had bunked from something, a meal or a lecture or something, and hidden under their beds. They got caught, and for punishment had to wear the doibies. Their CB punishment was brutal. They had to *op die looppas*, which meant they had to jog everywhere and all the time. They weren't allowed to walk. They weren't allowed to eat sitting down; they had to jog on the spot. Every hour on the hour they had to report to the hoofhek in full battle uniform. Even throughout the night, every hour on the hour, they had to go to the gate and get the lieutenant to sign that they had reported in, so they were not getting enough sleep. At any time, anywhere, any officer or NCO could stop them and tell them to drop and do 30 push-ups or whatever. It was inhumane. I got stuffed up in the army occasionally. I got a bossie, or a bosbus. That's when the major or colonel drives in a Ratel or Land Rover or something and you have to run and try to keep up with the vehicle while he shouts and tells you what to do and where to go. He might tell you to run up and back down a hill and all the while he's driving and you have to keep up. It absolutely killed you. He just kept driving and you would have to keep up. As tough as a bossie was, it still didn't affect us the way it did those two guys. I've never seen physical exertion affect anyone like that. They looked like scarecrows. The worse thing was, at the end of it all, they were chucked off the course, so the whole punishment was for nothing.   – Stof, age 24

Many of us came out of different homes, different circumstances and different upbringings. We felt differently about the war. Many of the troops didn't even want to hold a rifle, but I was very fortunate. I was very patriotic and, being in the State President's Unit, I was very lucky because being an instructor there meant I worked with guys with strength of character. They were fighters. They could go the whole night without sleeping, or go without food. I didn't have a problem like some of the other instructors did, with guys not wanting to fire a rifle. My troops wanted to. They wanted to protect the President. They wanted to do whatever it took to perform those duties. But there were stressful and difficult times. We had one guy who hanged himself in the shower and another who shot himself with his R4 while on guard duty. But I would rather tell you about the good times 'cause I prefer to remember those.   – Brett, age 18

It was primarily graduates who worked at Personnel Services. We were grouped together, and army life was made more bearable working alongside people who were intelligent and had some qualification or other. Unfortunately, not the same could be said of the corporals and lieutenants. We quickly learnt that if we stuck together as a group and did things together, they couldn't do much to us. So, if we were told to run to a fence and back in less than two minutes, we ran as a group, constantly reminding each other to stick together. We'd get back in two minutes and five seconds and be told to run again. This time we ran it in two minutes and ten seconds. Do it again. We took longer each time. Do it again. And so on, until we were all running it in three minutes. What could they do? We acted as a single unit. However, I recall this one time that even sticking together didn't help. While we were north of Pretoria doing bush exercises near Hammanskraal, there was a rail strike, so they couldn't get food to us. We were given what they had, tinned pickled fish, which after a while got a bit much. One afternoon we were told to report to the parade ground immediately. We decided that we weren't going to comply without having decent food for dinner first. So we sent our Bungalow Bill, who was pretty brave to do this, to tell the corporal that we weren't moving until we got some proper food. Next thing, the captain comes stomping down the path, yelling, 'This is not a fucking trade union movement! This is the army!' It was at this point that we realised that we had probably pushed matters a little too far, and that the captain and his staff really had the power, and could effectively do anything with us. Result: we got up smartly and marched to the parade ground. Later we had to put on a show as part of a competition, and our platoon won, even though we made some fun of the captain. I think he secretly admired how we stuck together.   — **Michael, age 21**

Because our tent was so far away from everyone else in the camp, and because we were hung-over, we didn't hear the Sunday morning reveille and missed church parade. The RSM came into our tent and screamed at us because we were late. As punishment he made us rake the parade ground. Not with a normal rake, but with a small one. It was so hot raking this bloody parade ground under the blazing sun and with a hangover. But we still managed to have fun and play around. We feng-shuied parts of that damn parade ground. I doubt any general had a little feng shui thingy on his desk, so I don't think that's where the little rake came from. We managed to enjoy ourselves. We played a lot, in a lot of places. They did try to break our spirit, but I think because we didn't have the seriousness of war to deal with and no running or push-ups and such, they could only mess us around with inspection and stuff like raking the parade ground. But we stayed strong for each other. The Sisterhood survived for the entire two years and some years after. It was an incredible bond. I can easily say that I have never experienced such strong friendships like the ones I had in the army.   — **Rick, age 18**

If you ask any guy who played rugby in the army, they'll tell you they were well looked after. If you played rugby, you were a god. Our colonel was rugby-befok. The very first day I arrived at the base, he said he wasn't interested in soldiers, he was only interested in rugby players, and if you were a rugby player, you were a natural leader. Rugby was life and death, the be-all and end-all of everything. They put all the rugby players in the same bungalow. We lived in rooms, five guys to a room, in a long bungalow with a room at the head for someone with rank. A corporal or someone had to sleep there every night to make sure we behaved ourselves. There was a standard command when someone with rank entered the bungalow and wanted everyone's attention, to issue orders, to report something or before we were marched somewhere. He would shout, 'Almal in die gang!' [Everyone in the passage!] Because of the pronunciation of *almal*, it sounded just like they were calling my surname, Hummel. So we all had this thing going, when they shouted, 'Almal in die gang!' Instead of everyone coming out of their room, only I would go out, and I'd say 'Hummel hier.' Everyone else just remained in their rooms, doing whatever they were doing. It really pissed them off! I think they were a bit nervous of us 'cause we were all rugby players, all big guys and all older than the usual 18-year-old recruit.

It really annoyed this one 17-year-old corporal, who hated me, probably because of that little trick, but also because I was English. I was one of only three guys out of 50 who were English. He would mess me around and instruct me to run up hills with the biggest rock and so on. We had this big rugby match coming up, and a few days before it, he told me to pick up this huge rock and run around with it. I picked it up and threw it down at his feet and told him that if I went to the colonel and told him he had fucked me up just before Saturday's big game, who did he think would be in the shit? I took a chance, but he did back off after that.

So on the one hand they did take care of you, but there was this one time our rugby-obsessed colonel took us to Potch to play in the SADF Rugby Week. It was a huge rugby event at the Olen Park Stadium, and every unit in the country sent a team. There must have been about 500 rugby players in the tournament. It was a knockout competition. We got through to the semi-finals and were up against Free State Command. We blew our first-half lead as André Joubert slotted six penalties in the last few minutes of the second half to beat us. It was hard, especially after we had been in control of the game till then. Now our colonel's life's dream was to win this SADF Rugby Week, and he wanted his little boys in Oudtshoorn to take out the big guns and beat units from Northern Transvaal, Free State Command and whatever. I thought we had done very well to get that far in the tournament, but we were out now. After our loss, we went back to the change rooms and the colonel comes in. He was apoplectic and going berserk; he was screaming and going absolutely mad. At the end of the ranting and raving, he locked us in the change room. We had left the field at about five o'clock, and only at about ten that night did someone realise that 21 guys were missing and they came looking for us. We had sat there for five hours with nothing to eat or drink. In those days there were no cellphones or anything, so we had to just sit until someone from the function realised where we were. Our colonel would have left us there the whole night. It shows how passionate he was about rugby.   – Stof, age 24

I was kla-ed on for KFC. We were at Maselspoort, a training ground about 20 kays from base, and four of us asked the OC for permission to run back rather than go with everyone else, as we were in training for the Comrades Marathon. We ran back in full kit, and when we got back the mess hall had closed and we were a-b-s-o-l-u-t-e-l-y starving. There was nowhere to get food on the base, but there was a KFC outlet not far away. We were not supposed to leave the base, because there was a curfew, but a few of us decided to scale the wall and go and buy Kentucky Fried Chicken. We did that, ate it, and afterwards we went back to our respective bungalows. Next thing the commandant came in and shouted, 'Walland, you cunt! Don't lie to me. Where have you been?' I knew that no one had seen us scale the wall, but what had happened was that one of the guys had split on me and told the commandant that I was involved. All I was trying to do was get food for us hungry guys. There was no sympathy, because we had decided to run back off our own bat. They removed the belt from my trousers and the shoelaces from my boots, and they locked me in the kas. I'd never been in a cell before. It is not somewhere you wanna be. There was one tiny barred window too high up to see out of. It was so bleak and I spent a horrible night. I was told I had committed a serious offence and I was being kla-ed aan and would be sent to DB in Pretoria after a trial in the morning. I was absolutely devastated. My OC, who despite having a very English name couldn't and wouldn't speak a word of English, liked me for some reason, and he pleaded my case before we were tried. He suggested hard labour rather than DB. I was stripped of rank, but at least I didn't get a record. All for scaling a wall to get Kentucky Fried Chicken.   – John, age 18

As religious objectors in prison, we were never really ill-treated as such. There were times when it was tough, but the hardship was mainly emotional, mental. They used to bolt our doors closed in the evenings, and all we had for a toilet was this little potty. There were three of us, all big guys, over six foot two. And Steve had the longest arms I've ever seen. He could reach through the bars above the door and slide open the bolt. Around two in the morning he would open our cell door. Then we would let everybody else out and all go to the toilet. One night, before I could get back to my cell, the guard came round with his Rottweilers. I flattened myself against the bathroom wall in terror. I think the only reason the dogs didn't smell me was because the guard was smoking.   – Alan, age 17

The World Outside

Jeremy, one of my best friends, died. But because I was doing Basics, we were not allowed *any* communication with the outside world. We were so isolated. The only information we were given was what they wanted us to know. Pretty quickly I would've believed anything they told us. If they had said there'd been a coup and we had to head out to quell it, I would've gone. I was later told about Jeremy's death and that I should've got the message, but that I wouldn't have been allowed to go anyway because he was not immediate family.

– Paul, age 17

There was this little line of phone boxes, tiekieboxes, next to the mess. I will never forget the sound of those *bee beep bee beeps* as the seconds counted down, knowing that the call to my mom or dad had only ten seconds, nine seconds, eight seconds before that dreaded *doo doo doo doo* ended it. The queues were not something that anyone can relate to today. There were only certain times that you could use the phone and there were hundreds of guys. Everybody wanted to use the phones. There was no allocation of time; it was a free-for-all, but if anyone took too long we would all start chirping. If we were loud enough and insistent enough, the guy would hang up. I'm also sad to say, but there were guys who really wanted to get out of home, not necessarily to the military, just out. It made me realise how fortunate I was to have the family I did. They never raised a hand to me.   – Paul, age 18

On the first Sunday, we were all called together on the parade ground. Instructions were shouted and the guys ran all over the place into new groups to go to church. I went to the nearest group, not knowing it was the NG Kerk. Picture this soutpiel with a red helmet in the NG Kerk. I never made it to the church – the rank pulled me out of the platoon and I was drilled until church finished. The dog tags I was issued for the Border read 'Baptist'. I had never seen the inside of a Baptist church in my life. Of course, they refused to change my denomination. — **Brett, age 18**

I was so happy on Sundays during Basic Training 'cause we all got out on church pass. This meant tea and cake. I was and still am Anglican. We were one of the smaller groups and used to attend the evening service. We had some time off to prepare, to shine our boots, to shower, and were then marched in our browns in our group right up to the church door, with the MPs driving up and down making sure we didn't disappear. After the service we got tea and cake. The grannies made us tea and cake. It was so — when you are in that military environment — I just don't think anyone will ever understand how it feels when you are so completely immersed, so surrounded by everything military and people with a military mentality, to be able to see a woman wearing normal clothes, even if it was the colonel's wife. It was an escape. An escape from the regime of discipline, the 'Ja Korporaal', 'Nee Korporaal'. — **Paul, age 18**

Each company had a *posparade* area. We would be called outside, and the corporals would get this big bag of mail. They were bastards. They would open our mail, and sometimes they would tear the letters in half, not into little pieces so you couldn't read it, just once in half. The guy's name would be read out, but before they gave you your post, you had to *sak* for push-ups. For every letter you got, you had to do push-ups. They made it very difficult for guys who got letters from girlfriends. Chicks would put lipstick kisses, or little sayings and things, on the backs of envelopes. I do recall them occasionally opening these letters and reading them out to us to embarrass the troep. It was hell hanging around until you got dismissed, 'cause you were not allowed to open them there. — **Paul, age 18**

One of the best, best, best days of my life at that time was 14 August 1983. My mom, dad, sister and brother came to visit me in Pretoria. You get Visitor's Day before you even get pass. This was the first and it was long overdue. They lined us up, and when they dismissed us, all 240 of us started running for the car park where our families were waiting. My mom started crying when she saw me. She had packed lunch, roast chicken and potatoes, and we picnicked on the rugby field. — **Nick, age 20**

I was so looking forward to seeing my parents and girlfriend. It was the first time they were allowed to visit us. We were to wear our summer step-outs, which always looked really smart: short-sleeved beige shirt, name badge on the chest, tailored coffee-coloured trousers with a smart bronze belt with a square buckle, green beret and smart shoes. Full step-outs also looked very cool. They comprised a long-sleeved shirt, tie, step-out jacket with large shiny convex silver buttons, and the shield-shaped unit flash – ours, 7 SAI, depicted a Rooikat – worn on the top of the arm, and the same green beret with the bokkop and unit balkie. But I didn't get to wear anything that made me look cool or smart. I got a fungal infection on my testicles, and when they came to visit I was lying in the hospital totally naked with my legs open. It was not lekker. — **Clint, age 18**

Luckily the possibility that a conscientious or religious objector would get six years didn't happen. After 1984 they made it six years, but three years of that was commuted. We never got leave or received any pay while we were in prison for those three years. We had a once-a-month family visit, which was for an hour, sometimes two, but sometimes reduced to 15 minutes. While I was in Bloemfontein, this was often at the whim of our sergeant major, who was an alcoholic. The one Christmas Day, there were about 15 of us, all Jehovah's Witnesses, and we were looking forward to seeing our families. We were also looking forward to the visit because it was the only time of year we were allowed sweets. Some of us had parents who had driven up from Durban, which was an eight-hour trip then. We were standing in front of the offices and could see our parents through the gate. Next thing, the sergeant major, who was stone drunk, comes up and tells us that the visit is off and we can't see our parents. You know we Jehovah's Witnesses are a peaceful bunch, but that was the closest I've ever seen any of us come to rioting!   – Alan, age 17

My greatest fear in the army was that leave would be cancelled. Weekend Pass meant everything, and if there was just one speck of dust in your rifle, it could be cancelled. Even after parade, just before you went on leave, you were still scared leave would be cancelled. Until you were out of the camp gates, you were scared.   – Paul, age 17

I was one of the few people to go home during Basics. It just so happened that I was awarded my Springbok Scout Award while we were away for the two weeks' compulsory bush training during Basics. So not only did I get to go home during Basics, but it was also while everyone was roughing it in the bush! I was allowed to go, but I had to go in browns. I remember thinking how paraat I already was, after only a few weeks in the military. Compared to the Scouts, we were the *manne*! Two nights in bed at home, hot showers, cooked meals, time to relax while all my mates were stuck in the bush. Part of you thinks, shame, but the other part thinks, uh-uh, self-preservation. If I can do something to make my life a little easier, fuck my mates. But I remember going back to hell. I'd been out of it for two and a half days. I'd got out of the cycle and everyone else was used to it by now. It was pouring with rain, it was wet, and we didn't have tents, only a groundsheet and a poncho. The transition from a nice cosy bed, having a lie-in, to that – it was like switching a switch from on to off.   – Paul, age 18

     AN UNPOPULAR WAR

The best thing about the army was being out on pass. You're young, you're fit, you've got no cares, and most people treat you really nicely because you are doing your bit for the country and they make allowances for you. If you get drunk and throw up on somebody's carpet, they'll say, 'Shame man, he's out on pass.' I found that even girls' parents were more accommodating.   – **Paul, age 17**

When I joined the army for three years' short service, I was young, dumb and full of cum. I was also 246 pounds and 5'11. After 12 weeks of training in Heidelberg, I went home to the farm for my first leave. One of the guys had an Opel Manta, and a bunch of us chipped in for petrol, which was difficult to get because of the petrol restrictions in the 1970s. We had to drive at 80 kph. Eventually, about 4 a.m., we got into Somerset East. My brother picked me up and took me home. My boet hadn't said a word to alert my folks. My ol' lady came to the door and said, 'Hi soldier, how are you?' I was then 6'3 and I'd lost 78 pounds. My old lady didn't know who the hell I was! I said, 'Hi mom,' and she burst into tears and said, 'What have they done to my little boy?' and all that sort of shit. The first thing she did was cook me a huge breakfast: bacon, eggs, sausage, toast and tomato. I think she tried to put those 78 pounds back immediately.
    – **Ric, age 18**

I was still a recruit and had only been in the army, in Oudtshoorn, for about two months. I was sent there because I was a teacher. All teachers, whether they had a degree or a diploma, were sent to Oudtshoorn to do the Officer's Course, the SADF mentality being that teachers were born leaders. If you were good enough to lead in the classroom, you were good enough to lead troops! During the JL phase of the course, they held rugby trials for the various units. They wanted to pick three sides to go to Port Elizabeth to play rugby for Infantry School as a pre-season opener. I made selection, and off we went to PE to play rugby for the weekend against EP Command. It was the first time I had left base other than to go to the Catholic church, which was off the base. It would be the first time I would see civilians! Women! Real life! We played the PE sides, and they let us go out that evening. I knew the area and we all went to Lilly's Pub at the Holiday Inn, where I got chatting to this girl, and, y'know, things went well. Very nice. But there was a problem. She didn't have her own place, neither of us had a car, and we needed somewhere to go. The only place was back on the base. EP Command was much slacker than Oudtshoorn regarding security, so it was easy to get her in through the main gate 'cause they had civilians in and out all the time and it was very, very late at night. We were staying in this long bungalow-like barracks, because we were just visitors to the base. So I took her into the dorm where all the guys were sleeping and we did the business as quietly as we could, somehow without waking up the other 29 guys. But now I had a big problem: how to get her home. She stayed in Northend, which was miles away, on the other side of PE. There was only one thing to do. The oke on duty had to know there were three visiting sides from Oudtshoorn, so I put on my overall and went to the gate and said to the guard on duty, 'Ek is Luitenant Hummel! Waar's die diensbestuurder?' [I am Lieutenant Hummel! Where's the duty driver?]. He came to attention, saluted me and said, 'Moenie worry nie, Luitenant, ek sal hom roep' [Don't worry, Lieutenant, I'll call him]. I instructed the duty driver to 'Vat hierdie meisie huis toe' [Take this girl home], and that's what happened. Just like that she was outta there and he took her all the way to her house about 30, 40 kilometres away. The story about me bringing a girl back into base, and me, with no rank whatsoever, impersonating an officer, got out, and I thought I was in for big shit. I could be thrown off the course and even sent to DB. The major who took us on our tour was a real hard-ass, and a few days after it had all happened, the story got back to him. He walked up to me, tapped me on the shoulder and said, 'Mooi gedoen' [Well done].   – **Stof, age 24**

There was this little hole-in-the-wall shop on the base in Voortrekker-hoogte. Absolutely tiny. A café we called die snoepie. It only opened at certain times and it ran out of everything all the time. They'd blow the whistle three times at the end of parade, and if you weren't one of the first troops of the hundreds and thousands rushing to buy Cokes and smokes, forget it. They had a telephone as well, but the bloody thing was always out of order.   – **Paul, age 18**

Fear and Loathing

On the second day of my army life, the sergeant major noticed that instead of one crease line down the front of my trouser leg, there were two or three lines. These 'tramlines', as he called them, caused the sergeant major to scream right into our ears about how he would 'sny jou keel, daarin afklim, en op jou hart kak' [cut your throat, climb down it, and shit on your heart]. Although we thought it was not a bad effort for our first attempt at ironing, his words inspired us to make sure our clothes were properly ironed. The next day he made us all 'march' through the dam and then 'swim' across the red sands of the parade ground – his idea of a joke. It was a rude and fast awakening to the complete power that those in charge were going to have over us for the next two years. Initially I thought these people were clowns, but, as time passed, I realised how they were able to take young men from all walks of life and mould us into like-minded characters. We soon believed that the good of the country took precedence over individual rights, and that all we had held sacred about our lives was under threat from the evil Communist empire that was brainwashing 'our blacks' to rise up against us.   **– Chris, age 17**

Our platoon sergeant was called Fires 'cause of his blood-red hair. He was Afrikaans, and he was particularly resentful that he was an NCO and hadn't been selected as an officer. The qualities necessary to be a leader are inborn; you can't take someone with minimum ability and transform him into a good leader. So he, as a failed officer and only an NCO, was particularly cruel. He liked to strip you of your dignity, and his training methods were very harsh. During them he liked to yell things like, 'Ek sal jou nek afsny en in jou keel afkots' [I'll slit your neck and vomit down your throat], or another favourite he yelled at you when you returned from leave was, 'Ek sal jou suster se vingers in vishoeke verander en hulle in jou neus opdruk en jou breins uitpluk' [I'll turn your sister's fingers into fish hooks and stick them up your nose and pull out your brains]. In our platoon we had this Portuguese guy. He was short, fat and unfit. We called him Vetseun. He was so big, he must have had a glandular problem or something. In training they always told us Vetseun had to come first. You can imagine how difficult this was. One day we were doing a section of the conventional warfare course, house penetrations and such, and were on a forced march in full battle gear, so we had everything with us and on us. We reach this bridge and wait for Vetseun, who is about 150 metres behind us. He is white, just these black eyes in his face, his steel helmet is skew on his head and hanging crookedly over one eye, he's dragging his rifle, sweating and, honestly, he looks like he's already dead. And Fires just strips. In one move he grabs Vetseun as he reaches us, and he whips a tokkeltou around Vetseun's neck as he kicks his legs out from under him and pushes him over the bridge. He had him hanging there for a good few seconds before some of the senior officers rushed over and told him to let him go. Fires drops him and Vetseun falls into the little stream below. It wasn't much of a distance, and I think the water revived him somewhat. This happened in front of about 30 guys, but not one of us said a word. Our training was already so ingrained, and we were so aware of the power that the NCOs had. Fires was busted down to a one-liner, and he lost his instructor status.   **– Clint, age 18**

Guys would shiver with fear when just talking about this sergeant major in Ladysmith. He was a maniac. We wore doibies with a big coloured mark on the front to depict which platoon we were with. Echo was yellow, Charlie was orange. The guys on light duty had white to say they were sickly boys and couldn't be chased around. We were drilling when I saw this sergeant major hit a guy so hard on his doibie that it broke. He had this gleam in his eyes, like an axe murderer. We were extremely scared of him.   **– Nick, age 20**

What stands out for me is that very young people were in charge. Our corporals and lieutenants were only 18, 19 years old, yet they were in charge of hundreds of men. The major was younger than 30. The other thing I recall was the instructors' lack of humanity. I could never drill a guy until he vomited, or shout at someone who was injured to keep going. We were very lucky in that we had a very decent instructor, a corporal from South West, who would group us together every night and have a chat to us, like a big brother. But as nice as he was at night, he was ruthless during the day. He had very shiny inner ears and we used to joke that he boned his ears! Then there was this other corporal, with short-man syndrome, I'm sure. He used to come up when we were standing at attention or during parade and whisper in our ear, 'Wil jy my moer?' [Do you want to hit me?]. The guys said no, of course, but the one time he asked me, and I replied, 'I'm not allowed to.' That just threw him. He said he'd take off his rank and meet me. I said, 'Corporal, make the date and time and I'll be there.' It never happened.   – **Tallies, age 17**

One of our majors was not particularly well liked. The guys thought his leadership was rather arrogant, but I thought he was an okay chap. We were jumping in this remote area and we all landed miles away from this small dam. Oddly enough, the major, who was using a steerable [parachute] landed far from all of us, right in the middle of the dam, and he drowned. It was very strange, because he had jettisoned his emergency chute – we found it at the edge of the dam – and there had been no wind to blow him off course. To this day we don't know the reason behind his freakish death. I heard that a whole company held a braai to celebrate his death. I found that quite disturbing.   – **John, age 18**

It couldn't have happened to a better – or rather a worse – person, and I swear it wasn't on purpose. I don't think. This lieutenant was hated, absolutely hated. He was such a dick. He just happened to be standing behind the Buffel I was driving. He was screaming at the troops lined up to get into the Buffel. The vehicle's exhaust stands quite high, and as he opened his mouth, I started the engine. This huge ball of wet black diesel belched out and covered the whole top of his body. You know those cartoons where there's just a black sooty face and gleaming white eyes and teeth? He looked just like that, like a cartoon. I laughed so hard I hit my head. He didn't find it so funny and jumped up on the wheel and klapped me with his fist. But it was worth it, he was such a dick.   – **Brett, age 18**

There was a huge competition between SSB – Panzer School – and Parabats. And the war between them involved putting anything heavy – irons, bricks, stones, anything like that – into your balsak and going over to beat the shit out of the guys. You had to be wearing your jumpers – these were very heavy boots, much heavier than the usual military issue boots – and you would climb over the wall to get them. Sometimes it was like a war, with one company attacking another. Both groups thought they were elite, but the Panzer guys weren't an elite unit; the Bats were the elite unit. I suppose jealousy sparked the fights.   – **John, age 18**

Sometimes you would get a guy who just wasn't performing or toeing the line or who didn't bathe – whatever – there was a problem with him. Then the guys would call a meeting. They'd put him in the middle and tell him that he had better listen up, 'cause he hadn't been keeping himself clean. 'Either you sort yourself out or tomorrow we are going to throw you in the shower and scrub you with the floor brushes.' It usually worked. But, if not, that guy could be sleeping and suddenly wake up to guys hitting him with a balsak filled with boots and stuff.   – **Nick, age 20**

We had a rat in our bungalow. This guy would rat on us to our platoon sergeant. But he went too far when he piemped us out for getting a few six-packs. It was the end of Basics, and to celebrate we were allowed two beers, but we had bartered and organised a six-pack for each of the six English-speaking members of the platoon. We had a contact in SAWI and he got the beers for us. This rat must have seen us take them into the bungalow, 'cause he wasn't around while we were drinking them. Of course, after Basics you are so fit and you haven't touched alcohol for six weeks, so you get absolutely trashed on just a few beers. I was finished after just my third. The corporals were smart. They waited until we had passed out and then woke us all around 2 a.m. We got such an opfok. From 3 a.m. until 10 a.m. the next morning we had to leopard-crawl in only our shorts and T-shirts, cradling our rifles. We had to crawl on the lower parade ground that was just sand, stones and thorns. My knees, elbows and toes were stuffed. The entire platoon got the opfok, during which the rat's name came out. We had our suspicions, but until then we hadn't known for certain who had ratted us out. Not being able to trust someone is a major problem in a bungalow where you depend on one another. We decided it was time for him to 'get an orientation'. That night each of us put a bar of soap into a sock and each person hit the rat just once. Twenty-nine hits were enough. Suffice to say he became a reasonable human being after that.   – Clint, age 18

Of course you must remember this was the early eighties. It was illegal to be a homosexual; you could be arrested for sodomy. I was so scared that my sexual orientation would be discovered. I also thought I was the only gay man in the world. I hadn't met others like me. I was terrified of being exposed, of being victimised, and I was even more terrified that the army would find out somehow. I went to see a doctor for some medical problem. I sensed that he was gay, and although I couldn't tell him I was gay, I knew he probably suspected it. So I told him I was fearful of going to the army without really revealing why. He wrote out a medical certificate for me, claiming that I suffered

AN UNPOPULAR WAR

from rheumatism in my joints. First prize was that this would get me a medical exemption from the two years' National Service. Second prize was to get a classification of G4K3. I got the latter, which meant I was exempt from physical training and was assigned only to light duties and admin work. Although I was issued a rifle, I spent two years in the army without firing a single shot, not even for training like target practice. It was a bit strange because I was there for two years, but never felt part of the game. I was assigned to a platoon in 1 SAI, HQ Company, in Bloemfontein. We were a company of failures, so we were told. We were all either not medically fit or unfit mentally for active duty.   – Rick, age 18

I would wake up and he would be in my bed. The first time he raped me was after a party. He was a married corporal. He even said that one of his children was 'ours', because he was thinking of me while he was having sex with his wife and the child was conceived. He said he knew me from Oudtshoorn. I recognised his face, but he hadn't been in the same bungalow as me. He remembered all sorts of details and incidents involving me, which I had no recollection of. I was too scared to report this corporal, because I knew being homosexual counted against me, and I knew my superiors would not believe it was rape. The only person I told was this social worker. It was strange, because she was counselling him and his wife because they were having marital problems, so she was able to advise me on how to handle certain things with him.

It was after this incident that I began a relationship with one of my troops. They were coloured and I was white. I had completed Junior Leadership and I chose to train coloured troops. I was a one-pip lieutenant who managed a section of the Cape Coloured Corps. It was the least popular posting. I chose it because I wanted to be close to Joburg, and Vereeniging is only an hour's drive from there, and because I had no desire to go to the Border. Most of the others chose a Border posting. They believed in the government, believed in why they were there, and they wanted to go to the Border to fight the enemy. I think they also wanted to go to the Border because there was a lot more freedom there. Also more drinking and more pay – they got danger pay – and they wanted to be able to say they had been on the Border. They were more paraat. But my motives were less political. When I was in Basics, I saw that the officers had better food and accommodation, and that's what I wanted. Something a little more civilised, something to remove me from the masses.

I immediately felt at home with my coloured troops because they were volunteers. They were not there because they believed in the war. They were there for financial reasons. Most of them were very poor and very poorly educated. They were often sole breadwinners. There was a lot of drug abuse and alcoholism. I became very involved in programmes to help them. I also took abuse for defending them and was called names like 'kafferboetie'. The coloured troops always came second to the white troops. They had to eat after the white troops; they were second for everything: the TV room and the telephones. I protected my troops. It was quite funny, really, from trying so hard to get out of being in the army, it became my life. I seldom even went home on weekends. I socialised with my troops and got to see what life was like across the colour bar. It got so that I never even saw people as different colours.

I guess I was trying to save this one guy. He had a lot of problems – drink, drugs – and because of the amount of time I spent with him and all the help he needed, we developed a relationship. It was exceptionally hard dealing with the corporal's sexual abuse when my troop, the one I was having a relationship with, had an accident. I had insisted that he go out on patrol. In those days we were deployed mainly to patrol in the townships, and I knew I could have easily got him out of it because he was experiencing withdrawal symptoms as he was coming off the drugs, but I said he had to go on patrol. I thought it was the best thing for him. There was some accident and he fell off the Samil.

He was taken to 1 Mil. His family flew up from Cape Town to see him, and it was really hard just being his lieutenant and not being able to tell them how much he meant to me. He died of his injuries. That was 20 years ago, and I haven't had a long-term relationship since then. The abuse from the corporal only ended when my National Service did. — **Anonymous**

The showers always ran out of hot water early, long before everyone had a chance to shower. If you were late, you got cold water. But we used to alert the guys who were showering and announce our presence by screaming and shouting that we were coming. It usually worked, and even the showers that were full were empty by the time we entered the place! If someone remained, we would give him 'the stare down there'. That usually worked, although some of our friends were beaten up for doing it. Talk about exploiting homophobia. — **Rick, age 18**

Ever heard of the Tempe Tigers? That was the name given to a girl's reformatory outside Bloemfontein. There were so many weird stories about them. Guys who had got too close to the fence and had been chained there and had their dicks cut off. Lots of strange stories about the Tempe Tigers! We used to run past their school and we were warned to never, ever go anywhere near the fence or them, or something awful would happen, like getting your dick bitten off. This was pre-Bobbitt days, but I never forgot all the wild stories about them! They were notorious. — **John, age 18**

One of my duties for a while was to assist the chaplain at 1 SAI. I ran the coffee bar next to the canteen and mess. The coffee was free and the room was a nice one, quiet and private. At the end of the evening, after the last troop had left, we – the Sisterhood, as we called ourselves – made the place our own. The room offered us gay guys, and the few straight guys who didn't mind being amongst us gays, the opportunity to just relax and be alone. We hung blankets over the windows because the curtains didn't close properly and people were always trying to peer in. We played music, played pool, chatted and enjoyed having time to ourselves. Then this rumour started that we were having orgies in there. I told the chaplain I would rather leave than bring shame to his office. I think he knew his clerk might be a homosexual, but he never said anything. That ended my short career working for Jesus.   – Rick, age 18

One time I went to the charge office to collect our letters. I witnessed a big prisoner beating up a smaller prisoner while the sergeant major looked on. There was just blood everywhere. The large prisoner looked at me; I looked at the sergeant major and just shook my head and turned around and walked away. I was so sickened by it. The next day the sergeant major came past our tent and said, 'Daardie vuilgoed is dood' [That rubbish is dead]. We knew he had been beaten to death, even though the official story was that he had hanged himself.

– Alan, age 17

Black and White

I volunteered for Parabats. The guys came around with their maroon berets and said we could be part of this elite unit. It was all a big adventure, and we bought into it. There were five requirements: you had to have a matric; you had to be G1K1; you had to belong to a recognised religious group, like Anglican, NGK or whatever – if you were atheist you were out – you had to pass the intreetoetse, which were physical fitness tests; and the fifth thing was an interview. You stood there in your underpants so they, a doctor and some PF officers, could look at your physique and check you didn't have flat feet or anything, and you answered their questions, like why you wanted to join. Oh, and if you had any tattoos, you were out. No tattoos. It was a 14-day selection course held at 1 Parachute Battalion in Bloemfontein. Physically it was very tough, but they did it in such a way that there was more opfok than rondfok. It really was unbelievably tough, but it was very positive. The whole objective was to weed out those less physically tough. Out of about 100 that started, there were about 27 left at the end of the PT course. Then there was the jump training, and after two months or so you got your wings and qualified as a paratrooper.

On the course was a coloured guy, a Captain C from the South African Coloured Corps. He was one of the 27 left, and his whole mission was to get into the Reconnaissance Regiment – the Recces. They told him that if he went and did the course and qualified as a paratrooper, they would then put his name forward to go to the Reconnaissance Regiment. Another of the 27 was Captain L, whose mission was to become the first South African to have two wings: air force wings and paratrooper wings. Captain L, who was a helicopter pilot, Captain C and myself became really good friends. When we finished the course and received our wings, I said let's go to the Spur in Bloemfontein for a burger and some beers, y'know, to celebrate.

And C said he didn't want to go. We said, no, come along, and he replied no. At first we thought it was maybe a money issue. He said, no, he doesn't want to go because he'd be embarrassed. We said, what the fuck do you mean you'd be embarrassed? And he said they won't let him into the Spur. So I said to him, kak man, but he insisted they wouldn't let him in. L, who was quite windgat, said he was a captain in the air force, and he would make such a scene that of course they would let him in. C said, no, what will happen is that there will be this huge palaver and issue, and he'd be too embarrassed because no ways would they let him into the Spur. And I thought, fuck, this is 1985 and they won't let him into the Spur 'cause he's coloured. I just thought, here is this guy who is a captain in the military who wants to become a Special Forces soldier and he's not allowed into the Spur! It was the first time it dawned on me that, fucking hell, this apartheid thing was a real issue.   – John, age 18

I was surprised at how racially integrated the army was. In the mid-eighties we shared all facilities – mess, ablutions, sleeping quarters – but the army still had its own form of segregation. We didn't shower or eat with other ranks, whether black or white. Black officers were few and far between, as most officers were white, but the segregation was only rank-wise. Admittedly, in the mess, blacks usually ate together, but there was just as much segregation between the SAAF and the Engineers. The air force guys sat at their own tables with their fresh bread and stuff.   – Paul, age 17

My crew on *Fleur*, a diving, training and torpedo recovery craft, were very tight. We looked out for one another. The crew went ashore in Port Elizabeth and I went off to join my girlfriend. Most of the crew went to a hotel bar to listen to a band. One of the coloured chefs could sing really well, and when the guys asked the band if they'd mind him singing a song, they said it would be great. So he's on the stage singing when the manager walks in and says, 'Get that kaffir off the stage.' Well, I tell you, the navy guys – coloured, Indian, white – took that bar apart. They trashed it completely and then bolted for the ship. We had a golden rule – always make it back to the ship. We could stay out all night, but we had to be back in time, looking presentable, for colours (raising of the flag) at 8 a.m. I got back to a dockside filled with police cars and flashing lights after my quiet romantic night out. All our guys had made it back from the hotel and were lined up at the ship's railing, looking down at the police, who were there wanting to arrest them. Guys in blue on one side, and guys in blue on another. But on a ship the captain has complete jurisdiction, and he decides whether or not to hand over crew. Needless to say, he didn't order anybody off the ship.   – Louis, age 17

Right down at the bottom of the barracks of Bravo Squadron of Tiffies in Voortrekkerhoogte there was a very nondescript but very important building on the edge of the lower parade ground. It was the Bravo Squadron donkey boiler. In those days we still had coal-fired water heating for our showers, and this building held the coal, the heaters and a small room for a black guy whose name I didn't even bother to find out, whose job it was to fire up the donkey boiler so that all the whitey conscripts could have some form of lukewarm water early in the morning and late at night. He was known as Kaffir. He wore an army overall, and whenever the water went cold, it was Kaffir's fault. I'll never forget the corporals – who were only one-liners – in Bravo and most of whom slept in the squadron bungalow – calling Kaffir out at all times of the day and night to fire up the donkey so they could have warm water. I was sitting next to my bungalow one day when I heard one of the corporals shouting for Kaffir to make the water warm. This old black guy, I reckon he was about 40, came out in an army overall; the corporal, who must have been 18, made him stand to attention in front of him and said to him, 'Wat is jy?' [What are you?]

And the elderly black guy said, 'Ek is 'n kaffer, Korporaal' [I am a kaffir, Corporal]. Everyone laughed, and the corporal said, 'Maak die water warm, kaffer' [Heat up the water, kaffir]. He said, 'Ja, ek sal dit doen want ek is 'n kaffer' [Yes, I'll do it because I am a kaffir]. He went and did it. I remember wondering a few hours later whether he took the abuse because he was in fact an ANC plant in the camp who was reporting on training and troop movements, and then I just thought, ag fuck it, it's not my problem.   – **Rob, age 19**

Propaganda and Subversion

Part of our re-training was a deeper level of indoctrination. I remember being shown two pictures. The first was of a beautiful African woman in tribal dress. At 17 years old and in an all-male environment, any bare breasts were enough to make you fall in love. The second photograph was of the same woman, except now she had no breasts – just two bloody cavities and her face grimaced in pain. The horror was nauseating. Of course, 'they' – the enemy – had done this to her. It was our duty to make sure this didn't and couldn't happen again, and it was our duty to make sure the enemy did not get to Johannesburg to do the same thing to our girlfriends and mothers.   **– Chris, age 17**

During the day, you were generally out doing mortar training, on the parade ground or whatever, but at times you were indoors, in the TV room, for Com Ops. This was the SADF's idea of indoctrination. Two Com Ops officers were attached to a company, and they had two slots a week to put across the political message of the day. It was meant to be Communications, but it was really just political indoctrination. They talked to us about the Red Threat – die Rooi Gevaar – gave history lessons on Communism in Angola, and told us how Africa was falling apart and what the threat was to South Africa. It was to justify why we were in the army.

The worst job must have been being a Com Ops officer having to address a group of teachers. The teachers, particularly those from Wits and other more liberal universities like Rhodes, gave them a lot of shit, like questioning why they were there. Then you had the teachers from Pukke or Tukkies, who were a lot more verkramp. To give them credit, the officers did try to promote dialogue, but they had a message to get across. A lot of guys were too scared to speak their minds or question things too closely, 'cause they might have been labelled as troublemakers and get kicked off the course. We were careful about what we said. I didn't contribute much, 'cause I didn't want to get into shit.

They used the TV to show us footage of trouble in the townships, necklacings and that sort of thing. They told us it was not the SADF doing those terrible things, it was the township people themselves doing it to one another: Xhosas versus Zulus and hostel dwellers versus the township residents. We saw quite a lot of videos justifying why the SADF presence was required in the townships. The video channel was linked so that five companies in different rooms could watch the same thing at the same time. Our group of 50 had finished listening to the lecture and was waiting for the video to start. The officer switched the TV on to the video channel and there was a porn video playing! The okes went berserk! You just heard every single bungalow full of men erupt into cheering. There was this shout of 'Yeah!' from all the companies watching. They were so chuffed! The English okes loved it. Some of the Afrikaans guys had never seen anything like it before, and they left the room. The Com Ops oke looked at it for a while before turning it off. I never forgot that particular Com Ops session! Rumour had it that it was the dominee watching it in the video centre!

– Stof, age 24

Just after Basics I was sitting in a bar. Booze was so cheap. Three shots of Kahlua were 15 cents and the milk was free. A Long Tom was 30 cents. On your birthday you had to drink a lit Sambuca. But if you left it too long the glass got very hot and burnt your lips, and you walked around camp with these blistered lips. Anyway, some Dutchman turns to me and says, 'Hierdie land sal regkom wanneer ons een Engelsman en twee kaffers elke dag kan doodskiet' [This country will come right when we can shoot one Englishman and two kaffirs every day]. The only reason it was two kaffirs was because there were more of them than us Englishmen. I just shrugged and had another beer.

– Paul, age 17

I always knew I was going to prison for three years. My parents were Jehovah's Witnesses and I became one in my teens. It was three years in prison for my older brother, then me, and then my younger brother. It must have been very hard on my parents. But, the psyche at that time was so different. There was so much paranoia in the 1980s. It was the height of the Swart Gevaar. If you weren't part of the military, you were unpatriotic, a Communist and a coward. We even viewed those who went to university just to avoid conscription as compromising their principles. I mean, what happens when you finish? We had been brought up not to see any difference between blacks and whites, and I knew my beliefs wouldn't change and nor would my approach. I recall this one captain having a full go at me, calling me a coward and a Communist. I asked him what he would do if a terrorist jumped over the wall into his yard. He said he would shoot him. And if ten terrorists jumped over? He said he would shoot them. And a hundred? Shoot them. And a thousand? Well then, they would kill me, he replied. I explained that my faith and trust in a higher power would not change, no matter what the threat. But his would have to. I had a similar discussion with an MP lieutenant whom I met again many years later. He said he remembered our discussion and that I had said I wouldn't have to change my view, and he acknowledged that he had had to. No one could ever, ever have imagined things would turn out the way they did.   – Alan, age 17

I was an extremely good shot and was one of the State President's Guards chosen as a sharpshooter within the State President's Unit. I was given this magnificent R1 with an extended barrel, and day, night and telescopic sights. I also had a motorbike and didn't have to wear a helmet all of the time. The President, who was then PW Botha, had his own bodyguards, but when he travelled, say, between Parliament and his house, I had to follow at a distance. Or if he was delivering a speech at a stadium or something, I would be set up there before he got there. I was an 18-year-old guy using a high-powered rifle to protect the President. I had the responsibility of the decision to pull the trigger or not. I could kill without worrying about taking the shot or about the consequences of killing someone. The funny thing is, people always think you'd be looking for a black guy, but it wasn't the case. A white person would be able to get much closer to the President than a black. It's very strange looking back on it now. I was Level One security; I could go just about anywhere, do anything and no one would stop me. Being with the SPG, no one ever questioned you; there was this autonomy. It was exciting then, but looking at it now, at how much power I had, I mean, how did they know *I* wouldn't shoot the President?   – Brett, age 18

I was a religious objector and one day this guy arrived. He was a true conscientious objector. As a Jehovah's Witness, the main thing is we are neutral and not politically involved in anything. We don't believe in the ethic of war, so it was more of a religious thing, but this guy was a pacifist and didn't agree with the government and what they were doing. There was so much hype when he was brought into the military prison, because he was 'a Communist and a terrible person'. When I saw him, there was this short little guy who looked a little bit like Cat Stevens, and I thought: who could this guy be harmful to?
                                                            – Alan, age 17

After the Basic Training phase, the entire 1 SAI Battalion had a variety concert to lift up the morale of the troeps. Each platoon had to participate, and it was up to them how many troeps were involved: it could be just one person or the entire platoon. You could do anything – sing, dance, music, drama, opera – as long as it was 'above the belt'. One of the platoons decided to perform 'Beds are Burning' by the Aussie band Midnight Oil. It was a huge hit then. It was very funny watching a fake band miming and pretending to be Midnight Oil while a thousand troeps went mad, dancing and singing every word of the song. What was even funnier was that I had heard that Midnight Oil had apparently donated money from sales of the album on which the 'Beds are Burning' song appeared to the ANC. There the troeps and the brass were, all going mal to a group that was supporting the enemy. We all danced while not the beds, but the borders, *were* in fact burning. I found it very ironic.   – **Rick, age 18**

In our own way we supported the End Conscription Campaign and managed to do so in the army newspaper, *Uniform*. We would do record reviews, and we always chose to review a record put out by Shifty Records. They were very active in the ECC and produced many albums and songs that were staunchly anti-establishment and anti-conscription. 'Hou My Vas Korporaal' was not a lovely song about the strong bond between a troep and his corporal! They never twigged that the Englishmen, who were all former Rhodes students, were promoting and giving publicity to records known for their strong anti-war lyrics and sentiment. We also refused to cover the townships, which we justified by using their own rigid structure of rules and regulations against them. If we wrote about the township operations, we might accidentally leak COIN information, and that could jeopardise lives. We also stated that we could not go into the townships because we had not received any urban warfare training and would therefore be a liability. Hmmm. Yes, of course not, they concurred. Meanwhile, we hadn't received any bush warfare training either, and shouldn't have been allowed on the Border. We also got free movie tickets and packs from Ster-Kinekor, UIP and Nu Metro. Every Friday the new movies came out, and although we didn't go to previews, we could go and see a movie the day it was released. If the colonel came around on a Friday morning the office was always empty – we were out on a story – ja right, sitting in the dark scoffing popcorn, drinking Coke and watching movies.

          – **David, age 22**

They called us blou-jobs, because of the blue overalls we had to wear. We didn't conform to the military's dress code or rank, and didn't march or salute, because we were never part of the military. Saluting was viewed as a form of worshipful honour and we didn't partake in it. This created some interesting incidents. Two stand out in my mind. The first was this young lieutenant, fresh out of Officer's School, who saluted us in front of regular troops. They smiled because they could see what was coming. He couldn't believe it when no one saluted him back. He screamed at us and asked us why we weren't saluting him. Everyone started laughing at him then. Our mediator explained that as religious objectors, we didn't salute. He threw a fit! Screaming and threatening all sorts of things, like he would double our sentences. We started laughing even more, because we knew he couldn't do that. Then our sergeant major walked out and said, 'Luitenant! Wat maak jy met my blou-jobs?' [Lieutenant! What are you doing with my blue jobs?] He left us alone after that.

The second incident occurred while we were at 2 Military Prison and Brigadier de Munnik was the Tempe base commander. For some reason he always saluted us. He saluted everyone; I guess his military protocol was instinctive. We, the blou-jobs, were working on the bowling green and some military prisoners, guys who had gone AWOL and such, were working adjacent to us on the golf course. I was pruning roses or something when the brigadier arrived in his car with the staff sergeant, who was his driver. He got out and I waved and said, 'Goeiemôre, Brigadier.' He replied 'Goeiemôre, boys,' and saluted me. The military prisoners' eyes nearly popped out of their heads! They had no idea who we were, but word got out, and for weeks afterwards everyone was snapping salutes at us. We had to collect supplies from a Parabat base. When we jumped off the back of the Bedford truck, it was amazing, everyone was saluting and strekking us! Even months later it still continued. Once the sergeant major sent a chap to come and call me. He scratched on the tent and when I opened it, there was this chap standing to attention. He was so scared he wouldn't even look at me as he strekked, saluted and gave me the message! — Alan, age 17

Gyppoing

We had to guard this ammunition dump outside Potchefstroom, and a big deal was made of the fact that you weren't supposed to sleep on guard duty. We put a trip wire across the road a few kilometres away from where we were, in case the captain drove up to check on us. If he did, his car would trip the wire, which had cans attached to it, and the guy who was manning the wire would alert us and we'd be awake and paraat by the time he reached us. So we all had a good sleep while on duty. The big thing was to gyppo. Everything was about that. How do you get out of things? What can you do to get out of things? How can you make things easier for yourself?

I looked at all the sports that were available during Basics and I joined the long-distance running team. I worked out that the long-distance circuit was about five kilometres, so I ran it once and worked out my time, and then for the rest of Basics I ran out with the others and then ducked off. We ran from Ladysmith base down to the river, where I would duck off and go and sleep. I calculated the time I was expected back, set my alarm for the right time to wake up, and promptly fell asleep. It got me out of a lot of running and effort and nonsense.

– Martin, age 23

I fell asleep while we were doing camouflage training. They just never found me. I must have woken up in the bush two hours later. I got away with it by saying it wasn't my fault that they couldn't find me – I'd listened and applied what they told me. I had slapped on my Black Beauty, this thick horrible cammo paint that came in communal tubs, or, if you were lucky, you got your own tube. I'd made the stripes run from top left to bottom right, because that's the way that people tend to look for things. If you are looking for something in the bush, you must look right to left because that's an abnormal movement. Anyway,

I was in my browns, I'd picked straw, leaves and grass, and stuck them in my hat and web belt. They walked and drove around but couldn't find me in the long grass. Thank God they didn't drive one of those Samils over me.   – Paul, age 18

I was the Sports Officer and my duties for the entire week could be done in three quarters of an hour. All I had to do was type up a Sports Order and give it to the Captain of the Sports Office. It told him who was playing what. That was it, the sum total of my job. I think I had the best second year in the army of any man alive. No work (well, less than an hour a week), playing sports, doing what I loved and getting paid for it! But being Sports Officer still meant that I was a National Serviceman, and when we went away on a sports tour a PF guy always had to accompany us. This was an official standing order: any touring side had to have a PF member in charge. National Servicemen weren't permitted to escort other National Servicemen out and off base. They didn't trust them out on their own, and rightly so. We were about to leave for a cricket trip to Cape Town when the PF captain who was to supervise us had to pull out at the last minute because his wife was ill. Amazingly, the captain put me and another lieutie in charge of the group, and off we went to Youngsfield Air Force Base for seven days to play the three or four games against Stellenbosch, Boland and whom-ever else he had organised. Fifteen guys in a big army bus and we hit Cape Town. We had our own driver and own army bus. It was great. That bus was parked at Clifton beach for four of those seven days! It was also waiting outside nightclubs in the early hours of the morning. We had such a good time and played exactly two games. There was a little bit of trouble, though. One guy, a mad Natal farm boy, came out of a club in Rondebosch, very pissed, and walked up to a policeman and pointed at his SAP badge and told him it stood for Soek Altyd Poes [Always looking for poes] and Poes Altyd Skaars [Poes always scarce]. The policeman grabbed him and locked him up for the night in the cells for drunk and disorderly behaviour. Fortunately, it didn't get back to base. I would have been in huge shit.   **– Stof, age 24**

The State President's Guard's uniforms were fantastic. For guard duty at the President's house, the opening of Parliament and ceremonies, et cetera, we would wear a grey formal uniform with gold and brass trims, and a special helmet. The weapon was an old .303 which could only fire blanks. Some of us were selected to perform in a special drill squad. In this squad we wore a green and gold uniform with a hackle, a black ostrich plume on the peak. This squad went through serious drilling and training, sometimes standing in the rain all night and not being allowed to move, in order to perform shows in front of visiting dignitaries and at various state functions. We probably looked like a drum majorette squad, only with rifles and bayonets. This one night we were in green and gold at the Pretoria Show, and instead of getting back on the bus, two of us sneaked off. I was with a chaplain's son, and he was really the wild one! We met these two girls and went on all the rides. There we were, in full State President's Guard uniform, going on the roller coaster. At that time it was against the law to wear this particular military uniform on civvy street. If you wore a combination of browns, cammo, or any military uniform, you could be arrested. But what the hell? We went off to Jacqueline's, an absolute classic nightclub in Pretoria. I still had my cap on, with the big ostrich plume. We got into several fights with the guys there. All the fights were about girls. We thought we were heroes. We caught a lift out of town to the base, and then we had to try to sneak into Voortrekkerhoogte; there's electrical fencing, lots of guards, everything. We found a place where there was a bit of a gap under the fence. So we took off our uniforms to keep them clean, and, dressed only in our underpants, we dug a hole under the fence big enough for us to get through. We still had to get past the guards. There was none of that 'stop, who goes there?' stuff then,

AN UNPOPULAR WAR

only trigger-happy *roofies* on guard duty. It was very exciting, but also very frightening. — **Brett, age 18**

It was always about manipulating the system – how to gyppo. Everyone did it. What varied was the degree of success. Some guys managed to gyppo and score an afternoon nap or extra food or avoid guard duty, something small like that. I outsmarted the system and scored a four-month-long beach holiday. I was at Port Elizabeth Air Force Base on behalf of *Uniform*, the army's in-house newspaper, and was actually walking to the Flossie that would take me back to HQ in Pretoria when a guy asked me if I was there to cover the story on the paddle-skiers. Interested in anything that would keep me out of the office, I said I was. But when I went to speak to the guy about the story, he thought I was there for the job of accompanying and reporting on the paddle-skiers' trip around South Africa's coast. How could I turn that down? I was one of five people who acted as the support group to the two paddle-skiers. They had sold their idea of paddling South Africa's entire coastline from Alexander Bay to Kosi Bay to the army under the pretence of breaking the open-water paddling record. I doubt such a record even existed. Their stated intention was that it would be good press, promote a healthy lifestyle and bring glowing commendations to the military. Their hidden intention was to spend their National Service doing something they loved. The army bought it, and we spent four months driving along the coastline to meet up with the paddle-skiers on hundreds of different beaches.

We were allowed into areas that were off-limits to the general public: missile-testing sites with pristine beaches littered with massive cowrie shells, beaches that no one ever visited. It was paradise on earth. We dived, snorkelled, fished, swam and gorged on freshly caught cray-fish. We grew our hair. We were tanned and fit and having a helluva lot of fun. We pooled our S&T and bought booze. I was filing stories to the newspapers and radio stations every day, and as our trip progressed and became more widely known, the reception committees grew larger. At Lambert's Bay there was a mayoral reception and they were so proud to serve us crayfish. We'd been eating crayfish for days, and what we really wanted was red meat. That's how spoilt we were. I remember that we could also eat free at the Spur, as they were one of the sponsors. I knew their menu backwards. Our trip had no hard and fast deadline; as long as they kept paddling and I kept filing stories, we were legitimately beating the system. We stayed on in Knysna for days. There was no set schedule. I remember filing a story about whales surfacing next to the paddle-skiers near the Storms River mouth, and it made the front page of the *Sunday Star*. I was putting my journalism degree to good use.

Once we stopped at a very secluded, densely wooded beach and put up the orange flags so the paddle-skiers could see us. When they pulled in, we hauled their double ski out of the sea and propped it, along with the spare ski, against a tree where we thought they wouldn't be found, and headed back to where we were staying. The next day was very windy and the guys said it was pointless trying to paddle, so we took a drive and heard on an East Coast Radio news bulletin that the two paddle-skiers were missing. Someone had found the paddle-skis and reported the paddlers missing. It was very weird hearing that on the radio. How could anyone think they were missing if they found the skis ashore? Idiots. We had to call the media and tell them that the paddle-skiers were fine. The army was not amused, and the Officer Commanding who was in charge of us got into serious shit.

I'll never forget the one hot morning we were lying in the shallows, with the warm waves lapping against us, and behind us lay a beautiful forest. It was paradise. There was no one around for miles, and I felt like I was in a Mainstay commercial. I looked at my watch. It was 10 a.m. I knew that back at HQ the troeps were on the hot, dusty parade ground being yelled at by a corporal, and there I was, lying in the warm sea. The funny thing was that if someone had come to me at that moment and told me I could leave the army but I had to go right then, I would have gone in an instant. I just hated being in the army so much. I would leave, even though I had the opportunity of months of doing nothing other than visiting pristine beaches, drinking and eating crayfish and touring around the coastline.

By the time we reached Port Elizabeth, the paddle-skiers' home town, there was a flotilla of small craft to welcome us. It was unbelievable; thousands of people were there. At first we thought it was just fortuitous that our arrival coincided with some large event, but we discovered that they were all there to welcome our paddle-skiers!

The end was a bit of an anti-climax. The finish was not far from the Mozambique border, and for security reasons they didn't want to let any of the support crew in. I said that as the journalist I had to be there. They escorted me in with 4x4s, and we were in a small inlet as the two guys paddled in. They pulled their paddle-ski up, looked around, and one of them said, 'Okay, let's go home.'

There is not a beach in South Africa that I haven't been to, courtesy of the Defence Force, and I'm sure my four-month-long gyppo was one of the longest. It sure beat merely gyppoing an afternoon nap.

– David, age 22

We had this surprise evaluation on our medical equipment and gear. This guy looks inside our ambulance. There are four bunks. On one bunk I had a surfboard and on another a dive kit. He was not impressed and gave me ten minutes to sort it out. I carried a dive kit with me 'cause my sergeant major was a diver and he could organise dives in the prohibited military area at Saldanha. They were very strict about who could dive and what you could bring out of the sea, but we managed to get permission to dive and bring out some crayfish. We wanted them for the dinner we were hosting for the evaluators that evening. We were hoping to impress them with a little crayfish cocktail. I pulled out a crayfish almost the length of a man's torso, so they got their crayfish and we passed our evaluation.   – Dave, age 19

We didn't grow dagga on the Border, but we used to sell it. You had to be careful. What we'd do was open up the bottom flap of a cardboard box of Omo – you know the side that is glued down – so that it didn't show. You then poured out the soap powder and filled it with dagga which had been mulled so fine – all the pips removed and so on – so that if they X-rayed it, nothing would show up. Then you carefully glued the bottom closed again. That's how we took kilos of dagga back up to the Border. Up there, you could sell a matchbox full for R10. That was a lot of money in the early eighties. We sold mainly to the SACC.   – Anthony, age 18

I swear if someone went and dug around the gardens in Voortrekker-hoogte they would still find all the literature we buried there. We were not allowed any literature apart from the Bible. So we used to sneak our Bible study books, magazines and *The Watchtower* in. We buried stuff all over the place for our Bible study meetings. We always knew when there was going to be a search; it's amazing how quickly information travels in a prison. We used to double-wrap our literature in two plastic bags, tie it tightly and then submerge it in our washing. We had buckets to wash our clothes in and a plunger – you know those toilet plungers? And we simply dropped the plastic bags into the soapy water. When the guards came in, there we were, just plunging away, doing our washing as they searched our cells. They never once found the stuff! All of us agreed that although it was skeef to smuggle literature in, it was justifiable. Smuggling out letters was different; that was a grey area. Some thought it was crossing the line. We were only allowed to write one letter per week, and the Military Police searched us for letters going out to our loved ones. There was this one guy, Jan, who just knew how to work the system. He was a skeef guy, Jan. That meant he went against the rules. Jan was a big guy, and he had this huge sombrero. No problem to him, he would joke and talk with the guards while they searched him, and all the time he had letters lying on top, on the rim of his sombrero!   – Alan, age 17

I had a military licence to drive a Unimog, a Land Rover and a Bedford, but no civvy licence for a car. A friend of mine was taking his old bombed-out Fiat to the testing station to get his licence. I said I'd go with him for moral support, but I had no intention whatsoever of getting my civilian driving licence. This woman, one of the testers at the grounds who looked old enough to be my mother, but who was probably under 30, comes up and says, 'Jirra, julle lyk pragtig in julle uniforms' [Jesus, you look beautiful in your uniforms]. We did look good in our maroon berets, but maybe it was because her husband was in the military and she was obviously fond of people in uniform. My friend got his licence and we said cheers and started to leave when she asked me if I wasn't going to get mine as well. I told her I didn't have a learner's licence and she said it wasn't a problem; she could sort it all out for me and I could do my tests all in one day. I sat and answered these questions, with her guiding me through them. Then she says, 'Het jy 'n kar hierso?' [Do you have a car here?] She said I would have been able to use hers, except that it had gone in for a service. I asked my friend if I could use his Fiat, which I was not familiar with at all. I knew there was a clutch and where the gears were and such, but not a great deal else. So there she is sitting next to me as I manage to pull off carefully in first and cross some railway lines. I'd only had my learner's for a few minutes, and before I can even change out of first gear, she says, 'C'mon! Send it! Second gear! Let's go!' I got my learner's and driver's in less than an hour. I'll never forget it. 　　　　　　　　　　　　　　　　　　　　　　 – John, age 18

Roofs worked long hours. When they were manning equipment, we didn't want to have to sit and supervise them the whole time. However, we were supposed to be watching them and making sure they didn't fall asleep. So, we wound yellow telex tape around their heads, stapled it tight, ran it to the next guy's head, did the same, and so on. If one guy fell asleep, his head would fall forward or backward and the tape would snap. We could then go off and relax – go to the bar or play table tennis or whatever. We looked for horrible things to do to *roofs*. It's what you did, because everyone was horrible to you.

– Andy, age 18

AN UNPOPULAR WAR

Training

We had people who would come to our camp and give us talks on various units within the SADF. We had a guy from Bats come and talk to us, and a guy from 1 South African Reconnaissance came too. I remember him, 'cause he said, 'Don't worry if you smoke dagga, 'cause I smoke dagga too.' There were rumours about joining the Recces, things like they make you kill a puppy to see if you have the mind for it. Despite that, 40 guys applied, but only one got in.

One day we were in a queue and these two guys were talking, and the one says, 'Nee, ek gaan SP Wag toe' [No, I'm going to the State President's Guard]. I asked them what it was, 'cause we'd never heard of it, and the guy says it's a very paraat elite unit. When I asked what they did, he says they drilled a lot, stood guard a lot, did demonstrations which involved throwing rifles around, and were guard of honour at Parliament. I said 'Where is it?' and he says 'Pretoria.' That was the magic word for me! Pretoria! The closest posting to home I could get. I was told I was tall so I would definitely get in. I had to do the 2,4 in less than 12 minutes, sit-ups, all sorts of drilling manoeuvres – omkeer, regsom – to qualify. I got in, and, yes, there was a lot of drilling, standing guard and so on, but the one day General Malan wanted his garden done, so we were sent to do his garden for him. And when the Prime Minister became State President, we had to go and lug all these personal belongings from Parliament. So we did furniture removals too. — **Nick, age 20**

I loved Mine Warfare and Dems. It was lekker to blow things up! I think most little boys like to blow things up – you know, make little forts and blow them up, light crackers and blow up little soldiers. Now I got to do it for real. I learnt all sorts of interesting stuff: half a kilo of PE4 blows a half-metre gap in a railway track, and how much cortex is needed to cut a tree down. We even simulated a small nuclear explosion, a few drums of diesel and ... sorry, I'd better not say what else, but it was all in the manual, so of course we had to try it out.   — Paul, age 17

All troops are given basic first-aid training. I trained further as an army ops medic with my battery. SAMS had just been formed, and we had it much tougher than those poofters. We did additional courses to qualify as much more than medics, things like a Signaller's course and courses on the 20-mill and 40-mill guns. The SAMS guys didn't even iron their browns. They said they were told they didn't have to because there was only one plug outlet in their bungalow. Ja, we also had only one electrical outlet in our bungalow, but we still had to iron our browns. Their Basics was also a walk in the park compared to ours.

As part of our training for a war situation we spent three months working in government hospitals, mainly doing stitching, drips and learning how to deliver babies. I'm proud to say I helped to deliver about ten babies. There were doctors around, but they were usually only involved if there was a problem. It was us army medics and the sisters that delivered the babies. The difference between the theory and the practical side of childbirth was ... amazing. I was only 19 and, boy, was it an experience and a half! Fortunately I'm not squeamish, so the process didn't worry me. I did query why we were learning to deliver babies, and was told we might have to help the plaaslike bevolking. I'm sure the troops were happy and reassured that we were learning how to deliver babies!

On Friday and Saturday nights we worked in the casualty section of numerous coloured hospitals, and stitched people up. There was a sign on the wall saying 'Only Doctors Can Stitch Faces', but the workload was enormous and we did plenty of stitching of faces. I wish I could have seen my finished healed product 'cause I was very careful and tried to make the stitches as neat and small as possible.

One night this guy comes in with a stab wound in his back. It was from something very slender, maybe a bicycle spoke or something like that. There was a huge haematoma, which we knew we had to empty before we could begin working on the wound. Because of the pressure, we knew it would burst and cover us in blood, so my mate, another army medic, and I discussed for ages which angle to squeeze it at, where we should stand, and so on. Eventually we were ready and positioned ourselves and what happened? We got covered. The blood just sprayed all over us. So much for our planning. We collapsed with laughter, and this guy was just complaining and telling us to get on with it.

– Dave, age 19

The mechanics were known as tiffies – they fixed up vehicles. I was in the medics and we were known as Tampax tiffies, because we fixed up guys – we stopped the cunts from bleeding.   – Paul, age 18

At Berede we were told to catch our horses. These horses hadn't been ridden for three years, so they were wild. The horses got three years' pasture and then were ridden for a year. The first horse you caught was the horse you were going to keep. Both the horse's spirit and the person's spirit were broken and then built up. With us, they did that through lack of sleep, lack of control, and having to get back on a horse that kept bucking you off over and over again. To break the horses it was a case of riding them bucking and kicking until they were exhausted and they stopped. Only after that did they start building you and your horse up as a team, and then as part of a larger team of around a dozen guys. I must say it worked. We were told the horses were more important than the stupid little troops. The Artillery guys were not far from where the horses were kept, and the one day this guy must have got his gun a few degrees out or something, 'cause next thing this shell exploded in a field next to us. I also remember one day they again miscalculated and blew up the stables and a couple of horses were killed. So much for the horses being more important than us!   — **Martin, age 23**

As Marines we had to practise beach landings, even though there weren't very many beaches for us to invade! This involved a great deal of running. And shouting. We were very used to the former because our base, Scala, was in two sections. We slept at the top of the hill, but all the amenities, like the canteen, were downhill at the lower base. We never walked anywhere, we always ran, and it was a kay between the two bases, and another 500 steps from the lower base to the beach. For our beach landings, we would set off from Simonstown in Delta boats and make our way to nearby beaches. The boats would go in as close as they could to shore without fouling their props, so we still had to jump into the water with our rifles held high above our heads to keep them dry. We would then charge up the beach with whistles blowing and much running and shouting. This was not as easy as it sounds, for there were always civilians. Charging up the beach in full kit, roaring at the top of your lungs was not a simple matter when you had to sidestep sunning grannies, little kids and their sandcastles, and lurking picnic baskets. It must have been rather startling for all of them to see two platoons of men suddenly come rushing ashore, their faces streaked with Black Is Beautiful and hitting the beach very hard. You can't dig a foxhole quickly on sandy beaches, so you had to push the sand forwards to create berm-like walls to hide behind. After enough practice you could ensure you hit the beach in such a way that your chest pushed up a fair amount of sand ahead of you. The warrant officer in charge was an ex-Parabat and, boy, was he gung-ho. He would check to see if anyone's head was visible, and if it was, he jumped on that person's back. Once he did this and the poor guy underneath him struck his head against his rifle sight and tore open his nostril.   — **Louis, age 17**

I had two horses. The first horse I rode was beautiful, but one day in training, she stepped in a hole and broke her leg. The horse medics came out and they looked at her but said she had to be put down. Then it was my right, my privilege and my duty as a soldier to shoot my own horse in the head. I used the lieutenant's revolver and they showed me exactly where to shoot her. It was horrific. It haunted me for quite a long time afterwards. I tell you, I could have done without that privilege, honour and right. You get very close to the animal. I mean, we lived with our horses. We ate our food with them, slept next to them, and when you spend so much time with them you learn that they are very intelligent and a lot like dogs. People normally only see their horse when they ride it, but we lived with ours, and you get to see just how intelligent they are. My second horse was a beautiful black stallion called Blikkies, but with the most uncomfortable trot!

Our training sessions involved diving off our horses at full gallop when the instructors shouted 'Kontak!', or just started shooting. I'm sure they'll say they used blank ammo, but when you see leaves and branches falling to the ground in front of you, you begin to wonder. We were in a rocky quartzite area, full of aloes, and we had to dive to the ground from a full gallop. You have no idea what that is like. I saw at least three guys bash their front teeth out. If you were clever, you learnt to dive and roll while holding the reins. That way you didn't have to run and catch your horse later. But it wasn't easy. You had a full pack on your back, a funny helmet that was always too big – nobody had the right size – and it kept falling down over your eyes so you couldn't see anything, and you had your gun in your hand. Your gun was upright at a 45-degree angle, resting on your hip, and you controlled the horse with one hand. On patrol, forget it – our rifles were slung across our packs.

When we were out, we carried rations for 24 hours for ourselves. In the evenings, the truck would arrive with lucerne for the horses and our ration packs. But I would say about 80 percent of the time, even though we weren't allowed to do it, we would end up at a farmer's place at night and the farmer would put on a nice spread for us – kill a sheep or something. But they would also lock up their daughters! We went to some sokkiejols on the weekend. And the girls there? You have no idea! I remember this one girl danced once around the floor with me – *langarm* – then asked me to go outside with her. I agreed to go but told her I wasn't going to do anything. She looked at me and said, 'Are you sure?' Halfway through the next circuit she'd gone on to someone else. After the sokkiejol the guys were comparing notes and were horrified to find that five of them had slept with that one girl.

– Martin, age 23

I had some of my guys doing exercises off the coast of northern Natal. We were going to practise Naval Gunfire Support and would fire from the ship to a naval firing range near Jozini. Some of the guys were going to deploy onto land from the smaller boats and call in the naval gunfire. It was a training exercise so that we could use that capability should we require it. I think these guys spent the entire journey, all the way from Durban to where we went ashore, hugging the heads. Another time I recall we were on a strike craft and heading out from Saldanha Bay northwards up the coast. As we turned out of the bay, the strike craft was lurching violently up and down. The sea was horrendous. We stayed out of the crew's way and lay low in our bunks. During the night I had to take a piss. I went down to the heads and was holding on to a pole, trying to aim as accurately as possible. I saw this guy come running down the steps, obviously going to be as sick as a dog. I knyped [pinched] off and moved back. He hurled, then I pissed, then he hurled, then I pissed again, and so we each took our turn at the heads. How's that for collaboration!

I used to run some of the sailing courses at 4 Recce Langebaan, and we had this 64-foot gaff-rigged schooner. The planned trip was from Langebaan, stopping in at Cape Town, Gordon's Bay and Hermanus, and then one shot back. On the course we had some Angolan blacks, and there was one guy who was a very famous black guy in Special Forces. It was around the time that Bertie Reed was sailing *Stabilo Boss.* And this guy says to me, 'Me and you are going to sail around the world together.' As we went out that night, we hit heavy seas. In ten minutes, everyone was hanging over the side. This went on the whole night. There were 11 on the yacht and only three men weren't sick. I knew it wasn't going to work, and the next morning I said we were going back. As he was getting off the yacht, this guy turned to me and joked, 'This thing is for white people, not kaffirs.' **– Anonymous**

We were on manoeuvres up the West Coast near Saldanha to test and be evaluated on these fancy new 35-mm twin-barrelled anti-aircraft guns connected to radar systems. The radar system could track and lock on to an aircraft and then the guns could follow and lock on to the aircraft. The chefs had not brought enough food, so we ran out after a few days and decided to shoot springbok. We pinched the spotlight off the top of an ambulance and smashed the protective coloured lens to fashion a spotlight. We set off and find them easily enough, because their eyes shine in the spotlight, and five of us (and I have to say there was rank there – two PF guys), we let off a volley with our R1s and 9-mills. But we never hit one Springbok. Next we tried to get a rabbit. Now, if you shine a light on a rabbit, it stays still. We pinned this one poor rabbit in our spotlight and the guys must have emptied about two magazines from their 9-mill pistols at it. It was sitting dead still and yet we missed it. Eventually one of the Bombardiers started up the Landie and hit the rabbit with the vehicle and killed it. Me, being the medic and the one with medical knowledge and sharp knives, had to skin it. I left it to hang overnight. The next day we bought geese from this coloured woman for about R2.50 each. She killed and plucked them and we cooked them and the rabbit. The rabbit was much better than the geese, which must have been old.   — **Dave, age 19**

I was so happy when I cleared out from the army's School of Armour, to join the air force. Euphoria, that's what I felt. The air force food was better and there was actually a choice. You didn't eat off varkpanne. You ate off white plates and there was cutlery on the table. They served the food up to you, politely asking if you would like some of this or some of that. They didn't just slop things onto your plate. We didn't have to walk around with our pikstel. Cutlery and crockery were washed for you, so we didn't have to wash our stuff in the 44-gallon drums outside the canteen, which, if you weren't there quickly, became filled with a layer of grease from everybody else's washing up. I suppose at some stage it must have been soapy water, but there was a lot of gippo guts going around. Major Mike Muller, we called him Major Triple M, called me in and said my signal had come in and I had to leave immediately. I was delighted. The downside was I didn't get to say goodbye to the guys I'd gone through Basics with, and we were very close, 'cause you form a very close bond when you go through tough times together. I gave back my rifle and got on a train. The upside was, when I arrived, an air force officer, a colonel, spoke to me like a human being, the way one person normally talks to another. I was treated so differently, like someone important. It was only a five-minute discussion, but the treatment and the way I was talked to still stand out in my mind.

There the PTIs were meant to be these superfit guys. During the two weeks of integration from the army to the air force, they supposedly make things tough for us. But, please, we only stood inspection at 7 a.m., compared to 05h30 in the army. The beds didn't have to be as square as they had to be in the army, so we became more relaxed. This one guy is sweeping out the bungalow, guiding the dust towards the door. As he sweeps it out, the corporal who was there to do the inspection appears at the base of the steps and the dust covers his boots! So this corporal decides he's going to give us the opfok of our lives. He says, 'Sien jy daardie boom [See that tree] … I'll give you one minute.' In the army it was ten seconds. We ran and were back with 45 seconds to spare. He wants 30 push-ups. In the army it would've been 120. So after 30 you stand up and you're not even tired. He tells us to put on our PT kit, as now we're gonna run the 2,4. In the army we ran the 2,4 in full kit, staaldak and poles, and we ran it in less than ten minutes. Now here we are in PT kit! Shame, he really tried so hard. To us it was a total jol.   – **Tallies, age 17**

To put it in a nutshell, becoming a JL meant you would become an instructor for the next intake. I'd had enough after Basics and thought I'd take the easy way out and become a chef. Chefs didn't drill or march. I was so cross that my dad went over my head because he thought JL was the way for me to go. He hopped on the phone and gave the colonel my background in Scouting and told me being a JL didn't mean you would become one of those corporals giving troops shit. I hated the corporals; they were uneducated, whiny 16-year-old dropouts with nothing higher than a Standard 8. I didn't want to become that. But JL could also get you to the position of lieutenant, which was attractive to me. My pay would go from R252 per month as a private to about R600. So off I went to Bourke's Luck on this course that was three times harder than Basics. There was obviously a lot of theory too. And again, insufficient sleep. I fell asleep standing upright between two guys while we were being taught the phonetic alphabet. And again it was this stupid corporal, 'Hey! Hey! Word wakker!' He thought he'd nail me 'cause we were only just learning the phonetic alphabet, but I knew it from my Scouting days. He was pissed off that I was sleeping and even more pissed off because I could answer his questions. That's what the corporals were like. They were not the brightest crayons in the box and hated you if you knew more than them.   – **Paul, age 18**

They had a very scientific approach to selecting people for Junior Leaders Course. Only two days into National Service you had to run across the rugby field with your kit to a certain group of officers and shout your number, rank and name, and by that they decided whether you went to do JLs, Officer's Course or remained in ordinary National Service. I have to say there must have been something about it that worked because the RTU rate was very low.   **– Tallies, age 17**

During OC everybody had to look the same. Eenvormigheid. Either everyone in the platoon wore jerseys or no one did. They'd been issued, but you weren't allowed to wear them until you'd 'earned' them. You did that by running the 2,4 in under a certain time. But it didn't help if only some of the guys ran it under the time, because they still couldn't wear their jerseys. The whole platoon had to do it. Winter was starting. It was almost May and we still didn't have our jerseys, so we went to the company commander and said we wanted to run the 2,4 to earn our jerseys. Everyone else already had theirs. He told us we couldn't do it during normal training times; we would have to run it after hours. So on a Saturday around lunchtime we went and ran an extra 2,4 to earn our jerseys. We fuckin' ran our guts out and we all made it with only about three seconds to spare. It had to be the whole platoon and we did it. We all earned our jerseys and that night we wore them. I will never forget it. That right to wear a jersey still remains one of the greatest 'prizes' I've ever won.   **– John, age 18**

I kinda had three Basic Training periods: my army Basics, then air force and then the air force OC. Hard, easy, very hard. I think the SAAF's OC was one of the toughest because they put you under a lot of pressure to ensure you were able to think and make decisions under very difficult circumstances. The pressure was both emotional and physical. I also found it tougher 'cause I was a lot older than I was when I did my army Basics. There's a training time called 'Gogga' –

because you're meant to be scared of it. They take you to a remote location and they push you for 36 hours without sleep. You run around with tyres and poles, and carry weights on your back, they make you pitch and strike and pitch and strike tents repeatedly – and these were huge canvas military tents. They'd let you sleep for ten minutes and then wake you up because you had gone to bed with boots on. 'An officer doesn't sleep like that!' they'd shout and give you an oppie and then make you strike and pitch the tent again. And again, because the tents weren't in a perfectly straight row. After 15 or 16 hours of physical pressure they let you sleep a bit, and then woke you and off you went to write an essay on Why You Want to Become an Officer. By then you are so tired you fall asleep while you are writing and your pen keeps sliding off the page. It was one thing after another, including the night march, which began at about 3 a.m. The guys are following the instructors and the rest are just holding onto the webbing of the guy in front so they don't get lost. I think it is possible to sleep while marching; you just go into zombie mode. You don't know where you're going or for how long you'll be marching. You just hold onto the guy in front of you. After Gogga you are allowed to wear your CO badges, a white little band on your epaulettes, which previously you were not worthy to wear.   – **Tallies, age 17**

There were lots of myths about becoming a Recce: you were given a puppy at the beginning of your training, and once you completed your training you had to kill it. If you didn't do these things, you failed. This was absolute bullshit. Utter nonsense. The focus of the training was to understand the capabilities of an individual to perform mentally and physically under the most extreme circumstances. There were various exercises which involved extreme physical stress. This translates into mental stress, but there were also mental exercises, problem-solving and such, which were actually very simple, but not in conjunction with sleep and food deprivation. As basic as the exercises were, they were effective in seeing how guys performed in small teams of four to six men. The combination of physical and mental tasks brought out the capabilities of each man. One of the mental tasks that the psychologists came up with involved a Lego man. One guy from the team goes and has a look at the Lego man. It is only two bricks high, but he may not touch it. He can only view it, see how it is built, and then he must return to his teammates and explain to the team how to build it so that it is exactly right. If they are going wrong, he must explain clearly what they must do to correct it. It's not nearly as easy as it sounds, 'cause you must remember the guy's brains are stuffed after extreme physical and mental strain. It's interesting and necessary to watch the interaction between the team members. This revealed how a person was capable of handling problem-solving when physically broken and shattered, and how they interacted with one another under stress. There were obstacle courses with sections that appeared to be absolutely impossible to overcome. Specific obstacles had specific problems and solutions. With the different aids provided, the team had to work things out in a limited time. For example, the whole team had to get themselves and some or other shit across a four-metre gap, using planks of varying lengths, without stopping at a certain point or touching the ground between certain platforms. It had to be done in, say, less than ten minutes. The pressure was the time constraint. The guys were constantly watched and evaluated. The actual evaluation period for selection was anything from two hours to 100 hours, but the training was a year. You were continually assessed on courses like Foreign Weapons, Demolitions, Seaborne Orientation, Parachute Course, Know Your Enemy, Bushcraft, Tracking & Survival, Minor Tactics and so on. The emphasis was on three things: how do the guys measure up on the physical side, on the mental side and on the teamwork side of things? The Recce training was completely different to any other SADF training. It involved assessing how a guy was going to fit into a small team under extreme combat and in difficult conditions. — **Anonymous**

I was called up to 1 SAI in Bloem, but spent only one week there before being chosen for Parabats when the selectors came through. When you first start training at 1 Parachute Battalion at Tempe outside Bloemfontein, you begin with six weeks of Basics, which is much harder than the normal SADF Basics. Sure, you run, do sit-ups and stuff like that, but you also do skaapdra. That's when you run around with this weight, this concrete block, and train carrying it around, in addition to all your kit. After that, there is a two-week PT course, and then a three-week hangar course. A lot of training is done in the hangar, where they have a mock-up of an aircraft interior, swings and other things to give you the feel of what the real thing will be like. One of the other training exercises is jumping off the 35-metre JP Louw Tower. This is one of the deciding points in your training, because the instructors know if you can't jump off the tower, you sure as hell aren't going to jump out of a plane. So if you don't jump, and without the slightest hesitation, you are off the Parabats course. Finally, you get into a plane, but you still don't jump. This particular exercise is called 'flight experience', but we called it 'fright experience'. When you are airborne you are watched carefully to see how you react when you have to move to the open door. They make you stick your head out of the doorway and look down. Your reaction is critical. If you seem afraid to move towards the door or pull back when you look down, you are off the course. Eight 1 000-foot jumps later, on a static line – stand up, hook up and jump, including a night jump – you qualify. Lastly, you do your 'glamour jump', so called because you get to show off your capabilities and jump in front of your parents. After nine jumps you are awarded your bronze wings, and after 50 jumps or more you are awarded silver wings. On my first jump, I received a GP+, which is the highest grading you can get. I was very chuffed, because it was a notoriously strict staff sergeant who gave me the grade. Staff Sergeant Landman was a legend there. You just knew if you did one wrong thing, he would chuck you off the course. And those guys had the power to do that. I was terrified of him, but I respected him; he was a disciplinarian and good at what he did. I remember on the one jump out of a Dakota, Staff shouted, 'Staan op!' and everyone stood up and I just couldn't get up. Now you haven't got much time; everything has to be executed with precision. I tried and tried but my legs wouldn't move. The whole stick is standing and he's still shouting at me to get up. I was so fearful of him and nervous, I thought it was nerves paralysing my legs. My brain was telling them to move but I just couldn't get up. I say, 'Ek kan nie! Ek kan nie!' [I can't! I can't!]. Then Staff points out that I hadn't released the safety harness across my lap!   – John, age 18

Even though I was a Parabat, I spent most of my time in the bush and never did one operational jump. So much for being afforded the nickname 'Vleisbom'. We'd been called out a few times, but never jumped. On a particular occasion we were deployed as a stopper group, which is very similar to an ambush group. You are effectively covering an envisaged escape route with the intention of inflicting casualties. We flew in in C-130s and C-160s, 64 people absolutely laden with equipment. We were so heavily laden down with radio, rifle ammunition, mortar bombs, landmines, ration packs and water that you needed to hang onto the overhead cable that secured the parachute static line just to keep yourself upright. Before you jump, you have your reserve parachute across your chest, your main parachute on your back and your equipment resting on your leg. Only once you exit the plane and have done your flight drills do you release your equipment so it hangs below you. Once you land, you ditch the parachutes and carry your equipment on your back or webbing belt. But this one time we couldn't find the drop zone for whatever reason, and the flight was taking longer than anticipated. It got to the point where the fear of having to execute the operation and jump into an enemy situation hanging underneath a parachute became less of an issue than the weight of the equipment. It felt like it was dragging you down into the fuselage of the plane, and the Black Is Beautiful was running into your eyes because you were sweating with the effort of remaining upright.   – **Dudley, age 21**

I thought, yeah, studying through the military was the way to go. The Military Academy was for the crème de la crème. I was to do a BMil degree. I was one of only four from the Medical Services to be selected. Although we were shown around Stellenbosch, we actually went to Saldanha Bay. Already on the Flossie from Pretoria to Cape Town I knew that I'd made a mistake. You know when you just don't fit in? I honestly believe a lot of them were doing it because it would give them a comfy, cushy job in the army for the next 20 years, or their pa was a colonel and they were expected to go to military school. When we got to Saldanha, the weather was miserable. It was freezing cold and there was nothing, nothing there. I had a wooden hut on Malgaskop and the area stank from these thousands of seagulls that nested there. The hut was so run-down you could see through the holes in the floor and the walls. I was expecting a more educational environment, but it was far more military than I had imagined. We had initiation, induction, and every morning at some ungodly hour we had to swim in that freezing cold West Coast sea. I cried myself to sleep, thinking, what had I done? The picture they had created and that I had created in my mind as to what the Military Academy was like and stood for didn't exist. All my mates had klaared out and I had committed myself to eight years PF. I could've already been out of the military, but there I was, 1 200 kays from home. Three days later I'd had enough. It was more difficult to get out than to get in. In the end it came down to this colonel who had recommended me to the Academy and heaped praise on me, to write a letter saying I could leave. Ten days later I could finally go. I felt like I had been let out of prison.

                                              – **Paul, age 18**

Boetie Gaan Border Toe

We were so disciplined after Basics. You did anything they said. When we were out on trains to go to the Border and they told us to put up the blinds – we just did it. I've no idea why. Protection? I have no idea, but we immediately closed the blinds. You were like that after Basics. When we got into Windhoek, we sat on the station platform for 16 hours just waiting for anybody to come and get us. We had no money to buy food or anything to drink. We only had our army pay books, but we couldn't use them. Eventually, the next morning, they came and fetched us and took us to the Windhoek base. Then it was back to the station and up to Grootfontein, to the Deurgangs camp. There we waited for two days. We were given rat packs. We didn't know what the hell they were or that they were supposed to last for an entire day. What did *we* know – we'd just completed Basics. We ate it all in one meal. They finally collected us in Buffels to drive us to Rundu. I was shitting myself. I knew how to make an oven in the veld, but here I was over the kaplyn without a rifle, clutching my balsak. I kept looking over the top, and every Ovambo I checked was a terrorist. There's one. There's one. There's one. You don't know what to expect. When I got to HQ there was no rest time or teatime; it's just *tree aan*. I was terrified; you've come from the city and the next thing you're in this godforsaken place. The camp was just sand and dust and thorn trees, acacias every-where, and more dust and no women anywhere. And the next thing you look and there's a goddamn swimming pool and squash courts! I thought, hey, this can't be that bad.   – Anthony, age 18

After my Basic Training in South Africa, I was sent to Rundu. We flew in, and as freshly arrived troops we were immediately lined up on the runway and issued with two compulsory malaria tablets. We were told these were special army tablets and of course that we were special to be given them, but they would only work if you chewed them. All this was bawled at you by a screaming corporal, and by now one had come to accept anything one was told, so the tablets were chewed, much to the merriment of all the spectators who had lined up to see the weekly comedy of the 'new arrivals' show. In less than a week, it would be my intake standing on the side laughing, because by then we had learnt to pretend to chew the tablets while surreptitiously spitting them into our hands. While we were almost vomiting from the tablets, we were ushered into a hall and given a wad of forms to sign. These included the State Security Act or some equally pompous document in which we swore not to divulge our activities to 'lesser mortals'. We also had to agree not to object to our personal letters being read by a clerk who wielded the awesome power of a wide black marker pen with which he could eradicate any portion of the letters he thought could give the enemy information about our super-duper fighting machine. I am still not sure why poetic descriptions of sunsets across the Kavango River were deemed worthy of erasure by the black pen.

– Chris, age 17

All that shit they taught you in Basics was good for discipline, but we didn't even iron our clothes, because it made them shine. However, we did take good care of our boots, because we walked a lot, sometimes 40–50 kilometres a day. We had Israeli Desert boots, but had to keep our leather boots in shape with wet newspaper and regular polish with Kiwi Military Tan. But they didn't last too long. We alternated pairs of boots, because you didn't want to have to wear in new boots and tried to make your old ones last as long as possible. There were some guys who enjoyed keeping their hands busy, polishing boots or whatever. We'd pay them with a packet of smokes. I smoked Texan Plain, 15 cents a packet of 20. This was around 1978. Hardly anyone smoked Camel, as they were too damn expensive – 25 cents a pack.

Ridiculous. Booze was cheap too, 10 cents a tot. Colddrinks were the most expensive, 20 cents a can.   **– Ric, age 18**

I wanted to go to the Border in my second year. I thought it was important for me because I would be required to lead troops then, and when I did camps at a later stage I wanted to be sure that I had some experience at least. We flew up to Mpacha just after New Year and landed around 2 p.m. As you step off that plane, the sun just hits you. It was hot, hot, hot and humid. You don't realise things can be as hot as that. I'd got some good advice – take a 9-mill – 'cause they don't have 9-mills on the Border, and wherever you go you have to take your weapon with you. A 9-mill is much easier to carry around than a rifle. But I didn't have any ammo. This fact didn't seem to matter. It's just that if the colonel catches you without your weapon, you're in serious trouble! We still had to drive from Mpacha to Katima. We hitched a lift on this Buffel going through, and I was very nervous. There I was with only a 9-mill and no ammo. The roads were tar, but the grass and bush grew right up to the edge of the road. Man, I was really scared. The terrs could hide in the bush and shoot at us. This was not lekker. I thought they should really cut the grass. If the guys are going to shoot at us, let it be from at least 50 or 100 metres away and not right on the edge of the road!   **– Paul, age 17**

We drove to a 32 Battalion training camp just west of Rundu. It was the Recce Team HQ, and even though it was a temporary base, it had clearly been in use for a long time. There were sandbags everywhere, underground bunkers and sand berms with machine-gun posts. These machine guns were real. They had ammo crates next to them and were clearly for use, as opposed to being there just for troeps to polish. When our Samil drove in, a wild man dressed only in SWAPO camouflage shorts and a headband greeted us at the re-training base. He was standing on a water tower. In one hand

AN UNPOPULAR WAR

he held a beer, in the other a heavy-calibre Russian machine gun, which he fired over our heads as we fell out of the truck. While we were grovelling in the sand, the captain, who was a hero then but has since been discarded, stood oblivious to the bullets and welcomed us to his base. Arriving at this base was a shock. Everything suddenly seemed very real. We were used to the general disorganisation of the army, but here there was a very strong sense of purpose. The soldiers all looked like real soldiers. Very hardcore. They looked like the pictures I had seen in newspapers and magazines of the RLI or Selous Scouts from the Rhodesian war. They had this very capable air about them. They didn't look like they were ready for a parade; they looked like they were dressed and ready for war. All the men seemed to be carrying rifles and ammo. There were guns everywhere, but we didn't have any, as ours hadn't been issued yet. These guys clearly knew what they were doing and why they were there. They had a swagger and an air of competence about them that I hadn't seen in the army before.

I was there to train as a real radio operator for 32 Battalion. Before, I had fiddled about on telex machines and hi-tech equipment, but I had done very little practical training. I had never even spoken or communicated in real radio talk – codes and such – to another person before. I would learn how to send and receive coded messages, how to transmit in Morse code, and also how to handle Russian military equipment like their machine guns and AK-47s. Four Reconnaissance guys trained us. It was quite something to see them strip and reassemble an AK-47 in less than 30 seconds – blindfolded. In less than two weeks we could also do that, even after a 10-kilometre run. Because everything in the camp was done for a purpose, I tried really hard. There was no rondfok. Nothing was formal in the camp. Even the one parade in the morning was only to tell you what you were going to do that day, not to mess you around. Things were done because they had to be. Even when I received my camouflage beret with the Buffalo insignia, it was nothing formal. I was so proud to wear my beret with my unit's insignia, as only members of that elite unit could wear them. It was the first time in my life that I was really good at something.   – Chris, age 18

In the Bush

Angola is an incredibly flat, dirty-coloured, sea-sand terrain with host upon host of haak-en-steek thorn trees and open shonas that are usually dry. Only in the rainy season do they become full of water. Under such circumstances one could liken them to the rice paddies of Vietnam. Subtle difference: 'Who stole the rice?' There was always an incredible shortage of water, although there were a few primitive dams and some square-shaped Portuguese dams. We called them that because you could see at one time the Portuguese had used them for watering their farmlands. Sometimes there were these little water wells close to a kraal. The water was invariably brown or green in colour, no matter where you got it. But it wasn't a huge issue. Initially you used your purification tablets, but soon that fell by the wayside and eventually you even stopped boiling the water. Your constitution does adapt. When scooping water out with your fire bucket and pouring it into your water bottle, the object was to try and avoid getting tadpoles in your drinking water. We also had these empty plastic sachets, part and parcel of your rat pack, and you emptied a naartjie- or strawberry-flavoured powder, whatever the wonderful flavoured variant was in those days, into it. When you added green or brown unpurified water, it didn't take on the colour of the powder but remained green or brown, but at least it tasted better. We didn't see many males around kraals, mainly females or younger children. They couldn't speak our language, so communication was always through an interpreter. I felt for them. They were beaten by SWAPO on one side and by us on the other, although I never allowed my troops to do that. Adjacent to the kraals were pens made of branches and thorn trees to house their livestock, and they cleared patches of land and grew mielies or mahango. There also seemed to be an abundance of watermelons. I never saw any game except kudu, once.   – **Dudley, age 21**

We were members from various Special Forces units doing patrol in western Angola, south of the town of Namibe. It was in a mountainous area of the western Angolan highlands and we were looking for specific enemy bases. Our job was not to attack the bases, but to gather information on them. We'd been deployed into the area in groups of six and carried with us what we could, as there was no possibility of re-supply. We deployed for about four to six weeks to walk around in the mountains and gather specifics on bases. We lived on rat packs and counted on finding a waterhole to replenish our initial water supply. It was incredibly hot, and to conserve energy we moved around mainly at night. We'd been out for about four weeks and hadn't spoken with anyone other than each other. I don't know if you can imagine what it is like not to have contact in any way with anybody else for a month. We also ran out of water and couldn't find any in the mountains. We got so thirsty our tongues swelled up. It's unbelievable how thick your tongue becomes when you dehydrate that badly. We even started drinking the drips from our medical supplies. It was rather challenging. This one night we were resting up in a hide, just prior to moving out, when we noticed that the sky looked strange. The moon was up but it looked weird. We couldn't understand what was happening. There was this funny light in the sky and we saw this apparition. We were convinced it was the end of the world and everybody had forgotten about us in those bloody highlands. It took us a while to click and realise what it was. An eclipse. If you are not aware that one is going to occur and have no prior knowledge whatsoever about it and all of a sudden it happens, under those circumstances, it can be rather unsettling. – **Anonymous**

We got a rat pack a day to survive on. I swear I only utilised about 10 percent of mine. If I had to eat another tin of mixed veg swimming in a kind of watered-down mayonnaise or eat another guava piel ... I hated that stuff. UNITA got these nice cammo packs that obviously came in from somewhere else. They had a nice variety and the stuff was more continental and exotic, with a Portuguese flair. Things like meatballs, and their bully beef was different to ours. What can I say, it was just tastier. We used to swop out packs. Of course, the first item I swopped out was my mixed veg. Our packs also had an energy bar, which was like synthetic plastic – it was quite nauseating. There was also that minced fruit rolled in sugar, which was not bad, and cheese in a tube, wrapped like polony in plastic. You'd cut off the end and suck the cheese out. All extremely synthetic and equally nauseating. Depending on which number rat pack you got, sometimes there was condensed milk. The packs were numbered one to five. No matter which number rat pack you got, you always got two coffees, two sugars and two dog biscuits. Those were nice. I used to boil up water in my fire bucket, throw in the sugar and coffee, and enjoy it with my dog biscuits. Towards the end, I didn't even eat the tinned food. For about the first three weeks we were in Angola we hadn't adapted and still craved meat; sometimes if the guys saw a buck, like a Steenbok, they shot it. We'd skin it and hang it out to dry before braaing it. I lost about 12 kilos in my time there.   – **Greg, age 25**

Amongst all the stuff we used to get in our rat packs was a plastic bag that you could make juice or coffee in. You squeezed your tube of condensed milk into it, threw in your powdered coffee and some water, sealed the bag, shook it up and drank it cold. Hey man, we were making Frappuccinos way back in those days!   – **Andy, age 18**

It was late in '81 and we were quite far into Angola, having been flown in to prevent terrorists from fleeing north. We were the front line on the northern side of a big operation. We had been there for three weeks. We were filthy and had been eating rat packs all this time. One day, while occupying one of the many temporary helicopter bases we had set up, a senior sergeant major and I'm pretty sure it was *the*

General Viljoen flew in on a helicopter for a visit. They brought with them boxes and boxes of T-bone steaks. It was fantastic! It was the first non-tinned food we had eaten in almost a month. There were only so many ways to heat and eat bully beef or meatballs. The steaks were enormous as only a South African farmer can make them and only the army could supply. There must have been about 100 of us and we each got a T-bone.   – **Chris, age 18**

We had been in the bush living off our rat packs for 40 days. They wanted to land a plane on the airstrip, but there were all these cattle. So they brought in the gunships, not to shoot them but to kind of scare them away, to herd them off the field. But one cow got shot, killed. We rushed onto the field with our knives and cut a leg off. We skinned it and hung it to cure. We had a braai for three nights in a row! That was a high point of my two years.   – **Andy, age 18**

On the Border we had this Buffel full of food and were stopped in a camp when these tired and hungry infantry guys came walking past. They stared at all our stuff and said, 'Check daardie rats' [Look at those rations]. We were very casual and said something like, 'Oh this? Here, have some,' and threw them a little tin of beans and a tiny packet of colddrink mix. The guys went crazy, stampeding as they tried to grab it. This poor one-liner was trying to control his guys and not lose face. We had fun like that sometimes.   – **Paul, age 17**

Army sleeping bags resemble cocoons. They taper at your feet and you can tie them so only your face sticks out. When we were in a TB we slept in our sleeping bags fully dressed and with our boots on. Our webbing was laid out in such a way that in one move we could wake up, roll out of the sleeping bag into our webbing, grab our rifle and be ready to go in seconds. We were moving through an area in which we knew there were terrs, so we were moving silently through haak-en-steek bushes. Perfectly named, because they haak you and steek you. Usually you carefully held a branch back so the person behind you could pass without getting snagged, but if there was a diknek behind you whom you didn't particularly like, you just let the branch whip back and catch him in the face. Of course, he couldn't scream or say anything, 'cause we had to be totally silent. At dawn, after a shake awake, one guy whispers that he can't get up because there's something at his feet inside his sleeping bag. Moving carefully and talking in whispers, we slowly unzip his sleeping bag. Two guys then grabbed his shoulders and two others carefully parted the sleeping bag at the bottom. In one move, and without anyone being able to make any sound, they opened the sleeping bag and yanked him out. It was a snake. We didn't kill it – we tried to leave wildlife alone – although I remember an accident involving baboons once. There was this model base on the Border in the Caprivi Strip. Visiting dignitaries flew in with SADF senior officers to see what a perfect base should be like and what life in the bush was like for a soldier. We had these demonstrations involving Impalas, wrecked tanks and white phosphorous grenades. But we didn't realise there was a troop of baboons in the area. The phosphorus is sticky, burns like hell and you can't get it off. Some of it landed on this one baboon's stomach and it was awful watching him ripping himself open trying to get the pain out of his stomach.   **– Clint, age 18**

The most awe-inspiring thing that happened to me was at a temporary base in western Zambia. At last light you take up your position, and at first light you get the hell out of there. The area was pretty flat, so there wasn't much of a vantage point, but we set up camp. I was only on third watch, so I went to sleep. Around 3 a.m. I was wakened and I noticed that it was pitch dark – when I'd gone to sleep there had been stars visible. I couldn't understand it. The guy who'd woken me put his face right next to mine and he said, 'We're surrounded.' And I thought, oh my God, and he told me to look. There was a herd of elephants around us. About 50 jumbo. But the scary part was that they were all looking in one direction, away from us. I told the guys we had to move. We moved about two kilometres and the elephants moved off too. At first light our previous position was mortared. To this day I believe those elephants warned us. — **Ric, age 18**

There were a lot of animals around where we were, a platoon base 100 kilometres west of Rundu. We had this little buck with big ears and called him Oortjies. He was still there when I left, and I still wonder what happened to him. The one time this civil engineer came up and we gave him a Land Rover to drive around in. It was lekker being able to tell him to go this way to see hippo and that way if he wanted to see elephant. But he got out of his vehicle to take photos and was killed by an elephant. Weird, hey. Myself and two NSMs once had a close call while collecting firewood. I could just hear one of them busy in the nearby bush – branches snapping and breaking. I thought, man, this guy is enthusiastic. Next thing I turn around to look and it's an elephant! Right there. We heard nothing, it never made a sound until it started feeding. It wasn't easy alerting the one guy to get away without attracting the attention of the elephant. We yelled a warning, but he didn't believe that there was an elephant just metres away. We ran. Another time I remember being in a trench and hearing these scratching sounds. I was so scared, because I had no idea what was making the sounds. Turned out it was a porcupine. We also fished with dynamite. It wasn't my fault or my idea! I saw them making a movie near Kroonstad and they wanted realistic explosions in the water. They used thunderflashes to do this, and I saw all these dead fish floating in the water afterwards. So I put it into practice on the river. We used PE4 and were fishing away when these civvies started shouting at us and telling us we couldn't fish like that 'cause we were killing everything. We told them, we're the ones with rifles – basically, piss off. Who the hell did these civvies think they were? Monday I get hauled in and told off about how I am ruining the military's name and how hard they've worked to have credibility in the area and now this. Turns out the civvies were Nature Conservation.　　　　　– **Paul, age** 17

You've got to picture the whole scene. You've got savannah bush with shonas and the ground is made up of this greyish sand, which is churned up by our vehicles. These were 10-ton vehicles, 50 or 60 of them. Then the choppers would come in at night, usually from Rundu, a field hospital in Sector 2Ø. They flew low to make it more difficult for a SAM-7 missile to shoot them down. It wasn't just one helicopter on its *eis*. It was a few of them. The Puma is a big helicopter; it can carry 20 people. It's a fair-sized machine with powerful rotors. We'd give our co-ords and there had to be a bit of a clearing, which had usually been burnt or *looied*, and when that thing landed, it was just a blizzard of black dust. A black snowstorm.　　　　　– **Greg, age** 25

We spent weeks in the bush, sometimes months, either in Angola or just out of base. Coming back, one always had to make adjustments to the relative civilisation of the base. I remember an occasion when the base doctor and a female nurse offered me a lift to my house. To this day, I can still recall, with absolute olfactory clarity, the incredible sensation of smelling the woman's perfume as it drifted back to me across the open Land Rover. It reminded me that there was still beauty in the world and that not all my appreciation for the softer side of human beings had been completely numbed. It was an intoxicating five-minute trip.　　　　　– **Chris, age** 18

For seven months, most of us never had the luxury of showering or bathing. Angola is mostly desert-like, with some bush and savannah grasslands. The sand is pretty much black from fires and the fighting, and there are these swamp-like areas called shonas. For obvious reasons we never wore rank, and our uniform was a T-shirt worn with either cammo or brown pants. I had two T-shirts and one pair of trousers. It doesn't take long for your clothes to get filthy. Our trousers were shiny, black and oily from the black sand and from wearing them every day. After a while your skin goes this dark grey colour and then goes black too. We had shaved our heads before leaving South West Africa, so my hair wasn't too bad. But we hadn't shaved, because there was not much water to spare. You all smell the same and you are all pitch black. After a while, though, you become so accustomed to the smell, you don't really notice it. We had been out of base for two weeks, when we stopped at this one shona. It was late afternoon; the sun was just going down. I took the gap and stripped off, removed my skeleton webbing, eight or ten magazines of 40 rounds, my R5, and had a wash. No soap or anything. I paid for my wash when a tsetse fly bit me on my inner thigh. Almost on my dick! The next time I managed to wash, it was the most unforgettable shower I've ever had in my life. It was months later and we flew out of Mavinga at midnight. We flew in Flossies, these amazing transport planes, Lockheed C-160s and C-130s, from the candle-lit runway. The planes flew late at night, with almost no lights. We flew to Rundu, Sector 2Ø's HQ. We arrived at 01h00, I reported to my OC, phoned my wife and then went to shower. I'll never forget it. I didn't know where to start. I stripped off my uniform, which I later burnt, as it was so filthy. I looked in the mirror at this animal-like creature that sort of resembled me. I had this reddish-brown beard that turned black closer to my face. I had to cut that before I could shave. And even then I must have shaved about three times. I'd had a Number One cut in Mavinga. That was a laugh. We all used the same barbers, who used electric razors, and you had to sit on a trommel. About 30 guys lined up at a time: black, white, UNITA, FNLA, us. And it's not like the officers went anywhere else for a cut; we all went to the trommel. I didn't see lice, but, man, I thought about them! It was very casual and reminded me of the barbers you see on the pavements in Joburg. So my hair wasn't too long, but I still had to wash it five times before it and my scalp felt clean. Then I washed and scrubbed with soap and a scrubbing brush to try and get my slightly cleaner skin free of all the impregnated sand and burnt offerings. I even used Handy Andy at one stage to try and get this black colour out. I finally got out of the shower at 05h30. A four-and-a-half-hour shower! It was a total transformation. I tell you, one thing I learnt from that whole experience – to appreciate things. In civvy street you are so used to just switching on a tap and there's clean, warm water. But when you go months without being able to wash or have clean clothes, you learn not to take it for granted. It's like sleeping on a Sealy Posturepedic every night; you never truly appreciate it. But if you sleep in a hole with a rock sticking into your side and it's raining, and you sleep like that for nights on end, when you do go to sleep on a Sealy, you really, really appreciate it. I learnt to truly appreciate a comfortable bed and sanitation. — **Greg, age 25**

Plaaslike Bevolking

We called it the Dead Zone. It was a strip of a few kilometres where nothing lived. We killed everything that moved. It was a scorched-earth policy. There was a sense that we could mete out any sort of justice to stop the violence there in South West Africa and ensure it didn't move south to our country. We were dressed in terrorist camouflage, with no identification on us, painted with Black Is Beautiful and using captured weapons. We dressed like SWAPO and carried terrorist weapons. If our helicopters had to extract us, the only way they would be able to tell us apart from terrorists was if we turned our hats inside out and they saw the bright orange patch inside our cammo bush hats. It showed up clearly, even through dust. We spent days in the bush or waiting at temporary helicopter bases, sleeping in narrow slit trenches, living off rat packs, helping ourselves to the odd cow belonging to the few locals brave enough to try and live in this Dead Zone. The very few villagers who stayed in the Dead Zone, probably because they had nowhere else to go, had the worst of both worlds. We would question them about their support for the terrorists, and if they gave the wrong answer or we thought they needed to be taught a lesson, we would destroy their bush huts and scatter or kill their livestock. Once we had been through, the terrorists – the other baddies – would go through raping and murdering, physically reminding everyone who they were.

– Chris, age 17

While we were still candidate officers we were sent up to the Border. We didn't have any contact with the enemy, but we did have to go around trying to get information. We had black translators, who were also trackers, with us. When we entered a village, they would ask for information. The people were always too scared to talk. If they didn't get co-operation, they would set fire to a hut or two. This usually

AN UNPOPULAR WAR

worked. I also saw them hitting villagers with rifle butts. When we moved on, the translators used to take a woman or two with them and some goats. The women had to slaughter and cook the goats for them, and I know they raped the women at night because I could hear those sounds. The moaning and crying. In the mornings we checked around the TB for tracks. There were always tracks, which I'm sure were from the husbands or men looking for their girlfriends. As we moved on, the black translators would let the women go and then do the same at the next village. I only talked about this with my buddy. Your buddy was the guy you ate with, talked with and who watched your back when you had to go to the toilet. We came from an academic background and had never seen this sort of behaviour. But it is funny what you soon accept as normal.   – Werner, age 21

We were in Angola. We entered a village to ask when last SWAPO had been through – don't know if we would ever have got a truthful answer. We got the medic to treat a small child who had fallen into a fire. We noticed some chickens running around, and after two weeks out we were tired of dry rations. The idea of roast chicken sounded good. We asked for a couple, but the villagers said no. We promptly selected a few chickens and loaded them up. There was a lot of noise from the locals, but they couldn't do much, could they? All the goodwill generated by the medical treatment destroyed in minutes. I felt entitled then to take what we did.   – Paul, age 17

It was difficult to differentiate between the civilians and the gooks, terrs or whatever we called them. However, if they took off their shirts, you might see if they had been carrying a heavy pack, as there'd be strap marks on their shoulders, or webbing marks across their middles. No calluses on their feet meant they'd been wearing boots. Signs, or rather the absence of signs, like that told you if someone was a civilian or not. Sometimes I had to get information. One time I injected a guy to make him talk, telling him it would eat him from the inside, but I had actually pumped him full of antibiotics. He talked and probably got rid of his VD and anything else. We also used to make out that a helicopter was flying 200 feet in the air, but it was only a foot or so off the ground. We'd throw one guy out and he'd scream, and as he hit the deck we would quickly shut him up. The other guy is sitting with a hood over his head and thinks his mate is dead, so maybe he should say something. Mind games. — **Ric, age 18**

In the Caprivi we used some of the local Ovambos to work with us. The one guy was a witchdoctor. I don't think he was a very good one. He'd pointed out somebody who had stolen a goat, so the police arrested him. There was a trial and it came out that there was no way this guy could've stolen the goat. The police had paid the witchdoctor two chickens to sniff out the guilty party, so now they wanted their chickens back. We had to have this hearing, me a one-pip lieutenant, supposedly a responsible person for whom the witchdoctor worked, and a policeman. We sat on chairs, the rest on the floor. They discussed all the evidence and I didn't understand a word, but it turns out the witchdoctor can't return the chickens 'cause he'd eaten them. We fixed a price on them, and I guaranteed that we would deduct an amount from his salary over the next two months to reimburse them.

— **Paul, age 17**

This black gentleman was walking through the Angolan bush in men's old-fashioned platform shoes. He was wearing a suit that was many sizes too small for him. The pants ended halfway between his ankles and his knees, and the jacket sleeves were also too short and just reached past his elbows. We stopped him, and it was incredible – he spoke Afrikaans! He had learnt it while working on a mine in Tsumeb. I never considered him a terrorist. A lot of the terrorists are barefoot, and you could see he had spent most of his life wearing boots, probably mine boots. He explained that he had been invited to a wedding and he was en route to another wyk, dressed in his best attire.

– **Dudley, age 21**

I will never forget this because I'm sure it came up in the TRC. We had set claymores in our doodsakker, and if anyone crossed into that and the trip flare was triggered, we were supposed to set them off. This one time the flare goes off and it turns out to be Bushmen. They tell us they are on their way home. Not long after that, these SWA Recces come in and say they are after the Bushies because they are AWOL. During the TRC hearings they talked about Bushmen being hunted, and I wonder. You can't believe something like that could ever happen, but I did immediately think of that instance.   – **Paul, age 17**

There was this huge fucking pot-bellied fucking pig of a major. A real fucking Dutchman from Military Intelligence. What he wanted was for us to go to these cuca shops … listen to how dof this is … and ask anyone who could potentially be a SWAPO guerrilla – which meant anyone who was black and between the ages of 18 and 70 – to come with us 'cause we wanted to ask them some questions about the degree and amount of support for SWAPO in the area. So we'd arrive at these cuca shops, armed to the teeth, and of course they wouldn't want to accompany us! Eventually we'd end up grabbing them at gunpoint, tying their hands behind their backs and blindfolding them before loading them onto a truck. They were screaming. It was a fucking nightmare. We loaded these poor fuckers, about 50 Ovambos, into the truck and started driving. At one stage one Ovambo jumped off the truck and this one PF piece of shit, the Military Intelligence officer, swings his rifle round and tries to shoot him. As he lifted up his rifle, one of my best friends, B, grabs the rifle barrel and depresses it as the round is fired. The shot went into the ground and B took the rifle away from him. We captured the Ovambo again and drove on to Eenhana, one of the fire support bases right near the Border. As we get into the camp, I took my magazine off and cleared my rifle. Now these poor fucking Ovambos on the back of the truck have already heard one shot being fired and they hear me cocking my rifle, clearing it, and the one guy says to me in Afrikaans, 'Ek het geweet julle sal ons doodskiet' [I knew you were going to shoot us]. They kept them all night, blind-folded and hands tied. The next morning they faced about a 10-kay walk back to where they had come from.   – **John, age 22**

We were on patrol in South West and had stopped in a village when these two Casspirs arrived, filled with black and white Koevoet guys. Like us, they were not wearing regular South African uniforms, but were in their own police cammo shorts and T-shirts. They were all fired up 'cause they had just been in a contact and killed 11 terrorists. They'd tied the bodies on the Casspir's mudguards, and they reminded me of deer carcasses strapped to truck bonnets by hunters. As the troops drove in, the freshly killed corpses bounced up and down and left a trail of blood in the dust. We all stood around and exchanged war stories about killing and also about rugby, all in the same breath. I think they came into the village to show the bodies to the locals, rather than us. The message on one level was, 'Look, you are safe now, the terrorists are dead,' and on a second level, 'Don't even think about being a terrorist 'cause you see what will happen to you.' We must have looked terrifying: we had not washed for weeks, were smeared in black camouflage paint, dressed in dirty, torn uniforms, and were bristling with weapons. Some village children were crying, but others were playing in the dust, using sticks to draw lines around the pools of blood gathering under the corpses.   – **Chris, age 17**

I was fortunate to have the opportunity to work with Koevoet and 101 Battalion troops for a week. The latter wore South West African uniforms with diamonds instead of stars to depict rank. I was one of seven guys in a reaction platoon. We were part of a stopper group assigned to help them with an extradition from Angola and prevent the terrs they were chasing from escaping when they went in after them. They were going into Angola to catch specific terrs that had been identified and targeted. We all crossed the jati into Angola. The jati was an area a few kilometres wide and it ran for a few kays before ending at the Angolan border. It was an area of nothingness – everything had been flattened so that anything moving was visible. The Koevoet and 101 Battalion guys caught the terrs they were after and then gave them what we call a bosbus. They tied the terrs spread-eagled on the bonnet of the Casspirs and drove through the thickest and thorniest bush they could find. I enjoyed talking with the Koevoet guys – they were a law unto themselves. Unless you were with them and part of what was happening, they never talked about their experiences. The 101 guys were very quiet and kept to themselves.   **– Clint, age 18**

It was usual to bring terr bodies back to base after a contact, and there was a reason for this: to win the hearts and minds of the locals. We were in the base, Nkongo, when a terr was brought in strapped to a Casspir. He was still alive, and the Koevoet guys had given him a bosbus on the way back. The medics treated him for an abdominal gunshot wound. They didn't use morphine but, rather, Sosenol as a painkiller. He was then taken down into the interrogation tent for a chat. I got to meet him later, because we used to take it in turns to stand guard over prisoners. Guard duty was limited to a half-hour stretch – brass didn't want any extended contact between us and the prisoner and therefore no bond could form. He spoke English and I got talking to him. We spoke about how we missed home, and I gathered from what he said that SWAPO soldiers were not treated as well or as humanely as we were in day-to-day military life. But he was well trained and didn't divulge any critical information. Many of the terrorists were very well educated and spoke English. A lot of them had travelled extensively: Cuba, Russia, China and Central African countries. They were often exceptionally well trained and had some of the best equipment in the world. They had good medical equipment, and although the AK-47 may not have been the best rifle in the world, it was incredibly tough: you could throw it in the mud and it still worked, or drive over it with a Samil and it would still fire. This guy was dressed in what we called rice-fleck cammo. The terrs wore cammo that was very distinctive from ours. He only wore trousers, and they were a grey, purple colour with small dark grey flecks that resembled grains of rice. He opened up a little booklet and showed us photos of his girlfriend and letters from his family. He was a human being just like us.

The next morning, he was dead. He had died from his gunshot wound. While we were having breakfast, we saw them drag his body up from the tent and, as was usual with all terr bodies, he was dumped in the middle of the camp to lie in the sun to bloat. Just before last light we were instructed to load him onto the flatbed Unimog that was used for menial tasks and take him to the kakgat area for disposal. Six of us loaded him, six spades and a 44-gallon drum of A1 jet fuel on to the vehicle, and then drove out the gates with a driver and an interpreter. We stopped at the village, which was right outside Ngongo Base, and called everyone over to gather around outside the school-house. About 50 people lived in the village and there were a lot of children around. Who knows what they thought as the interpreter briefly told them to look at the body and, if they supported SWAPO, this is what would happen to them. We then drove on into a dip, which is where the kakgat was. This was an area with holes for various types of rubbish. The villagers could only see the tops of our heads as we moved around, but they knew what was going on. We followed the instructions to dig a shallow grave, only about three feet deep, and were specifically told to place the body face down in the ground. I'll tell you why later. Then we poured the entire barrel of fuel over him and lit it. Our instructions were clear – we must leave no evidence of the body. It was a relatively clean affair – no weird Afrikaners or Koevoet guys came out with us to set fire to the body. I think your mind suppresses what you are actually doing. You can't act negatively in front of the others, but you have no bad dreams, no regrets, you don't feel bad about what you are doing or anything regarding that day. That all comes later, years later.

A few days after this, we were sent on patrol. Patrol was either for seven or 14 days; it wasn't usual to go out for 21 days, although it was a possibility. You never left through the camp's main gate; when you went on patrol you went over the wall. So off we go, past the kakgat and out into the bush. We walked about 60 kilometres, and on the third day stopped at last light to set up a TB. The area was hot – we knew there were terrorists there – and we had been criss-crossing, moving from reference point to reference point all day. There were about 25 of us, and we moved in a classic V-formation. The two Bushmen trackers and a guy and his dog from the dog unit – to help sniff out tracks – in front, and then whoever had been causing the most kak in the unit had to walk point with them. The others spread out behind and outwards, and the support guys – the corporal, signaller, 1 and 2 mortars, medic and 2nd lieutenant – in the middle. The last guys at the end of each point of the V were the light machine-gunners and lance corporal. Then there was a back line of guys. When you set up a TB, you sleep in a largish circle and there is only one entry point. Even if you have to go to the toilet, which is not a private affair, 'cause you have to go with your buddy, you exit and enter the TB through the same point. At night, everyone other than the support guys is tied to one another with a light cord so that when you change guard duty you don't have to make a sound, you just tug on the cord. We copied the Bushmen, who scraped the top layer, about 15 centimetres, off the surface of the packed earth into a rough pillow. Then we propped our webbing against that, climbed into the sleeping bag and tied the drawstring firmly around our neck to keep out the night crawlers. You could sleep fairly comfortably. We buried our water to chill it. The purified water was revolting, but at least tasted better when ice cold.

That night the Bushmen trackers practically dug trenches to sleep in, telling us they were convinced the terrs were going to attack. Sure enough, about 1 a.m. we hear the mortar pipes going off in the distance. They overshoot us completely, 'cause they don't know exactly where we are. We sit *vas* and go back to sleep. They know we're in the area, so they start walking, looking for us. They walk right through the TB. We didn't hear them and they didn't see us. Only very early the next morning, when we saw their tracks, did we discover that they'd been right through the middle of the TB. The Bushmen trackers followed the spoor and we ambushed the terrs at first light. It was a very short contact. You don't see much happen 'cause you fight from a distance. There were only five of them; we neutralised three of them and two got away. We radioed for the Pumas and they came in and extracted us and the bodies of the terrs. We get back to base and the bodies are left in the sun. At the end of the day we are told to take them to the kakgat. No winning of hearts and minds this time – just straight to the kakgat. We used to say some of our guys had no culture, only agriculture, and a bunch of those types came along. We dug three shallow graves and put the bodies in, but this time there was no dignity. The guys were messing around and making fun of the bodies by sticking cigarettes in their ears and noses. Then they placed them face up in the graves, poured fuel on them and lit the bodies. When a body burns, the skin goes black and then white as it burns off. A burning body's muscles contract and often cause the body to sit up and move, which is why we were told to place bodies face down before lighting them. The one body sat up and a guy swung his spade at the head, decapitating it.

I fired mortars in the army. Just by looking at a terr and the trees near to him and so on, I could almost instantly determine how far away he was. I could land a mortar within a square metre over 1 200 metres; I would fire and a figure would drop to the ground. Death was always distant. But this was different. Burning bodies made death more real to me than anything else I ever saw. **– Van, age 19**

...gun, and these two... around. The guy who was supposed to have been on the weapon was on a guilt trip, thinking if he had been doing what he was supposed to, this wouldn't have happened. The guy who was using it was on a guilt trip because he hadn't cleared the weapon properly, and I was on a guilt trip because I had made the assumption that all weapons had been cleared and made safe. It traumatised all of us involved, but counselling in those days was minimal - you're fucked up, that's all there is to it. – Anonymous

It was a Sunday afternoon, 1978, in Ondangwa, and I was having a nap. I woke up to this tremendous explosion – it was as loud as the dynamite explosions used in the mining industry. This nearby camp, allegedly a Recce camp with alleged explosive experts working at defusing Black Widows, POM-Z and Claymore mines, just went up with this 'boom'. We were told that two guys had been blown to smithereens. About a week later, in one of the Afrikaans newspapers that made it up to the Border, I read this detailed account of how these two guys had been killed in a follow-up operation. The whole story was contrived. I knew the names, and it was the same two guys who had been blown up. There is this whole blab that had no bearing or connection to what had actually happened. I know 'cause I had been present when it happened. I saw the propaganda machine in action, and it taught me that 'seeing is believing'. – John, age 18

Once, while waiting around for a personnel changeover, we snuck away from our outpost base to buy beers from one of the local cuca shops. We were mellowing out in the cuca shop garden, pretending to be civilians for the afternoon, when we heard a mighty explosion

Contact

Running in lines from east to west were kaplyne. These were long sandy 'roads' stretching for miles, which were impossible to cross without leaving a sign. There were no overhanging trees, no rocks, no branches, no patches of grass, nothing – just sand. They lay in a band between the Border and just north of the farming areas, like Tsumeb, and often ran between farming fences. The army used a Buffel to drag a tree so that the kaplyne were swept clear daily and we could check for fresh spoor. We could easily spot any tracks from terrs who might have crossed the kaplyn the night before. It was impossible to cross these stretches of swept sand without leaving a trace. Bushmen trackers from 101 and SWA Territorial Forces used to sit on the front of the Buffel looking for signs of a crossing or mine-laying activity. Usually the terrs would cross into South West in large groups of anything from 50 to 200 guys and then they would bombshell into smaller groups, as few as three or five. The trick was to catch them when the group was still large. And these guys would run – not walk, but run. Sometimes Intel would be given information and we would know when to expect a crossing and from which base in Angola the guys were coming. These guys were skinny guys and carried minimum dry rats: a few tins of Russian tuna and some mielie meal. But they came in carrying as much kit as they could: Black Widows, cheese mines, RPGs, RPDs, ammo, and they all had AK-47s. Some were given a few South African rands.

My clearest memories are of the first few contacts we had inside South West. I recall these SWAPO incursions more than our ops into Angola. We were spending our time doing patrols with little purpose really, just walking from A to B and making ourselves visible to the locals. We were based not far north of Oshivelo, and that evening we were given the opportunity to travel to Tsumeb for a Geraldine concert.

She was a corny country and western singer who was a big hit with the troops. I think one of her songs was 'Baby Makes Her Blue Jeans Talk'. Anyway, about 150 of us are sitting in the dark, watching the show, when the lights go on and we're told there's been an insurgency and everyone must get back to their vehicles immediately. We leave Geraldine and her blue jeans behind and head off for one of the kaplyne. We are to form a stopper group on a fence line just off to the south of one of the kaplyne. We form a long line of guys, about five to ten metres apart. There are also these large observation towers and the guys in them have night-vision equipment. It's pitch dark and completely silent. Nothing happens. We see no one. The next morning we are back in Ratels, about 12 of them in Alpha Company. We check out an area further west down the kaplyn from where we had been the night before. The trackers pick up where terrs had crossed. They all wore Russian boots with very distinctive spoor: a couple of V-shaped notches facing the front of the boot. I'm sitting on the front of the Ratel, and E, a guy from the Eastern Cape, is walking around looking at where the guys had come through the fence and crossed the line. He shouldn't have been there, on the ground, walking around. There was this *boom!* and smoke and dust as he stepped on a Black Widow. I was sprayed with sand and he collapsed with one leg blown off. We couldn't find any part of his leg, only a corner from the back of his boot. The wound wasn't bleeding much. The edges were ragged and partly sealed from the heat of the blast. He was lying there, conscious but completely quiet. No screaming or shouting. The medic treated him while we waited for a chopper to casevac him out. It felt like we waited forever. I was lucky, because that type of mine is a small concentrated charge, designed not to kill a person but to maim, and this one was buried in soft sand, which absorbed some of the charge. When one goes off, injuring someone, it has a demoralising effect on the rest of us. One minute we were in a hall in Tsumeb being entertained by the sexy singer Geraldine belting out country and western hits, and now this.

WE flew out, and some time later we picked up more spoor on the swept kaplyn. One of the Ratels, two behind 13 Bravo, the one I was in, was told to follow the tracks. It hit a sharp right, went straight over farm fences and flattened bushes and trees, 'cause that's how we drove up there, driving right on top of the tracks. The rest of us kept on, moving westwards down the kaplyn. Suddenly we hear a massive gunfight. There's just the noise of explosions and rounds going off. We immediately call for gunships and start to turn around, get into platoon attack formation and make our way back towards the Ratel that had turned off. We can't see it, but we know where it is by the terrific noise. We come into a shona and in the middle of it is this huge blaze. It was the Ratel. Bodies were lying around, some on fire and some squirming around. I've never seen such a terrible sight. The terrs had set up an ambush on the south side of the shona, and as the Ratel drove into the open clearing, they had opened fire with rockets, RPDs, which have armour-piercing rounds, rifle grenades and AK-47s. Following our training, the objective is to actually pass right through the kill zone of an ambush to the far side to take out the terrs if they are there. So we had to cross the shona, past the burning Ratel, the burning men and the injured, and check the far side before coming back into the kill zone to see if we could do anything. We'd come in in the Ratels and now we had to jump out and start 'vuur en beweging' [fire and movement]. I've never been so afraid. It was the most terrifying thing to have to move around in that open clearing expecting to be shot or blown up any minute. At that point we didn't know if there were any terrs still in the area. There was still ammo going off when we got there, but it was from the burning Ratel. A Ratel carries 11 people; a driver, a gunner, a commander, a tail gunner, two mortars and five riflemen. Some of the troops had been riding on the outside of the Ratel, and one guy who'd been sitting on the Ratel's spare tyre had been blown off. He lost the back of his legs and most of his arse, but at least he survived.

Although the gunships had got a few of the terrs, we went out the next day with Casspirs, ten Bushmen trackers in each, to pick up the spoor from the kaplyn again. The terrs who had ambushed us had bombshelled completely, so we went back to the kaplyn looking for a larger group to track. We preferred to track a bunch of at least three or more rather than individuals. We found spoor from a small group and then two of the trackers ran in front. Once they had the spoor they would keep on it, rotating trackers every hour or so, so that they were always fresh and fast. It was called hot pursuit. If we picked up tracks that were maybe 12 hours old we could catch up fast, and by the end of the day we would only be an hour or two behind. If we couldn't catch them that day, we camped for the night. Naturally the terrs didn't stop to sleep or eat but kept going. Of course, this meant that by morning we were back to a 12-hour-old track. But the terrs knew if they crossed another kaplyn, we would not be far behind them. As they became more tired they started dropping equipment, discarding whatever wasn't essential.

When we were only minutes behind, we called in the spotter plane. It could fly very slowly and very low, and it was fairly easy for the pilot to spot a person. When he spotted the guys we were chasing, he dropped a white phosphorous grenade as a marker. This rose and expanded and was easy to see over a fair distance. We put foot. All the trackers back on board the Casspir, and it was a flat-out rush to reach that white cloud as fast as possible. We caught up with the terrs, four of them. The contact was brief. They were exhausted; they'd been running for days, so it was over quickly. When the shooting stopped, it was a mad rush to reach the bodies to see what we could take off them. We took stuff as souvenirs: their equipment, uniforms, and of course the first person there usually got the money. It was only about R20 or so, but when you only got paid about R70, that was a lot of money. I ran up to one of the bodies, propped up against a tree. He was a young, skinny black guy with light brown army pants and a civvy shirt. I started going through his pockets, looking for the money when he started making these wheezing, gurgling sounds. Man! He was still alive! I stepped back and – *bam bam bam!* – I emptied half a magazine into his chest, then stepped forward and continued going through his pockets. I clearly remember finding a couple of crisp, brand new R20s. I split them with an oke from 101 who was next to me. **– Anonymous**

Three incidents concerning death stand out in my mind. It was strange: we saw an awful lot of action for a six-month period only, and then, after that, nothing but patrols, patrols, patrols. The first incident involved this big Dutchman. The biggest guys carried the LMG, and this one particular guy was large, windgat and a bully. We had got into a bit of an unusual situation in that we were in a more conventional contact. We were slowly working our way through a small town, building by building, doing house clearing. There was a lot going on. This LMG guy was standing in a small, low tree, his feet braced on a thick branch while firing his machine gun over the top of the wall. We ran around to be on the same side of the wall as him, and as we come around, we see this terr fire an anti-personnel grenade at our LMG's back. But it doesn't detonate. It lodges in the wall (which consists mainly of mud) right between the LMG guy's legs. He swings around, because there is a very heavy recoil and a fierce noise when this type of grenade is launched, looks over his right shoulder and sees us two very tanned Englishmen. It was quite funny. For a split second we could see him thinking and wondering if we had shot at him, but before anything else happened, the lieutenant shot the terr. The LMG guy then looked over his other shoulder and saw the terr who had tried to shoot him. He went as white as a sheet and looked like a *nagapie*, his eyes were so huge. That guy changed completely that day. He became a humble and nice human being.

In the second incident, as part of the mortar team, we were on the high ground overlooking a village. We received information that there was a cache of terrorist weapons hidden in the village. The platoon had been split into three groups – two stopper groups and one attacking group – and they were busy in and around the village. We hadn't even started firing mortars down onto the village when a PKM opened up. A PKM has the most unbelievable cyclic rate – it fires a staggering amount of rounds per minute – and because of that it has a very distinctive sound. It opened up from the high ground on the opposite side of the village and it shredded everything around us. I couldn't believe that they hit every tree, bush, shrub, everything, but somehow missed us. There were leaves and twigs falling all around us and we were covered in a dusty cloud from the dirt that the rounds kicked up. We were in the open with no cover, and everything around us shot to pieces, but none of us were hit. We did find the weapons, buried in a grondseil in the middle of three scattered huts.

The third experience occurred during a helicopter assault. If we knew where a terrorist base was, we could drop an HE bomb the size of a soccer ball right onto it. The weight of the bomb allowed it to penetrate right through the roof and it would detonate underground, destroying bunkers, tunnels and whatever else was down there. We came flying in on the Pumas. I loved to sit in the doorway with my feet on the step and look straight down at the ground as the helicopters banked steeply and only the G-force kept me safely suspended. The Puma didn't land; it hovered just off the ground as we jumped out. I was one of the first to exit because of where I liked to sit. As my feet touched the earth, it gave way and I fell straight through the roof of a tunnel. We had been dropped right on top of a hidden base. The terrs could build an entire base underground, even housing T-34 tanks, and you wouldn't even know it was there 'cause nothing showed above ground. I was completely disorientated when I landed on the tunnel floor. You can imagine: you think you are jumping onto solid ground but end up falling through the air, and you suddenly go from bright sunshine to darkness. I was very fortunate – we all were – that the base was abandoned. — **Clint, age 18**

I was with a mobile signals unit. We operated on a certain grid pattern; extending out from Grootfontein up towards the Border. We had our guys at various points, all of us waiting to pick up a transmission. When we did, we could plot it and move into that area of about 40 square kilometres, and then we had to wait again for a signal, cross-reference that and move in closer again. When we picked up that tap-tap Morse code again and were real close, the guys went in on foot in a line searching for this one terr. You had to look really hard and it could take ages to find the guy. This one wasn't transmitting frequently, and when we found the area he was in, it was really difficult to locate him 'cause he was in cammo, under camouflage netting in a pit dug into the ground, and his aerial was cleverly disguised in a tree. He was the leader of one of the regional detachments. Next thing we could hear gunfire and the Morse code still transmitting. He was frantically signalling that he was under attack. The Morse code kept going and so did the gunfire, and next thing there was just this long unbroken signal. He must have been shot and fallen forward onto his transmission key. — **Anonymous**

I lost three colleagues in one day. One guy was a HQ signaller who wasn't even meant to go out. The usual guy had flu, so he had replaced him. They were out on patrol, led by Section Leader Klopper, and they hit a contact. Klopper survived unscathed, even though all the guys around him, my three friends, were killed. His life was spared big time. Two years after Klopper left the army, he was in a car accident. The vehicle rolled, and even though he was not seriously injured, he lay on the side of the road in mid-winter for so long that he went into shock and got hypothermia. Complications set in, and although he was taken to hospital, he died. He had cheated death twice, once on the Border, and again in the car crash, but finally it was the cold that got him. **– John, age 19**

I was a very diligent officer, and if I was told to patrol in a specific direction for a specific distance, I would do so. I enforced my own personal discipline to ensure that the people I was responsible for adhered to what was expected of them and to make sure they respected the environment in which they operated. If you become blasé, you pick up problems. One particular day during rainy season, we picked up tracks, enemy footprints, on this dirt road. Having spent time up there, you got to recognise the different types of boots and what type of prints they left. I knew these were not ours. The prints were fresh, and I saw this as an opportunity to rest up for the day, as it was a prefect reason to justify a stop and to set up an observation post without me being negligent or neglecting my duties as an officer. Although not a hundred percent certain, I thought there was a possibility the enemy might come back along the same route. So we set up a well-concealed post, but in such a manner that the three guys in it could see the road clearly. The rest of the group moved about 150 metres away. I instructed the three individuals who were in the observation post that if they didn't come back with a strike rate of 75 percent – that is, if four people walk into the ambush and they don't take out a minimum of three out of four – then they mustn't come back at all. They must just pick up their bags without saying a word and head south. I waited with the others. One of the guys watching the road tried to make radio contact with me, but he was whispering and I couldn't hear what he was attempting to communicate. I said to him, 'Either speak up or revisit your volume control.' A firefight ensued with three terrorists. One got away only because he was lagging behind the others. He 'packed out swastikas' and escaped. Basically, we took out two enemy soldiers because of laziness, wanting to rest. It wouldn't have happened otherwise. It really excited the people back at base – the enemy had been engaged and they had two dead to report. I found it rather humorous that this effectively resulted in me being transferred to the Pathfinders for the next year.   **– Dudley, age 21**

Ballas Bak

I was on an island in the south of the Caprivi doing some monitoring work with five other guys, watching for infiltration of people. It was a beautiful island, like being in the Okavango Delta. Work was great, life was easy, although we didn't get replenished often, so we lived off the land 90 percent of the time. We didn't have cigarettes, so we smoked wild tobacco, and the only paper we had was the Bible. I smoked from Genesis to Revelations. — **Ric, age 18**

Ja, there were times of pure terror, but there were also times of extreme boredom. To relieve the boredom we graded flies. There was the small, the medium and the large. The small was this fruit fly type of thing, irritating as hell. They loved moisture, so they would sit in the corner of your eye or crawl up your nose. They were very persistent. You couldn't just flap them away – you literally had to scratch or squash them, which was not a good idea, 'cause then it burnt like hell. The medium was the standard persistent little shit, the normal common fly. Then there were the large, the serious horseflies. We would watch the flies, grade the flies, talk about the flies. If we could catch them, we'd pull their wings off, just to get our own back. But I think they must have got blown up, 'cause they seemed to get fewer and fewer with time. — **Greg, age 25**

We were bored, and killed time by making ornaments out of shell casings. We made wine glasses, dinner bells, sugar scoops and other rudimentary things out of the brass. One day the guys showed me something they were working on, and I wondered where they had got the casing from, as we hadn't shot for a while. I asked them where they'd got it from, and they told me they had cut the live head off with a hacksaw. The head can be triggered by heat, and there they were, sawing a 40-millimetre round apart! — **Dave, age 19**

There was a lull on the Border when the seasons changed. This was tanning time. During wet season we couldn't really undertake major operations into Angola, because the heavy equipment would get bogged down, so we didn't do much with regard to ground forces, as it wasn't conducive to conventional attacks. This was the time the terrs crossed in from Angola, heading for the farming community and such, to carry out attacks. We moved north in the dry season and they infiltrated south in the wet season. Kinda like tides. In the gap between the changing of the seasons, things were generally quieter and we could do some tanning. We'd put on our red joggers, which were hideous. They were these shiny red fabric shorts displaying the unit logo, edged with white piping and a slit up the side. Terrible, but, I suppose, quite fashionable at the time. Then we'd slap on brake fluid or ATF, that red liquid you use for power steering and such. Beautiful. We'd smear it on and lie in the sun for hours. **– Christian, age 18**

If you were off duty, you often tanned. We never took our malaria tablets, 'cause they made your skin go this horrible yellow colour, and we heard that when taken long term, they weakened your liver. So we never took them, and tanned using diesel oil. I got a great tan and no malaria. **– John, age 19**

We used to sit in the operating theatre with the medics, experimenting with combinations of oxygen and laughing gas. But first choice was Sosenol, a morphine derivative which put you on a plak and made you comfortably numb. The advantage was that no one could prove you had used up the supply on recreational purposes, 'cause it was used in the field as a painkiller. There was also dope on the Border. Some bases were so strict and the discipline so enforced that you never got away with it. Other bases were more lax and it was very easy to get dope and to use it. As long as you functioned and weren't blatant about smoking dagga, they ignored it. We had a few petrol heads come through our camp once. These were usually support troops, like mechanics, who sniffed petrol in order to get a buzz going. I wasn't big on it, 'cause it gave me a shit headache, but I remember the one night some of us tried sniffing carbon tetrachloride, the stuff you use to clean records. None of us had tried this before, so we all had a good sniff. We shat ourselves when one of the guys said that even one sniff was enough to make one impotent for life. At our base all the nurses were officers, and no way could we approach a female officer without getting fucked up by the male officers for trying to fraternise with them. We spent half an hour trying to secretly attract the attention of the base nurse while she was having a party with the officers. I'm sure we thought we were being careful and quiet, but we were probably making a helluva racket throwing stones at the window and psssst-ing when we saw her on the balcony. Finally she noticed us and came over. We told her our concerns and she told us that we were stupid, but it was unlikely that we had sniffed enough to be impotent.

– Chris, age 17

When we were bored, we used to stick a piece of rolled-up toilet paper between a guy's toes and light it. Once I did it to a guy under a mozzie net, and that caught fire too! The other thing was to hold a lit cigarette just above the toenail. It would heat up, and even when the guy jumped up it would continue to burn, 'cause the nail was still so hot. Man, we had some fun. **– Anthony, age 18**

There was a lot of horseplay, and once back in the States, at Swartkops, it was teatime and we were sitting playing bridge. I saw this hand come around the corner holding a black tin with a red cap. I saw the sleeve was green like a pilot's overall. I knew it was tear gas and tried to run, but I still got caught. We thought it was the pilots, so we got a small canister of tear gas and sprayed it into the pilots' tearoom. They, in turn, thought it was 44 Squadron, so they tear-gassed them. And so it went around. Everybody sprayed everybody, but it was always the wrong group. Eventually we found out it was this flight engineer. We waited until he went to the toilet. When we heard he was busy with a number two, we sprayed tear gas under the door. He couldn't go anywhere! He got what was coming to him!   – **Tallies, age 17**

We were *bos oupas*, as opposed to *ou manne*, who were in any camp but not on the Border. Whenever *roofs* came up, we did the same thing that was done to us – we made them chew their Daraclor, their malaria tabs. It is the most awful fucking taste in the world. And no matter how much you chewed and rinsed your mouth, there would always be some little piece left that fell out from between your teeth during parade when there was no water.   – **Andy, age 18**

We had two Paracats. They were called Bliksem and Streeps. We used to strap parachutes from the flares around them and drop them off from the top of the tower and they'd float down. Two chutes to a cat were best. We learnt this the hard way when Bliksem's one chute failed to open properly and he spiralled down, bounced on a tent roof and then fell onto a sandbag. I love cats and I thought, oh my God, I am going to have to shoot this cat. I got down the tower so fast that when I got there he had just stood up and was shaking himself and the harness off. Luckily he was fine. They never ran away, so I guess they enjoyed being Paracats.   – **Dave, age 19**

We were up in Mongua in Angola, in trenches around the HQ Bunker, the communication centre and where the commandant and sergeant major housed themselves. We decided to play Bolland's 'You're in the Army Now' over the guard radio. As soon as the sergeant major had the opportunity to get on the radio, because we'd effectively blocked it by keying and keeping the mike open while playing the song, he demanded that the individual or individuals responsible present themselves at the bunker, as in yesterday. As we were officers – lieutenants – the two of us figure we couldn't let the troops take the knock for it, and so we headed off to the bunker to present ourselves. The commandant looks at us and asks us, in Afrikaans, what we are doing there. He thought we had come for some other reason, and when we told him we were the two individuals responsible for playing the song, you could see he wanted to smile. He told us to go back to the trenches, think of a suitable punishment and inform him of that punishment the next morning. We wracked our brains but couldn't think of a suitable punishment, and he never pursued it any further.

– **Dudley, age 21**

Being in the army could teach you a lack of accountability. I would be working on road construction somewhere and would send the driver in the truck to go 20 kays to get me a 20-cent packet of chips and bring it back to me. The amount of diesel required to do that … but you had this perception, well, the army supplies the diesel, so it just doesn't cost anything. – **Paul, age 17**

I was on the Border – near Okalongo, I think it was – with Erich, whose nickname was Half-a-Bee, after a ridiculous Monty Python song. The irony was that Erich couldn't even say 'hello' in English if he tried. We were on patrol, and before settling down for the night, we'd pair off so that one could have a shit, clean his rifle or whatever while the other was on guard. I wanted to have a shit, so Half-a-Bee says he'll be on lookout. Now this whole fuckin' area is full of fuckin' dung beetles. I don't know if you've seen them. They are the most kakly designed insect in the world, 'cause it doesn't land, it crashes. And when they want to take off, they have to buzz around, gathering momentum before they go off. So I dig a hole, and have a shit. You probably don't know, but when you eat rat packs for a long time your shit goes this green colour. Anyway, this dung beetle comes *vvvvrrrr*-ing past, crash lands, climbs into the hole, puts his feet on the green shit, and he turns around and fucks off! Half-a-Bee turns around to me and says, 'Jy weet wat? Hulle eet net nie mis, hulle eet nie kak nie' [You know what? They only eat dung, they don't eat shit]. – **John, age 18**

Music and alcohol were a form of escapism. In the first year, you get a seven-day pass, and a 14-day pass in the second year. My first pass was over Christmas, and then I had to be back in camp before New Year to stand guard. When my mom and dad took me back, I sat in the car and just bawled. I couldn't handle it. When I got back to the bungalow, my mate had a Walkman and was passing it around. I escaped to Lionel Ritchie's 'Dancing on the Ceiling'. I never drank in the army. But a lot of guys did and drank a lot. The pub would open between five and nine, and some guys would drink 17 beers in that time. I asked this one guy, 'Hoekom drink jy so baie?' [Why do you drink so much?] 'Ek verlang' [I yearn], was his simple reply. – **Nick, age 20**

There was this path from the one bar at Ondangwa to the quarters, and across this path was a stormwater drain. It was about a metre and a half deep and a metre wide. Across the drain was a metal plate. As long as you walked straight down the path you could cross the drain safely. However, because at night the area was pitch dark and it was on the path from the bar, many people misjudged where the plate was and, being intoxicated, fell into the stormwater drain. It didn't help that every now and again, just for a laugh, some guys would remove the plate. We came up with the idea of welding a railing to the plate so you knew as long as you held onto the railing and crossed to the right of it, you were safely on the plate. So what did the guys do? They turned the whole thing around so the plate lay to the left of the railing. Often a guy was found the next morning curled up in a foetal position against the cold. – **Tallies, age 17**

I played golf. You had to see it to believe it. It was hilarious. There was a golf course, with a club house built by the army, in Rundu town, which was a base town. We could only go there if our sergeant major took us. Anyway, he liked to play golf, so I went along – anything to get out of camp. I'd offer to go with him 'cause he was a golf fanatic. Man, he played like shit. But fortunately I played such kak golf that I played as badly as him. The fairways were desert, the rough was thorn trees, and the greens were the nicest pieces of sand you've ever seen. They were slightly higher than the surrounding desert, flat and with a little Ovambo standing there with a pole and a flat piece of metal on the end so that he could smooth a path for your ball. He would make a straight line from your ball to the hole and you would basically hit it as hard as you could. If you played like that on a real green, you'd hit the ball 100 metres. I swear that's how I got rank, my first stripe, and my pay increase – playing golf with my sergeant major. I didn't suffer through JLs or anything, but I showed commitment on the golf course.   **– Anthony, age 18**

I and three others were hoping to run Comrades, even though we were stuck on the Border and even though we had done no hill training, run any other marathon races or done any of the other stuff they say you should do in preparation for Comrades. We were only able to train when we were off duty or at the weekends, and it was always hot, very hot. We trained by running around and around the – flat – perimeter of Ondangwa Air Force Base. I didn't think about it at the time, but thinking about it now, I realise we were such vulnerable targets. We ran right on the fence line. I couldn't believe it, but the commandant organised for us to run Comrades, and shortly before the race he organised us a flight on a C-130 from Ondangwa to Waterkloof. I know the Defence Force took pride in its athletes, but, man, just the four of us rattling around in this huge plane? It was amazing that we could do that at the government's expense! We did all right and finished in about eight hours.   **– John, age 19**

We were approached the one day by an officer and asked if we knew how to play cricket. We said we did and that we were bloody good cricketers. I'm a ... for God's sake, I know how to play cricket! We knew being in a cricket team meant we might be able to get away for a couple of days. We formed the Sector 7Ø cricket side, which I captained, and got a cricket mat and some old kit so we could practise and play on the parade ground. We had to go to Windhoek for a tournament, and from there they were going to choose the South African Defence Force cricket side. It was serious stuff. We get into a Dakota with all our hidden rations, a bottle of booze, smokes and whatever else we could shove into our kitbags. All 12 of us fly from Mpacha in the Caprivi to Windhoek, playing bridge all the way, drinking and having fun. We get to Windhoek and check into a *motel* nogal! The Safari Motel. And the next day we start our tournament. We're playing against the likes of Keppler Wessels – all these guys who are playing in the home units, in Pretoria, Johannesburg and the Northern Transvaal. We're these bushmen. The only thing we've got going for us is that we've got guts and we are as fit as fiddles and the word *no* is not in our vocabulary. We do very well: first game we played, we won. Then we get told by this big knob of a colonel that we had to be back at the motel before 10 p.m. Ten o'clock is ridiculous. We're not going to go to bed at that time. So we go out that night and end up at the Kalahari Sands at the disco at the top of the hotel. Needless to say, three of us got home as the sun was coming up. We decided that we should delay the start of the game, 'cause we were tired. So we turned on the hosepipe and put it under the cover of the cricket pitch. Play was delayed for at least two hours. The bragging side of that day was that even with that headache and babalaas, I took seven wickets for 11 runs in 14 overs. The only reason we lost that game that day was because I was too hung-over to bat. We still thought a few of us would be selected, me for my bowling and Jimmy for his batting. But some little jerk had ratted us out to the colonel, and when he was handing out the colours to everyone and announcing the South African Defence Force Team, he said, 'Due to ill discipline, the following players were not even considered …' So that night we went back to the Kalahari Sands.   – Ric, age 18

One Saturday we were told that those who wanted to experience a rough ride in a Ratel could take a ride as there was one lined up. So there we were, six bright-eyed gay guys going for a ride in the back of the Ratel. You can just imagine the shrieks and screams as we bounced across the veld! We were all laughing and shouting out, 'Watch out girls!' to each other and things like, 'Look out boys, here we come!' This one guy had been a koffiemoffie with South African Airways before the army and he stood up and did this marvellous charade, pretending that we were passengers on board a plane. 'Welcome to flight such and such, your captain today is the gorgeous so and so, and in the event of an emergency, please make your way to the nearest exits, which are now being pointed out to you.' He pointed to the imaginary exits to the front, middle and rear of the vehicle. I laughed so much I peed in my pants.   – Rick, age 18

Our base at Ongiva was at this old commercial airport terminal building. We were having a formal dinner for NCOs and commissioned officers. There were approximately 45 people in attendance. There were fancy serviettes, plates, cutlery and even a Choc-Kits biscuit right above the dessert spoon, everything. It didn't take long for a surreptitious food fight to start. We threw the biscuits at one another and then veggies wrapped in the serviettes, and a few of us accessed eggs from the chef's ration tent and were throwing those. The South African flag was hanging on the wall behind the commandant and he stood up and proposed a toast, saying that to the best of his knowledge this was the first time the South African flag had been raised in Angola and we all had to toast it. Then he turned around and saw the flag covered in egg yolk. It did dampen his spirit, but I'm sure that he realised that the intention was not malicious but merely a bit of fun being had by individuals on a tour of duty. The evening ended up with us pouring orange juice concentrate over one another. We went swimming in our drinking water, which was in these large open bladders, to clean up, and to top it all, our troops, who were guarding the terminal, had seen the entire escapade through their night-vision sights. **– Dudley, age 21**

Sundays were always very boring in 1 SAI. So we decided to liven things up and hold a fashion parade. We made dresses out of sheets, and the chefs, who had access to mutton cloth, made dresses from that. There was this conference-type room with a huge U-shaped table. The army used it for strategic planning and meetings about all things military. Not today! We managed to get the keys to this room at the centre and proceeded to use the large U-shaped table as a catwalk. We paraded and modelled our way down this table. We really strutted our stuff in our improvised dresses. It was hilarious to think of all those butch soldiers sitting around the very same table, all serious, on Monday morning, strategising and making plans for war, all while seated around our catwalk! **– Rick, age 18**

AN UNPOPULAR WAR

Where We Weren't

We were part of an assault group assigned to destroy a strategic enemy position in southern Angola. The operation was afforded the name Operation Protea. We initiated contact with the enemy at a town called Xangongo, a small town positioned alongside the Kunene River. We met with very little resistance and took it quickly because we enjoyed support in the form of Ratels, Mirages, Eland 90s – Noddy Cars – and artillery batteries. The enemy had dug in and had a complex network of trenches and bunkers, a number of tanks – T-34s, specifically – and some artillery pieces. Only a small amount of the available weaponry was utilised to resist our onslaught, and the enemy basically decided to live and fight another day by heading north. In our entire company of paratroopers we had only three non-serious casualties, which were as a result of shrapnel from a mortar. It was difficult to say whether the injuries were inflicted by the enemy or our own forces. From there we moved on through Mongua and on towards Ongiva, with very little resistance. We'd been travelling for quite a while. The plan was to attack Ongiva from the north as opposed to the south, the reason being that their defence infrastructure layout was in anticipation of an attack from the south. After about 75 kilometres, we took up temporary base outside Ongiva for the night. A temporary base can be compared to the old laager configuration – with all the vehicles and soldiers on the perimeter, facing outwards to defend what's on the inside. Ongiva was a small town, but it had banks, roads and shops. Obviously, those with some form of rank had looted the town. It was common knowledge that money had been removed from the bank and appliances from various trading stores. We laid our hands on small transistor radios. Those were the spoils for those in the military with lesser rank. As we passed through the town, we simply jumped off the vehicles, ran into the ransacked shops, and grabbed the radios. That night in the temporary base we were in our sleeping bags in the trenches with our groundsheets over us to form a shelter. And the irony of the story is that we turned on the stolen radio and unbelievably we caught a broadcast from the RSA and heard PW Botha categorically denying to the world that there were any South African forces in Angola.

– **Dudley, age 21**

We were in the Congo and were obviously there with the full knowledge and support of our then government. In return for certain favours, we were allowed access to certain things. One of the things we were having a look at was to see if some of the town or areas could be used as potential staging positions from which to launch attacks against the ANC in Tanzania. We flew into Kinshasa in a Learjet and were collected by some local and regional security forces guys. We eventually ended up in a town called Goma on Lake Kivu. We had some time there, and the local guys we were with were pressurising us to go out with them on one of their jols. Our seniors tasked two of us, the most junior officers of the group, with the duty of accompanying our hosts to a disco in Goma. I tell you, we stood out like sore thumbs. We were the only two whites in this nightclub in the middle of Africa. None of the locals were dancing, even though some of them clearly had their women with them. When we asked why they weren't dancing, they said they were waiting for us to dance first. The guy who headed up the security in the area had a very light-skinned Mulatto woman who was his wife. She could almost pass as white. I asked him if I could dance with her and he said it was fine. We danced and then I sat down. Then this nubile young black woman comes and sits on my lap! You must remember this was around 1985 – this wasn't something I was used to! She asks me to dance, and I do. Next thing the music changes to a slow dance and she is clinging onto me with her arms wrapped around me and I am just looking heavenwards with my eyes firmly fixed on the ceiling, thinking, 'Oh boy, if my mates could see me now!' We were not accustomed to this type of behaviour. After the dance she wanted a beer and asked me something in French, and when it was translated I discovered she'd asked me if I wanted to sleep with her. That's when we decided it was time to leave and ran back to the hotel. It was quite funny – running away from a woman! But the situation was just not something we had ever been exposed to before. I swear the guys from Zaire had set everything up with that woman and done it all on purpose. The next morning the senior officers were extremely inquisitive as to what had happened the night before, but we told them nothing. We just left them in the dark.

– **Anonymous**

In the early hours of the morning we boarded a chopper and headed out over the Kruger National Park. We landed in Mozambique, where we met up with a reconnaissance unit. They gave us a whole lot of boxes to load into the chopper. We then flew back to Phalaborwa. I don't know what was in them. Perhaps documents? It was rather strange. **– Clint, age 18**

It was 1982, and we flew out from Swartkops AFB to a destination defined only by co-ordinates. It ended up being a farmer's field in the Orange Free State. We landed the two Pumas carrying Special Forces generals near a big shed. When we entered it, it was filled with about 70 black Recces dressed in Basotho blankets. On the wall was a huge enlarged map showing Maseru in great detail. We were all told that that night, at H-hour, we were to hit a dozen or so targets in Maseru. These were safe houses used by the ANC, and the Recces hoped to remain undetected and move among the local population for as long as possible. We were shown photos of the houses, photos of those living there, and were given details of exactly who they were. The Recces were going to cross the Caledon River in inflatables and attack various targets simultaneously. As a helicopter pilot I was on standby in case a hot extraction was required. A C-160 was our telstar. A telstar is any aircraft that acts as a repeater station providing communications between various points. The Orange Free State farm was our HAG, and was so close to the border we could see Maseru's lights reflected in the sky.

The Recces left, and it was after midnight when we got the call to scramble. One of the guys had thrown a bomb through a window, but the walls were prefab and he was badly injured in the blast. The flight up into the mountains was hazardous. It was pitch dark and we couldn't use lights, 'cause we would make ourselves targets. We flew over our troops trying to make their way back to the river – they were to exit Lesotho where they had entered, and they were under attack from Lesotho forces, who must have known that they were heading for the river. We were shot at and took fire, even when we came in to land and pick up the injured Recce and his teammates. When we landed back at the HAG in SA, outside the farmer's big shed, the ground crew couldn't believe we had made it back, because small arms fire had ruptured a hydraulic pipe and there was this mist of hydraulic fluid spraying everywhere. **– Anonymous**

We had to get across to this one place, Cuito Cuanavale, which was very far into Angola. There was a large bridge that crossed the Cuito River and spanned a gorge. The enemy had a large air base, lots of support and infrastructure there, and we needed to blow up this bridge before they could get equipment and tanks across the river. The bridge was where they would cross to come south. It wasn't easy to approach the bridge because of the terrain. So we sent in Recce Operators. These are Special Forces guys, like the SAS or Selous Scouts. They are trained extensively in a lot of unconventional tactics, and they undergo training in diving, weapons, unarmed combat, interrogation and such. Only once they graduate and if they are the best, the cream of the crop, are they then classified as Recce Operators. Anyway, a small group, three or four, set off at night in canoes towards the bridge. When they were close, the guys scuba-ed the rest of the way, laid charges and blew the bridge to shit. It was an amazing operation, which the guys did helluva well. Unfortunately, on the way back, one of the guys was attacked by a croc. He was bitten on the ass and mauled across his thigh and waist and almost lost his dick. Not humorous for him at the time, but he survived, and apparently they sorted the croc out.

– **Greg, age 25**

There were three of us in each inflatable, and we had deployed from a submarine off the Angolan coast, travelling in two inflatables parallel to the Angolan coastline and heading for a specific harbour town. Once there, we were to measure strategic installations and calculate the distances, heights of buildings, distances between them and so on, to get a full understanding of what went on in that environment. This information would be used to assess when and how we should launch activities there. It would enable us to work out time frames and equipment required. If there was climbing to be done and you are going to launch activities into that site, you needed to know what distances were to be taken into consideration, the number of troops to be deployed and withdrawal options. For example, if there was an eight-metre-high wall, you would need ropes of a suitable length. The object was to get in, get the full picture, take photos and get out without being observed. No one should ever know you were even in these areas. The minute they know you've been in the area, they will heighten security, and you don't want them to do that when you are coming in with a large operation. It was night and we were moving just outside the breaker line. You always think you are extremely visible on the water, but you are not. We were very tense and alert, very on edge, as you can imagine. As we cruised past this one part of the town, there was a party going on. We were crouched down low, just passing it, when shots were fired. I tell you, we nearly fell out of the boat! We froze, thinking they had seen us and were shooting at us. They weren't. They were just partying and firing shots in the air. We slowed down, checked that the boats hadn't been hit, waited a little, watched, and then carried on to the harbour, where we continued with our work, obtaining the information that we required.

After that, but before we launched our attack, I took a 're-affirm' trip to ensure that nothing had changed that could jeopardise the operation. I also had to take a team on an orientation trip – a boat ride through the harbour at night to show them drop-off points and orientate them with the layout of the harbour. Two or three days later, our Special Forces hit the place. They blew up major installations, oil farms, railway lines and 'dropped' quite a few Russian ships. I was proud of the fact that the operations that I had planned and implemented were completed successfully and without compromise.

– **Anonymous**

The States

One of the most exciting days of my life was when we were hoping to go home for Christmas. I hadn't been home since January. Our sergeant wouldn't tell us if we had pass or not. We were in Oshakati driving southwards in Casspirs, and we didn't know if we were going home or to Grootfontein, where we could be sent all over the place. There's a point on the road where you either turn off to Ondangwa, to the air force base where we fly home from, or keep going to Grootfontein. The suspense was unbelievable. The intersection came up, and the driver continued on to the Grootfontein road, then laughed and pulled it back onto the Ondangwa road. This meant my first leave of seven days, and it was to be my only leave in two years. Maybe that's why they left me alone and I never got called up for camps or anything. I still get goosebumps when I remember the excitement of going home.　　　　　　　　　　　　　　　　　　**– Andy, age 18**

You flew up from and back to the States on this white aircraft called the Rum Run, so called because it flew up all the booze. It was also called the Milk Run, because of the colour of the aircraft – or maybe it was only the dominee who called it that. You went up to Ondangwa for three months and got on the Rum Run to fly home only once your release, another aircraft mechanic, arrived. He was your replacement. Usually when he arrived, there was a two-day handover and then off you went. I was missing my wife so much and couldn't wait to get back. This specific Thursday I was on the tarmac waiting and my release didn't get off the aircraft. I called and spoke to the sergeant major, and asked where was this guy who was supposed to be relieving me? Why wasn't he on the plane? He said he wouldn't be coming, because he had committed suicide. I waited an extra two weeks until the next guy arrived.　　　　　　　　　　　　　　**– Tallies, age 23**

Eenhana was classified as a red base, because it was attacked frequently. It was also the place where my letters and packages from home became legendary. I had a girlfriend who used to write me three letters a day. We hadn't had mail for six weeks, so you can imagine how much post I got when it finally came in on a Dak. They used to bundle the letters and call your name and toss you the bundle. Lots of guys got nothing – ever. I got 10 or 15 bundles and two huge packages from my mom. Inside she'd packed Marie biscuits, Romany Creams, sweets, cartons and cartons of Camel Plain cigarettes, for my own use and for bartering, and my personal favourite, Southern Comfort. My mom could have worked for MI6. She'd decant the alcohol into old Jik plastic containers. She'd also send Aromat, which was a necessity to improve skrapnel (corned beef and onion in gravy). We cooked our tins of skrapnel on an Esbit stove. This was metal and shaped like a packet of cigarettes. It had two flaps that you pulled up; you put an Esbit, which looked like a big white pill, in the middle, lit it and heated up the tin. The Esbit was also known as a PB Sweet. Legend had it that some crazy Dutchmen used to give the plaaslike bevolking these toxic white tables instead of the orange glucose sweets in our rat packs, which we usually gave to village kids. The glucose sweets were just as gross, as far as I was concerned. So the name, PB Sweet, stuck.

My girlfriend had numbered all the letters, so that I could read them in the order she'd written them, and sprayed some with perfume. That was a big thing to get: perfumed letters. The guys never teased me, 'cause so many of them got nothing, no letters or packages. I would go down into our tent – the tents at Eenhana were actually pitched under the surface of the ground, with only the roof sticking out and lots of sandbags stacked around the edges – and lie on my bed and read them. Guys would come and sit by my bed, desperate for news about anything back home. I read them excerpts from my letters – not the personal stuff, just the general news. Once I was reading about the snow that had fallen over Joburg in September and there was a picture

AN UNPOPULAR WAR

of my girlfriend standing outside the Carlton Centre in the snow. I had mopane flies buzzing around my face and it must have been about 40 degrees, but just reading about how cold it was and looking at that picture made me feel cooler. **– Clint, age 18**

It was the saddest day of my life. She was my school girlfriend and we had been going out since I was in Standard 8. She hurt me, man. I will be honest and say she did hurt me. I loved her. She was in matric and I'd been on the Border doing my army for six months. Women are very clever. She knew that a mate of mine, whom she was now seeing, was coming up to the Border and I'd find out, from him or somehow. So just before he got there, she wrote me a Dear John letter. I'll never forget the way it started; she wrote: 'This is very hard for me to say …' and she wrote some little poem, lyrics or some shit from a Lionel Ritchie song. I was devastated, heartbroken. I thought I was going to die. We were all guys up there, so you couldn't cry. This gay chef came up to me and put his arm around my shoulders and said I should go on my own and cry. But you don't, you're too proud. You keep everything in. I got totally drunk. I never picked up a pen and wrote back. I never contacted her again. **– Anthony, age 18**

We were resting up in a large temporary base after chasing the terrs for a change. Just near where I was lying there was this little helicopter, an Alouette. Flight Sergeant Soutie was there. I'll never forget him as long as I live. He had a handlebar moustache that looked like Harley-Davidson handlebars. I was lying in the shade of the helicopter and he said to me, 'Sargie, are you all right?' I was exhausted. We had been chasing terrs for days. I hadn't seen clean water, a bed or a razor for two weeks. But I said to him, 'Flight, I'm fine, I'm just missing home.' He said, 'Ja, I can see that. Wanna talk to your folks?' Of course I said yes, I would love to talk to them, thinking he was pulling the piss. He said, 'Come.' We get into the helicopter. He switches on the radio and gets onto Radiospoor in Walvis Bay. This woman with the sexiest voice I'd ever heard comes on. It was soft. Flight asks for my home telephone number and we get connected. And there, in the middle of the Operational Area, I hear my mom's voice and I say, 'Mom.' I just started to cry. I spoke with my dad too, and I realised nothing else mattered, everything became irrelevant. I was talking to the two most important people in my life. Flight Sergeant Soutie had made that possible for me.   – Ric, age 18

It was very easy to hitch-hike in those days, and especially if you were in uniform. People picked you up very quickly. I think people also stopped if you had a maroon beret because they wanted to talk about your experiences as a Parabat. This one old guy and his wife must have been moving home, 'cause he had everything but the kitchen sink in his car. They stopped for me and somehow I managed to squeeze in. Near Cradock there were always speed traps and, sure enough, this poor guy got caught. Three times. And three times he gave different excuses. His wife was pregnant, I had to get back to camp and so on, but it didn't work and he got fined three times. I never forgot it because he was not even supposed to be on that road. He had detoured from his intended destination of Cape Town to drop me off in PE. I never saw him again, but I never forgot his kindness.   – John, age 19

I was called up for a three-month Border camp during varsity holidays at the end of 1987. I didn't want to go. I took my call-up papers to the Dean of the faculty at Wits, and I asked him to write me a letter to say that I had vacation work to do and that I must be exempted from the camp. He looked at me and said that it was not his problem, and that it was my own fault for getting 'involved in these things'. I thought, what a doos, had he forgotten that this was all compulsory? All I wanted from him was a letter to send to the army so I did not have to go on the camp. A few years later I read in the *Citizen* that the professor had jumped from the Parktonian Hotel in Braamfontein and had greased himself. My eyes were very dry.

So, on 1 December, there I was flying into Ondangwa. We were doing fire force from there at the time of Operation Modular, Hooper and Packer, which were taking place in Angola around Cuito. I was up there for three months and of course had this serious tan. On the 14th of February 1988, I'm back at Wits and sitting by the Wits pool, and this very gay guy comes up to me and says, 'You are so tanned! You must have been in Plett.' I had such a kak houding at the time that I thought I was going to drown him in the fucking pool.

– John, age 22

Oh My Fok

I swear most fatalities or injuries in the army were because of stupid accidents rather than combat. One of the guys in our bungalow had to be put in a neck brace because he was injured when the corporal overturned his bed. Guys got injured when vehicles rolled. There were these three guys who called themselves the A-Team. We were on this range where you throw grenades, fire mortars and everything. During a rest period, they wandered off. One of them picked up unexploded ordnance, a practice hand grenade, one of those blue ones where the detonator explodes but the grenade isn't filled with explosives. This guy wanted to pick it up and pull the pin with his teeth. The pin sometimes catches, and this one came loose and went off. It blew a hole in his hand and took off most of his thumb. I'll never forget them running back towards us, this guy with a mutilated hand bleeding everywhere, screaming for an ambulance. Blatant stupidity from the A-Team. — **Nick, age 20**

I was a young officer, a 2nd lieutenant, only 18 years old, when I had a troop killed right in front of me. We were in Oshivello, not far from Grootfontein, doing fire and movement exercises. It was final touch-up training prior to being sent to the Operational Area. We had just finished and were sitting talking in a group, in the veld. I switched the radio frequency to the company net just as they were talking about an accident in which someone had been injured. I held up the receiver and said to the guys, 'This is how easily these things can happen.' As I said that, a shot went off. The guy next to me slumped down dead. He'd taken a round from a machine gun in the temple. The weapon was standing on its tripod and another guy had noticed that it hadn't been cleared properly. As he touched it, the expended cartridge dropped clear, allowing the working parts to move forward with a round, and it fired. It was very traumatic, both professionally and personally, for the guys who witnessed it. But it was especially difficult for the guys who had handled the machine gun. There are two men assigned to each machine gun, and these two had swopped around. The guy who was supposed to have been on the weapon was on a guilt trip, thinking if he had been doing what he was supposed to, this wouldn't have happened. The guy who was using it was on a guilt trip because he hadn't cleared the weapon properly, and I was on a guilt trip because I had made the assumption that all weapons had been cleared and made safe. It traumatised all of us involved, but counselling in those days was minimal – you're fucked up, that's all there is to it.   – **Anonymous**

It was a Sunday afternoon, 1978, in Ondangwa, and I was having a nap. I woke up to this tremendous explosion – it was as loud as the dynamite explosions used in the mining industry. This nearby camp, allegedly a Recce camp with alleged explosive experts working at defusing Black Widows, POM-Z and Claymore mines, just went up with this 'boom'. We were told that two guys had been blown to smithereens. About a week later, in one of the Afrikaans newspapers that made it up to the Border, I read this detailed account of how these two guys had been killed in a follow-up operation. The whole story was contrived. I knew the names, and it was the same two guys who had been blown up. There is this whole blab that had no bearing or connection to what had actually happened. I know 'cause I had been present when it happened. I saw the propaganda machine in action, and it taught me that 'seeing is believing'.   – **John, age 18**

Once, while waiting around for a personnel changeover, we snuck away from our outpost base to buy beers from one of the local cuca shops. We were mellowing out in the cuca shop garden, pretending to be civilians for the afternoon, when we heard a mighty explosion and saw a pall of black smoke rising from the base. We rushed back and found the tent alongside ours burning. The air stank of foam and burning flesh. While we were gone, new troops and post had arrived. One of our troops had just read a letter saying that a certain soldier had had an affair with his wife while he was away. The husband then walked into the tent where his wife's lover was lying on a bed. He threw a white phosphorous grenade into the tent, burning the lover to death and covering another seven soldiers in burning phosphorus. We spent the rest of the day checking drips and administering painkillers while waiting to evacuate the wounded. Who knows if the husband was ever tried for murder?   – Chris, age 17

We manned the big 40-mm Bofors guns on top of the towers around towns. The towers looked like those big steel scaffolding water towers that you'd see on farms. They were about 40 feet high, and we had the big World War II anti-aircraft guns, which we used for ground attacks, on top of them. One guy was on watch 24/7, and if he saw the so-called enemy coming he would radio it in, and three of us would run up to join him and man the guns. There was a barrel-shaped hessian-covered cage-like structure over the length of the metal ladder so no one could see us using it. Three people manned the guns: one checked elevation, another checked direction or bearings, and one guy loaded in these clips of four rounds. And there was one guy to give commands. At night-time we used night-vision sights. We never saw the enemy, and our only wartime experience was when a parcel bomb exploded one night in the nearby post office and blew a hole in the roof.

Another time we thought we would see action was when we were told to get ready as there was trouble. We were so hyped and so pumped full of adrenaline that we were not even afraid. We had our rifles ready, full ammo, and were ready to go. We leapt into the Buffel and charged off, expecting action. We headed for a tower next to a Koevoet base where this trouble allegedly was. Turns out this one Koevoet guy is threatening to blow up the tower because one of the Artillery guys has stolen a Koevoet sandbag. We thought we were going to fight terrorists and meantime we were there to sort out a fight about a sandbag! What a waste of time.

The only shots we fired were practice rounds – once a week. We shot across the main road just outside of Oshakati and hit our targets, which were burnt-out old trucks piled in a heap on what used to be the golf course. We usually did this at night, using HE tracer rounds, which were really loud and provided a very impressive explosion, which was to impress the plaaslike bevolking. There was no warning, so they never knew when it was coming. We'd just get a call on the radio telling us it was our time to go, and we'd go up the tower and fire. There was this bunch of campers standing guard – sleeping, more likely – near the main gate of Oshakati. We get the call to fire, and we run up and start turning the wheels to set the sights. Now we are supposed to check one another. So the guy doing the bearings is checked by the guy doing the elevation and vice versa. We both said that everything was fine, but the round explodes in the sand embankment on the opposite side of the road and nowhere near the target on the old golf course. Only then do I realise that my sight was a bit loose, so I tighten it, raise the elevation and we fire another round, this time hitting what we were supposed to. The radio starts squawking and the guys at the gate are shouting and screaming that they are under attack. Meantime it's us! Their officer said we had endangered his men, but it wasn't really dangerous, as his guys were about 200 metres away. We were nowhere near them. Honestly.   – **Dave, age 19**

On our way back into South West from Angola, my troops wanted to fire the RPGs at these watermelons growing at a riverside. It's awesome shooting an RPG. You look through the sight, pull the trigger, and whatever you are looking at disappears. I said it was a bad idea in case we needed the rockets later. I told them, once we were back in camp, then they could let off a few RPG bombs. Now, if you returned to camp at any other time than first thing in the morning, you had to work the rest of the day. So we positioned ourselves not far from Oshakati Base and decided to clean our equipment, repack things neatly, and enter base first thing the following morning. However, that night the base was attacked. In the event of that happening you are supposed to look for the flashes from the terrs' weapons and engage them. When all this broke loose, I said I would shoot the first person to move. It could've been a mock attack, anything. So we sat *vas*. At daybreak the Bosbok was up looking for the terrs. Then one of my guys lets off a Mindae flare. It's a 1 000-foot flare with a little PE4 and it makes a huge bang. Not ten minutes later, these Koevoet Casspirs roared up, MAGs pointed at us, and the Koevoet guys screamed that we'd tried to bring down the Bosbok and wanted the person in charge. I didn't have rank on, because we never did when we were in Angola, and we all just looked around and said we didn't know where he was. It was very tense. Luckily, we could honestly say we had all our ammo and our RPGs could all be accounted for. They screamed off, looking for the terrs, and we quickly counted our RPGs. We only found five of the six. I thought, that's it, I'm going to be court-martialled and shot for treason. But we eventually found it amongst the stuff we had already packed up. I still think about what would've happened to me if we'd fired the RPGs at the watermelons and come up short on the ammo count. — **Paul, age 24**

I travelled around the country doing weapon shows for the military. We'd have a huge stand at places like the Rand Easter Show. It was to show the public what South Africa was doing. Of course it was a whole propaganda thing. They gave me an Olifant tank, a Ratel, Buffel, G6 and a G5. We had limpet mines, and hundreds and hundreds of different SADF and terrorist weapons. We'd set up cammo netting, have troops talking to the civilians about the weapons, and the public could go inside the trucks. So many guys had been in the army, and they would come around with their families and show them an actual AK-47, which they could hold. They could even fire an R1 or R4, using blank rounds. We even offered civilians rides around the showgrounds in a Ratel which fired blank rounds.

This one night, we were at the Brits show, where they had a Miss Brits Competition. She was going to arrive by chopper. We had a whole motorbike squad, who, instead of patrolling borders and such, spent a lot of their time doing shows. I suppose the Brits show was a really large event and a PR exercise for the SADF, so maybe it's understandable. I took this 1 000-foot flare and put a thunderflash in it. It was supposed to go straight up and go off, but the bloody thing veered off and hit a bank of stadium lights. Well, there was a helluva explosion and glass everywhere. The audience loved it! They cheered and clapped and thought it was all part of the show. My troops looked at me, and we just thought, oh man, we fucked up.   **– Brett, age 18**

If your horse ran away, you had to go and fetch it. We used to hobble our horses, but this one guy's horse kept getting away. So he decides to tie his horse to himself. We all told him it was a bad idea, but, no, he had to go ahead and do it. In the middle of the night we hear this screaming and the sound of a horse galloping away. This guy is dragged about half a kilometre through the bush. We all woke up and looked at one another, and there was a general consensus because he hadn't listened to us when we told him not to do it: we thought, stuff that, and we just left him. The next morning they found him and took him off to hospital. That was an example of our attitude.

– Martin, age 23

The G6 had technology beyond belief. But it wasn't just the firepower; it was the capabilities of the vehicle itself which were awesome. It could go anywhere, over any terrain. It had six gears, and you could throw it into reverse from sixth gear and you'd just hear it winding and slowing down and then it was ready to go. It never fell over and it never got stuck. Unfortunately I couldn't drive it around, but I did have this Olifant tank, a 60-something-ton tank. The way it turns is remarkable: one track remains stationary while the other moves. I decided to do a 360, but I turned it so hard it was almost on its side and it ripped up huge chunks of this public road in Witbank. I was always in trouble, so this was just one more time.   – Brett, age 18

C was a rather controversial helicopter pilot with us at Ysterplaat. In order to remain current on all aspects of helicopter flying, a certain amount of flying hours had to be flown every three months. A request was submitted the day before, and in the morning off you went. There'd been a heavy snowfall on the mountains around Franschhoek, and everyone wanted to put in for mountain flying. C and his flight engineer flew off and decided to land in the snow and build a snow-man. They then decided it would be a great idea to bring a snowball back to Cape Town as a prank. They made one that stood about half a metre tall and flew it back. They radioed ahead to Ysterplaat and told everyone to come outside and watch their fly-past, meaning to drop the snowball on everyone as a joke. It backfired, because in the 20-minute flight back from the mountains the inside of the snowball had solidified, so when they dropped it, it hit a female corporal and broke her jaw and a few ribs. C was grounded and sent to Southern Air Command to fly a desk.   – Anonymous

We jumped with a PWC – personal weapons container – a canvas rucksack in which you usually kept all your ammo, goods and equip-ment required when going into operations. We also trained with a concrete block, which weighed somewhere around 60 kilograms, in our backpacks. We were doing this night jump at 600 feet and jumped out in the usual way, releasing our individual PWC so that it was suspended beneath us on a cord as we parachuted down. But I hadn't fastened mine correctly, and when I tried to jettison it so that it fell clear of me and hung below, the whole thing came loose and it fell away completely. When I landed, I used my torch to look for it and I found a huge crater in the ground. A lot of my equipment was stuffed; my dixies were completely flattened and unrecognisable. People were still landing all around me and I couldn't believe no one had been hit. I was a bit freaked out that I could've killed somebody. I would have been in such shit if my PWC had struck somebody. For punishment, the major told me to find my own way back with my flattened equipment and my concrete block, which he signed to make sure I didn't gyppo and simply collect someone else's when I got back to camp. I didn't have a compass and it was freezing. There were no space blankets or anything like that in '77.   – John, age 18

I was tasked with lifting a huge 40-mm Bofors anti-aircraft gun from one of the towers in Oshakati. It had a crack in the breech and needed to be replaced. It would be removed and taken to Ondangwa, where it would be stripped down and repaired. We had another one, in perfect condition, still covered in protective grease, ready to replace it. I knew the weight of the massive gun, 5 000 pounds, was close to the limit that my Puma could lift, but it could be done. Everything was unbolted on the damaged gun, and as I hovered above the 75-foot tower, the cables were fastened and I lifted the Bofors off with no problem. I gently set it down and moved the helicopter over to the replacement gun. They connected that up, and I slowly rose with this massive weight suspended beneath the Puma. I started to move the helicopter sideways, thumbing the trim button and watching the shadows where I could see the shape of my helicopter and the Bofors beneath it. As I touched the trim button, I felt my finger touch the cargo jettison, and in a split second I saw the two shadows separate as we suddenly shot up several hundred feet into the air and the 5 000-pound Bofors crashed to the ground. It landed on the unit's entertainment tent, right on top of the only snooker table in the area. Man, were they pissed off! 'Kaptein, wat de fok het jy gedoen? Kyk ons snooker tafel!' [Captain, what the fuck did you do? Look at our snooker table!] I told them it had been an electrical fault, but when I got back to Ondangwa and the colonel wanted an explanation, I couldn't lie. I said that I had just pushed the wrong button. He told me I was an honest boy and I never heard anything about it again.

– Anonymous

We were in a HAG in Angola when a call came in that there was a contact. When that happened it was a mad rush and the pilots scrambled to the helicopters to get airborne as soon as possible. There's a small inspection window, and as the pilot starts up the engines, the flight engineer looks through it to check there is no fuel leak and everything is okay. Although he's outside the helicopter, he's plugged in and has comms with the pilot and he can tell him it's all clear before jumping in too. The contact was very close to our HAG, so I was extra keen to get up and out there. I take off and scream over to where the contact is. I see the terrs and bank sideways, screaming at my flight engineer to open up and get them! Nothing happens. I look back and the chopper is empty. No one is behind the machine gun! The cabin is empty. I'd left in such a hurry that he had fallen out of the helicopter just as he was climbing in after the inspection. Luckily he wasn't hurt. I picked him up and went straight back to the contact.

– Trevor, age 25

Coming out of Angola, we used the Santa Clara water tower as a landmark and flew our helicopters past it, and we often used the road from Santa Clara to Ondangwa as the route back to base. T was excited 'cause he's been in the bush for two and a half weeks and he was looking forward to a cold beer. The child in him came out when, in the distance, he saw a black guy pedalling along the road, and he decides to give him a fright. He'll descend between the trees, onto the road, and then when this guy comes around the corner, he'll get a helluva fright. As he manoeuvres down he hits a telephone wire, which wraps around the tail rotor. Just before it crashes to the ground he manages to bring the helicopter down without damaging it. He was so lucky. He knew if anything had gone wrong, he couldn't explain what he had been doing there or why he had landed. As he's unravelling the telephone wire he looks up and sees the black guy standing next to his bicycle just looking at him, checking out the scene.

– Anonymous

The navy was environmentally aware. We had to keep our distance from whales and other marine life, which was not always easy. Dolphins loved to play in the bow spray, and whales loved the bubbles and spray kicked up by the Voith Schneiders. Trying to outrun a whale was not easy, and manoeuvring among them when trying to get into harbour was sometimes impossible. Sometimes you came into the harbour with a whale following like a puppy. However, I do recall an unfortunate incident that wasn't in line with the navy's green reputation. We were far off the Garden Route coastline and about six boats were preparing to refuel from the *Tafelberg*. It's quite an involved procedure. The *Tafelberg* trails cables and lines about 100 metres behind her, and the smaller vessels have to hook onto one of these, attach bollards, and then it is literally towed behind the *Tafelberg* while the fuel lines are fastened and the fuel pumped on board. Because we were in the smallest ship, we went in first. The smallest boat usually tested the waters, so to speak, for the larger vessels. For example, in a convoy, the smallest boat hugs the coastline, which means we are closest to the rocks too! Small craft are usually the first to leave the harbour and the first to tackle refuelling. We went in and connected and pumped about 4 000 gallons of fuel and disconnected in less than ten minutes. It was pretty smooth and we got a Bravo Zulu – a well done – from the admiral. Next up was a sweeper, which snagged the cables, fouled the props and became entangled in the lines. Divers had to go down and sort everything out. The admiral was pissed off and sent it to the back of the queue. Yes, there are politics even out there! The next ship that went in caught the tow but broke away from the fuel couplings before they were disconnected properly. There's a lot of fuel in those pipelines, and it went straight into the sea. I actually think there was a problem with one of the *Tafelberg's* fuel tanks, because they often had oil in their drinking water. I was hoisted by helicopter to the *Tafelberg* for a debrief, and when I was there I went into the engine rooms – what a rusty archaic mess that was. So I wouldn't be surprised if the oil leak came from a leaky fuel tank and not only from the botched refuelling. My captain and I had to race back to shore to handle the media queries about the oil spill. Once again the small ship had to do the dirty work.   – **Louis, age 17**

H was a huge guy. He played prop forward for the air force, so you can imagine what a big guy he was. He was G's flight engineer, and we went out to assist with a contact. Normally, immediately after a contact we'd push off back to HAG. This time they were circling and looking down at all the bodies lying around. G suggests to H that they go down and look for souvenirs: money, belts, buckles, boots, things like that. They land in the middle of the dead bodies, and H hops out and runs over to a dead guy and starts pulling off his belt. Suddenly the guy jumps up – he was only faking being dead. They fought, and it was rough. It was a fight to the death. G couldn't go and help, 'cause you can't leave an Alouette's controls while the engine is still turning. They fought, but, like I said, H was a huge guy. He managed to draw his 9-mill and he shot the terr in the head. He ran back to the helicopter, without the belt, and his face was completely white with shock.

I bumped into H again when we were both on board SS *Tafelberg*. A request would come in for such and such a number of helicopters and pilots on specified dates, and we would fly and land on the *Tafelberg* when we had to. We never knew where we were going or what we would be required to do. I hated it, because you could be steaming along for weeks, not knowing anything. We could be off the coast of Angola to carry out operations with the Special Forces or off the coast of Mozambique cargo-slinging supplies to RENAMO. We were 50 miles off the coast one night and it was pitch black. We had been doing Dark Moon Operations, no moon so no one could see us, and no lights other than two small ones mounted on the helicopter roof. They shone straight up and couldn't be seen from below. We'd just landed back on the ship's helipad, and H was standing with one foot on one of the nets. The nets were dropped out horizontally from the helipad during take-offs and landings, and extended over the sea while the crew hosed down the helicopters with fresh water and chained them down. Things corroded quickly, and with the embargo we couldn't afford to be careless with our equipment.

The net broke, and H fell 50 feet off the side of the ship into the pitch-dark, cold ocean. We were travelling at about ten knots – heading for who knows where – and it took a while to turn the ship. Meanwhile, we jumped into the choppers and were quickly airborne. We searched but couldn't see anything: the spray from the rotors threw up salt water and obscured the windows, and the spotlights reflected off the water, blinding us. I radioed back and said they'd have to launch boats to look for him. As we landed, they were launching a Delta boat. Two cables are used to lower the boat, and one snapped. The two guys were hanging on for dear life as they swung the boat back onto the ship. They were lucky they didn't fall off into the ocean.

H had been in the water about 20 minutes by now. As was often the case, there were Special Forces on board the ship, and the Recces watching all this said they'd handle it. They rapidly launched – no, dropped is a better way to describe it – a Namacurra ski boat. The boat fell about 30 feet, and when it hit the water those big engines were already going and the guys shot off into the dark. It took seconds. And they found him. When they got back to the ship, they said they'd screamed up to the area they reckoned he would be and switched off to listen for him calling. They'd stopped right next to him. He didn't even have to call out. He'd gone under for the second time and was contemplating just drowning and no longer fighting to stay afloat, but he kicked up once more and surfaced right next to the boat. They just leant over and pulled him on board. It was a miracle. A miracle that they had stopped at exactly the right spot, a miracle that they hadn't run over him, a miracle that he hadn't died of hypothermia and a miracle that he hadn't drowned.   **– Anonymous**

We resurfaced the Congolese navy. An entire convoy sailed up the west coast of Africa to the main naval port on the Congo River called Banana. There we raised two Osa-class strike craft. The Congolese navy guys didn't know how careful you had to be with ships. That's why there are duty watches. If a valve goes at night, your ship could sink alongside (in harbour). There was always somebody on watch, day and night. The Congolese guys would go off for three days, leaving their boats completely unattended, and then be surprised when they returned to find nothing but masts sticking out of the water! You can't do that.

– Louis, age 17

We received a Mayday call from some Koevoet guys. They were north of Etosha and an elephant had charged their Casspir. It rammed the front of the vehicle and broke off a tusk in the radiator, and then had really gone crazy and rammed into the side of the vehicle. Eight guys were trapped in the back of the Casspir. A Koevoet colonel came running into the SAAF HQ revetment at Oshakati wanting us to task a gunship to fly to the scene and shoot the elephant before it killed someone. There wasn't one available, but there was an Alouette Trooper at Ondangwa. It didn't have a 20-mm cannon like the gunship, it only had a .303 machine gun. But that was all there was. Bernie was a big game hunter and he figured he'd go out there and shoot the elephant from the helicopter. The only rifle he could find at such short notice was a 30.06, which is far too small to go elephant hunting with, but off he went. Wynand, the pilot from Ondangwa, flies in, picks him up and off the pair of them go. But they haven't communicated properly with one another, and Wynand doesn't realise that Bernie wants to shoot the elephant from the air. They find the Casspir and the elephant in an open shona, and Wynand lands and screams at Bernie to get out. He had to take off before the elephant charged the helicopter. Bernie leaps out and manages to get behind a little tree. The elephant is still going mad and is irritated by the chopper, which is now orbiting above its head, trying to distract it. Bernie gets off a few rounds and the elephant's back legs give way. He said it then looked like the elephant had been given a litre shot of adrenalin, 'cause it realised where the shots were coming from and charges. Bernie gets off a few more shots, which have no impact whatsoever, before realising he'd better run for his life. He runs away, firing blindly over his shoulder, trying to scare off this crazed elephant that is chasing him. He then tries to duck behind one of the massive termite mounds, hoping the elephant would run past and he can shoot it from the rear, but it sees him. He says it was so close he could hear the huffing and snorting, and just when he thought it was all over, the Alouette Trooper comes around the termite mound, flying sideways, blades thwacking the air, and it empties its machine gun into the elephant. It finally fell because the rounds caught its legs, and it collapsed just metres away from Bernie, who finished it off with a few more rounds.   **– Anonymous**

We had a small contingent of MLOS Mirage pilots with us. Although we had no air support, they were there to work with the Intelligence guys. We had very sophisticated radio equipment, and between them and the interpreters, they would tune in to the MPLA, East German and Russian frequencies and listen in. They had MiG 21s and MiG 23s, which could take out F-14s without any problem. The Russians had the most experienced pilots flying the most sophisticated planes. As you went down the scale, you had the Cuban, who could fly reasonably well, but the lowest or worst were the MPLA pilots, who didn't have the expertise or the skill of the others. We could tell who they were by the language they were speaking when they communicated with each other or the control tower. If the Russian or East German pilots were coming at you, you knew you were in a lot of shit, 'cause they were very good and very accurate. If you heard it was an MPLA pilot, you didn't really shit yourself too much. Once we heard this MPLA pilot coming in to land in his MiG 21, and he didn't deploy the parachute to slow the plane down and crashed off the end of the runway. We were all laughing and clapping; one MiG down the drain at however many millions of dollars. It was nice to have something to laugh about at their expense.   – Greg, age 25

Armscor were doing some tests and they needed some volunteers. We had no idea what they were testing or what they needed us for, but three of us went to the medics for a check-up, signed an indemnity form, and off we went to Armscor. They had this huge glass freezer, like a massive meat freezer but with glass walls, and they were using it to test uniforms, sleeping bags, all sorts of stuff, but all for extreme cold weather. We got dressed in the uniforms and had holes in our boots for them to place thermometers. They placed thermometers at various strategic points all over our bodies, including an internal thermometer that was up your bum. There was another just above the knee, and what they did was insert a little wire just under the skin so that they could disconnect and connect you up again more easily to a monitoring thermometer. We had to stand at a certain place in the freezer for a certain amount of time, sometimes until we fell down. It was pretty difficult at times. To avoid frostbite they had doctors come in to check us. Of course the doctors wore special suits 'cause it was bloody freezing in there. We were told it was for various reasons: a pilot having to eject, if we had to send troops to the South Pole or had to assist the British in South America. It was so cold and painful you couldn't talk when you first came out, but there was a full medical team on standby. We did it for five days.

I also tested vehicles for landmine resistance. I drove over anti-personnel limpet mines, not the huge limpet mines. What we were testing and checking after the blast was the wiring and water tanks underneath the vehicles. The tanks provide water and absorb the impact of shrapnel. We also had to see to what degree a vehicle could tilt before it rolled over, what tyres were best and how well protected the electrical systems were from a blast. It wasn't very dangerous. You really could only get hurt from being knocked around in the cab; sore elbows and such. — Brett, age 18

During our braais, I'd be barman. I used to over-pour and overfill the glasses, and then I'd sip the drinks before giving them to the guys. My sergeant major told me I was drunk. I insisted I wasn't, and told him I could drink him under the table and was even capable of running the 2,4. He ordered me to do it. In the middle of the night, there's me running and falling and running and falling, and the sergeant major is behind me in a Bedford. But he's also pissed, and if it hadn't been for my sober friend who kept stretching over and hitting the brakes when I fell, the sergeant major would have run me over. I always wondered how we won the war. The guys drank a lot. — Dave, age 19

Late one Saturday night, after a particularly wild night in the bar, we'd gone back to our house to continue the party. Suddenly the doctor appeared, asking to use the radio to order a helicopter to evacuate a badly wounded woman. She was married to a sergeant who had discovered that she was having an affair, so he had set a claymore mine in a tree outside their married quarters. She was still alive but needed to be taken to the closest hospital. Only the base commander could authorise a helicopter to be dispatched, but when we found the major, he was in an alcoholic stupor and still clutching an empty bottle of brandy. When we tried to wake him, he seemed to think he was a steamboat captain. So we pretended to be him over the radio – anything is possible with a bit of mis-tuning. Two hours later, the helicopter arrived and the woman was flown off to hospital. The next day we were called up on orders in front of the now sober major, not because we had impersonated an officer and ordered a helicopter, but because his wife had wanted it to fly to town to do some shopping. When we started to explain why we had done what we did, he quickly chased us out his office, saying, 'Moenie 'n fokkin' woord vir iemand sê nie' [Don't say a fucking word to anyone about this]. Ja well no fine.

– Chris, age 18

One night a big rainstorm hit Bloemfontein, and we were so energised that we decided to strip and run naked around 1 SAI to bless the camp with some gay power. We were not allowed to do any physical activities, so we would really be in trouble if they caught us running – and in the nude! We managed to get halfway round the camp but then reached the main gate, where the guards on duty spotted us and chased us. You can imagine five naked screaming queens with these butch army guys chasing us. Our fear of being caught managed to make us faster and we got away. – Rick, age 18

We had just been on a bombing raid into Angola and had dropped our four 125-kg bombs on some target outside a small town and were returning back to base. We usually flew the Impalas back at a sedate speed, but Ricky comes over the radio and says, 'Leader, this is Number Two. Can we expedite our return?' This means he wants to head back at full power. 'What's the problem?' Lead asked. Ricky replied that he had gippo guts. During operations, jet jocks wear a flying overall, a G-suit and a survival jacket with all the kit like radio, pistol, some food and signalling equipment attached. It's not quick or easy to get out of all that gear. We all took buster power and screamed off towards Ondangwa. We always used to do an initial low-level approach over the runway past the tower, bank and go around again, and then come in and land. Ricky comes on the radio again, 'Leader, can we skip initial approach? I need to get down asap.' As the first Impala lands, Ricky is coming in, and we just hear this 'Moenie worry nie, dis te laat' [Don't worry, it is too late]. It wasn't funny then, but it was funny that night in the pub.

– **Anonymous**

Japie was this very gullible aircraft mechanic. You could tell him anything, and he would believe it. Before he came up to do his tour of duty, the guys told him that Grootfontein was very dangerous: there was a lot of shooting up there, the food was very bad and you were only allowed to take your browns. So he packed only browns, half a balsak of tinned food and his .22 handgun, which he planned to sleep with. Grootfontein was like a civilian town, where you wear civilian clothes after hours. So poor Japie didn't have any. Another time, Japie says he's going off to the toilets. Grootfontein had a row of toilets with a service corridor behind them where the cisterns were. So we told Japie that there were a lot of ghosts at Grootfontein because a lot of people had died there. Off he goes, and I sneak into the service way and listen, until I know which specific toilet he is busy on. I open the cistern lid and pull the plug, flushing Japie's toilet. I run back, but there's no sign of Japie. We only saw him after lunch. He tells us he was sitting on the toilet and all of a sudden it mysteriously flushed. He stood up in such a hurry, the turd dropped into his overall. He tried to take it out but couldn't, and he had to walk all the way back to the living quarters with his overalls half on. He then had to wash them and put on fresh ones. To this day he doesn't know it was me. — Tallies, age 19

I hated guard duty, but one time really stands out for me. We watched the first part of the horror film *Carrie* with all the guys, but then we had to walk beat. So two hours later we come back, and watch the rest of the film. Our base was an old convent and we had a great pub. It was a de-sanctified chapel and the altar was the bar. That was the nice part. It also had a cemetery, where the nuns were buried. Remember, in the film, how terrifying it was when she goes to put flowers on the grave and that hand comes out and grabs her? Let me tell you, there was no way we were going to walk through a cemetery on a pitch-black night after watching *Carrie*! We hid away.

— Paul, age 24

Stripes and Stars

My first impression of my battalion sergeant major was that everything about him was immaculate and impressive. He was a tall, thin Afrikaans guy with perfectly ironed browns; his boots were polished so much that they were bright and shiny. Even his moustache was impressive: it was one of those old-fashioned ones that looked like it had been waxed at the ends. You could tell just by looking at him that he was hardcore. He had faded combat browns with lines ironed across the back of his shirt to represent the number of Border tours he had completed. We were not allowed to call our NCOs 'sir'. They said they worked for a living, unlike the officers, who were privileged and lazy. Faded browns as opposed to crisp new ones were a status symbol. Up on the Border it didn't take long for them to fade 'cause of the way we had to wash them: by hand with a bar of Sunlight soap and a corrugated washboard.

— **Clint, age 18**

Training is critical. It makes one respond instinctively. If someone tells you to hit the deck, you must do so without asking why. It also drums into you the privilege and importance of rank. I never felt it as strongly as when one of my mates was killed. This RSM walked by and said — and I can quote him verbatim, because I never forgot his words — 'Verwyder die fokkin' ding, dis net 'n lyf' [Remove that fucking thing, it's only a body]. But rank works both ways, and unfortunately for him the commandant overheard his remark and lost it completely. We all wanted to kill this guy. That's when training comes in. It wasn't just the shock at what he had said, but the fact that he was an RSM and I wasn't an officer that meant I didn't deck him. He deserved his nickname Hägar the Horrible: he was an insult to humanity.

— **Ric, age 18**

'I have often been asked why we do not have a medal for the wife of a soldier. The answer is simple: a medal worthy of a wife of a soldier has yet to be minted.' That was a speech known by troops in the early eighties at Northern Transvaal Command as Speech 3B by the Command OC. He spouted this bullshit at every medal parade he presided over. We used to stand at these endless parades as he outlined the contributions made by various force members and the reasons why they were being given these medals. In most cases they were over-weight quartermasters who had served 20 years and for the last ten had made sure that the best cuts of meat had been sent to their homes. Or in one case a PF corporal – yes, can you believe it, a Permanent Force corporal – was getting his ten-year service medal. Most of us who were called up, if we wanted to be instructors, got to that rank in one year! He was a two-liner and had been in the army for ten years! What was worse was that he wasn't even an instructor! This man, whose wife the army could not mint a medal for, had given ten years' service and was a fucking two-liner chef in the tiffies mess! Can you fucking believe it! I wanted to weep.   – Jay, age 18

There was this paraplegic captain in SAMS. He'd fallen out of a Samil and I was his run-around aide. One day we got a call from his wife to say that his Staffies were fighting. We rushed to his house and the dogs were tearing chunks out of each other. We tried everything to make them stop: hitting them, turning the hose on them – everything. Next thing he takes his gun out and shoots his one dog. He shot it twice. I think he was extremely frustrated.   – Paul, age 18

The mess at Ondangwa was a tented-off area, and we had a problem with wild and feral animals like stray cats and dogs, meerkats and jackals that used to come in and pinch food. One night the sergeant major said he was going to set an ambush and put out bait to lure the animals in. He was then going to 'take them out' with his 9-mill. I had

AN UNPOPULAR WAR

a sleepless night, because all I heard was this *dwar dwar dwar*, all night long. When we went through for breakfast, there was this pile – and I'm not joking – a massive pile of dead dogs, cats, and everything. They were stacked and their mouths hung open, blood and flies everywhere. That was how he thought he should deal with the problem. He was very proud of himself. He thought he was such a hero. The whole experience, from lack of sleep, to the pile of dead animals, to the stench at breakfast time, was very unsettling.   – **John, age 18**

We had this arrogant, bombastic commandant at Ondangwa. Everyone hated him. One night, after a drinking session in Chopper Corner (our place to de-stress and dop), we returned to our living area to braai. All the pilots' – Impala, Light Aircraft, Alouette, Puma – accommodation was in terrapins clustered around a swimming pool. We usually headed back after drinking in the pub, to have a braai on the sundeck or boma belonging to the Light Aircraft guys. We drank together, even though there was professional jealousy between the jet pilots and the chopper pilots. They said we got pissed and flew while drunk, and we said we had to babysit them. We were the ones who had to go and fetch them when they ejected or crashed. That particular night, Roelof, who had very powerful family connections, decided it was time to get his own back on this commandant. In those days all the pillows were feather ones. He took one and filled it with a dozen eggs and a thunderflash. He threw it into the room where the commandant was sleeping. There was this tremendous bang, and the commandant came flying out, covered in eggs and feathers! You can imagine what a mess he looked. He was furious. He told us he would court-martial all of us if he didn't find out who it was. Roelof owned up, and the next day he was on a Flossie back to the States to be court-martialled. But because of his family connections, in less than two weeks the case was squashed.   – **Anonymous**

I was on the bridge of a minehunter as we were coming alongside to berth in Port Elizabeth. The minehunters had Voith Schneider propulsion: the propellers were inside the hull, and instead of turning like a regular boat's, the propulsion system operated more like twin egg-beaters. This meant it was a highly manoeuvrable boat, like a heli-ship. But in addition to trying to berth between ships, I had the captain who was down below watching Wimbledon on a TV with poor reception. He kept calling instructions up to me to swivel the ship to improve the signal: 'Yes! No! Go! Stop! Yes! Yes! Right there! Yes! Yes! That's it! You got it!' It sounded like sex.   – Louis, age 17

There was mutual dislike and disrespect between this Afrikaans adjutant officer and myself. An adjutant officer enjoyed the rank of captain and was responsible for the disciplining of fellow officers, amongst other responsibilities. I was an English-speaking lieutenant with a reasonable amount to say for myself, and even though he was senior to me, I had very little respect for him. Not so much because he was Afrikaans, but given my operational experience and parachute qualifications, I got the distinct impression that I was being victimised for the fact that I spoke English and was not impressed with the fact he had not yet qualified as a jumper. The two of us were sent down to Oudtshoorn on a three-month mortar-training course, and there we shared a room. Over one of the weekends that we were afforded pass, a few of us drove down to Hartenbos to go and enjoy ourselves at the beach. I was a passenger in the adjutant's vehicle. Everyone had a few beers under the belt. The vehicle in front of us slowed, and I could see that this captain had quite possibly not noticed and showed no intention of slowing. I wondered if I should draw it to his attention, or would he pull rank on me? I elected to say nothing and just braced myself for impact, which I did. There was impact. We got out of the car, assessed the damage, and he went to his boot and pulled out my military sleeping bag. He started tearing the straps off it so he could

AN UNPOPULAR WAR

tie his bonnet down. I said to him. 'With all due respect, why are you tearing up my sleeping bag?' He apologised and said he had not realised it was mine, and that he was more concerned about what his wife would say about the damage to the car. From then on, we forged a wonderful friendship. In life, when there is a dislike between individuals who do not know each other, but then they actually get to know and like one another, it seems to forge an even stronger bond than a meeting which is amicable from the start.

However, not long after we became friends, he was taken up to the Border as an Intelligence officer. He missed my 21st birthday at Free State Command. It was Bloemfontein and freezing. I got horribly drunk and apparently lit a fire on the floor, to which I wanted to add a guitar and sheets and things. My friends stopped me from doing too much damage and convinced me that what I had going already was sufficient to keep me warm. I did make it to the unit for parade the next morning, but was called back to Free State HQ because a cleaner had complained that some drunken officer had lit a fire on the mess floor and damaged it. The commandant asked me to explain the damage, and he basically told me that if I wanted to avoid being charged, I would have to replace the floor in totality. I then proceeded to clean those Marley tiles with Brasso to the best of my ability. Coincidentally, he was the father of my friend, the captain who had recently gone to the Border. Over the period that this was all happening, I heard that my friend, the captain who had gone up to the Operational Area, had been shot and killed trying to flush a SWAPO terrorist from a hut. I think he was killed as a result of not having had all the right information. His body was brought back for burial. It's certainly not compulsory, but it is a sign of respect to salute at the head of the grave during an officer's funeral. I went and did this, and, as I was saluting, I coincidently happened to make eye contact with his father. I'm sure that is why the whole damaged floor saga was swept under the carpet. No pun intended.   **– Dudley, age 21**

We revered the helicopter guys because they were there to get us out of trouble. We revered them because they often put their lives on the line. We revered them because they used to pick us up sometimes and give us a lift so we didn't have to walk three days back home. We revered them because if guys got into shit they just went in and got them out, and they were like, hey, it's our job. I think they went through more shit than anybody realises. They just went into troubled areas again and again and again. They took bullets through their helicopters and bullets through themselves and they got shot out of the sky. We revered them because they never acted as though they were superior to anyone else. Never. Never. Ever.   – Ric, age 18

We were fortunate, as we were 'in' with the air force guys. The Pumas used to come in to casevac guys out, and we had this code that enabled us to get goodies in. We would radio base on our VHF radios and ask for legit medical supplies like Plasmalite A or B, but then we would also ask for Plasmalite C, which doesn't exist. There's no such thing. It was a code for goodies like a six-pack of Amstels, dry wors, chocolate – stuff like that. So we would go, 'Two boxes of Plasmalite C,' and they would include goodies for us the next time they flew in. We kept the beers reasonably cold by wrapping them in toilet paper, which we would dampen with water. We left them under the vehicle overnight and the evaporation process would cool it a little, so that you could enjoy a fairly cool, not cold, beer.   – Greg, age 25

The army taught me to rely on others. On my buddies. It taught me self-discipline and to control and focus my mind. But it really was a major war, there was a shitload of stuff going on, and most South Africans didn't know. The guy driving his Mercedes around Sandton had no idea that men were dying or being maimed, losing limbs. Not just ours, but Angolan men, women and children too.

– Greg, age 25

My trip to the Skeleton Coast was the most awesome trip of my life. We were to go ahead and set up camp for all the OCs from every base in Sector 2Ø. This was not a Mickey Mouse trip. There was a signaller's truck and all its equipment, a chef's truck, a field kitchen on the back of a Samil 100, gas, food, freezers, generators, water, wood, everything. I was the only National Serviceman on the trip and I had two Ovambos to help me in the kitchen. We had two Samils, a bakkie and a Unimog, and drove them from Grootfontein, right through Etosha, over the pan and through the Petrified Forest and on to the coast. We were just going. When you get to that Skeleton Coast, everything changes – the world is so different. It's just desert, no more trees, nothing but dunes. It is so beautiful. We hit the coast and turned north towards Angola. At Möwe Bay we checked in with the ranger and his wife, showed him our permits, and he told us when and where to drive, because sometimes we had to wait for the tides to be able to drive on the beach. It was awesome: we'd been driving on tracks, but soon even those disappeared. Then we were driving on the beach and we passed thousands and thousands of seals. They were barking at us and I was thinking, should I shoot them? Remember, I was a chef and I'd never had a chance to fire my rifle. In the end I settled for looking for diamonds! Some of the big bulls started chasing the trucks! It was the most beautiful place I'd ever seen.

When we turned slightly inland, we got stuck. All because the stupid sergeant major didn't listen to me. He wanted to go slow and I told him to go go go. So we get stuck. For a day and a half. Now we knew we had to get there and set up camp at Rocky Point before the colonel and everybody arrived. That's where we were heading. So we set up camp and we were braaing meat and all these jackals were around us. You must remember I was a city boy, so I was awake the whole night. You could hear them and see them, and I kept throwing wood on the fire, thinking, why the hell are they coming here? They're supposed to be scared of the fire, but obviously they smelt the meat. We had to dig and stick dry seaweed and shells under the wheels of the truck, and eventually we got out – a day and a half later. I was a chef, for goodness' sake, and here I was with blisters on my hands!

As we got to Rocky Point, this Flossie came in, roaring low over the desert, and landed. We had been stuck for a day and a half in the sand and here this Flossie just lands in the desert and turns around like it's on a runway! The Unimog and bakkie went off to fetch the guys. We had slogged through desert for three days with all their shit, and these bastards just walked off the plane with nothing but their toothbrushes and fishing rods. Boy, they were happy! We were supposed to have set up camp at this permanent site. But because of our delay, the camp wasn't ready yet. The area was a fenced-in area with a gate and prefab bungalows inside. It looked like it had been there for years. The guys arrived, and every single one of them had a moustache. I'll never forget that. I didn't know which way to salute first. I was in my vest and browns, 'cause I was told not to wear a beret or uniform. They were all very relaxed and happy and shouted 'Korporaal! Maak die vuur' [Corporal! Make the fire], and they all helped set up camp. Within three hours everyone, including those with rank, had helped set up everything: camp and signals equipment. My sergeant major was going around giving everyone Old Brown Sherry. I wasn't sure why they were all there, but it sure looked like just fishing to me. I went fishing with them and caught 11 fish in one day: kolster and kabeljou. I'll never forget it. The seals would come right up on the rocks while you were fishing. The beauty was unbelievable. All I had to do was make brunch. They would wake up at five o'clock in the morning. I could sleep, they didn't bug me. They went fishing with their rods and Hanepoot. They drank so much Hanepoot, 'cause it was so cold in the morning. I made brunch for 12 people, but only at ten o'clock. How easy was that? I made omelettes, bacon, boerewors, toast, sausages. Dutchmen like that kinda shit. They just wanted a big breakfast. I would drive onto the beach, set up the table, lay out the food and whistle, and these big important guys would come running. It was so cool. I would whistle and they would come and eat my food. And I was their Rooinek. We would pick snails and mussels fresh off the rocks, and I made garlic snails and stuff for dinner. They taught me how to gut a fish, how to open it and how to cook it on a fire, using the skin and natural oils, no tinfoil or anything. They all cooked their own catch. The Ovambos cooked pap. I just made sure everything was clean. I was there for about two weeks. It was my best ever.

I remember the one night the signaller came to tell them that this well-known terrorist, Plat Pote, had been shot dead. He was an awesome terrorist. He was brilliant. They'd been after him for ages, and they eventually found out he used to run along fences. Right on the top of barbed wire fences – barefoot. The Bushmen trackers figured it out; they were brilliant too. So that night when we heard he'd been shot, there was a big chug chug. They were, 'Hey, they got the oke!' But yet there was respect. It wasn't like 'we'd killed a kaffir' or anything like that. Even though we had killed him, there was still admiration for him. Maybe it was an officer's way of doing things, but I never forgot it. It was strange. They were happy that the fucker was dead, you gotta understand – they drank toasts to his death – but they were still respectful.

I've still got a piece of petrified tree I picked up when we drove through the forest. I'd like to go back to Rocky Point again.

– Anthony, age 18

Somewhere on the Border

I was casevaced from the Border twice. The first time I collapsed from heat stroke while on patrol. That was really weird, 'cause I had an out-of-body experience and remember watching a mate of mine, an ops medic, talking to me and trying to raise a vein. It was only when a doctor treated me at Oshakati that they found out I had hepatitis. During my first night in the hospital there was an attack on a nearby base. Around 4 a.m. they started wheeling casualties, many of them terrs, into the general ward where I was. I wasn't impressed when they parked a gurney with a groaning terr close to my bed. He was singed and all scrunched up: lying on his back, but with his knees and elbows bent and sticking up into the air. As they were tending to him, a young lieutenant covered in blood and dust came in and I asked him what had happened. He told me a base had been mortared and rocketed. I asked him what happened to the terr, who looked like he'd seized up, and he told me that the guy had been standing behind his mate when he fired an RPG. Ja, a rocket launcher has a back blast of note!

I'll never forget the second time I was casevaced from the Border to Pretoria's 1 Mil, because it occurred shortly after I met Jonas Savimbi. I was with the SA Irish, a unit I was very proud to belong to. On our berets we wore an Irish harp and a hackle – a plume of green feathers – and our boots weren't brown, they were black. This came from the Second World War, when the unit was artillery but was completely annihilated at Sidi Rezegh in Egypt. It was reformed as part of a mechanised infantry division, and in memory of fallen comrades, our boots were black. We had driven from Oshakati to Alpha Tower. The base was situated on a dry riverbed and a bridge spanned across into Angola. There was an MPLA camp on the other side. At last light both camps fired their mortars, not at each other, but merely to say they were awake, alert – there and ready. Every morning after breakfast five guys from each side would meet on the bridge and exchange pleasantries. It was just general chit-chat about what time they would be firing-in weapons that evening and so on. Ten days after we arrived, there was a huge commotion. At first we thought they were just firing-in weapons – we couldn't see, as it was dark – all we could see were flashes lighting the sky. Unbeknownst to us, it was Jonas Savimbi himself! The next morning we walked onto the bridge and instead of the usual five MPLA guys, Jonas Savimbi and nine UNITA soldiers strolled onto the bridge. He was a big man and was grinning like a Cheshire cat. They all seemed very pleased with themselves. Savimbi was very neatly dressed in full uniform, but the other characters were a colourful ragtag bunch in cut-off T-shirts, bandannas, sunglasses and carrying a mixed assortment of weapons. All, including Savimbi, were laughing. Initially Savimbi spoke Portuguese to our interpreter, but switched to English after telling him they had klapped the MPLA base the night before. He was very charismatic and confident, and I felt I was in the presence of someone important and great. He shook hands with all of us, and when he did, his troops on the far side all started cheering and waving their rifles above their heads. You could easily see he was extremely popular with his men. When he shook my hand, I was dumbstruck – all I managed to stutter was, 'Morning sir.' I felt he was really someone of substance and great standing. He was still laughing. What a larger-than-life character.

That night I was in agony. It started as a dull ache, like a badly bruised rib. But then the pain became so intense that I pulled two bars out of my army cot's headboard. Okay, they were only screwed in, but still, it convinced the lieutenant that I was in excruciating pain. He radioed for a helicopter to casevac me out, but not one of them would fly out to Alpha Tower at night. Eventually, at 3 a.m., a Buffel arrived to take me to Etale. They filled the footwell with ammo crates to make enough level floor space for two mattresses for me to lie on. The doc there gave me two vials of Sosenol. He couldn't believe one was not enough and that I was still in pain. Turned out I had a kidney stone. Eventually I was taken by helicopter to Ondangwa, and then on a Flossie to Pretoria. On both flights there was a dude from the Coloured Corps. How's this for coincidence? He was goalie for the CC in a soccer match, but he had been a lousy goalie and they lost the game. He'd been standing naked, about to get in the shower, when one of his teammates ran in and stabbed him repeatedly in the bum with a pikstel fork! And who did they play against in the soccer match? The SA Irish!   – **Clint, age 21**

For some reason, along the Mozambican border, we knew the enemy as dissidents, not terrorists. And they were not nearly as confrontational as those from Angola. They were usually teenage boys, often by themselves and armed with AK-47s. They would usually surrender quickly. We had certain rules to put in place when we encountered a dissident. We were usually in a Buffel or Ratel. We would stop a short distance away. You never approached them on foot, because there could be landmines. He had to put his rifle down and leopard-crawl towards you for at least 10 metres before standing up. We'd then arrest him and do a light interrogation, using the trackers as interpreters. This would include a threatening tactic – something like a gun against the head. Strong-arm tactics involved holding a guy down and putting your foot on his throat. But they were very submissive. Generally you could see if they were hiding information, as they were not trained spies. They are looking for refuge – often these guys hadn't had water or proper food for a long time and wanted some badly. We'd use cable ties or tie them up with a seat belt in the vehicle and take them back to the base.   – **Brett, age 18**

Impalela Island, about 180 kays from Katima Mulilo, was a dry base. No alcohol. 'Cause the guys caused trouble and were shooting at game. It was quite isolated, right in the middle of the Chobe River between

Zambia, Bots and South West. There wasn't much there, just the animals and a water-tower type thing. I arrived back on the Border and the major said to me, 'Het jy beheer oor jou troepe?' [Do you have control over your troops?] Obviously the correct answer was that of course I had absolute control over my troops. What else did he expect me to say? 'Dan hoekom sit een van jou troepe in die tronk in Botswana?' [Then why is one of your troops sitting in jail in Botswana?], he then asked me. The troop's excuse was that he was merely helping out civilians whose boat had broken down. He'd towed them back to Chobe Lodge in Bots and they insisted on buying him a drink. That's all. The police version was that he'd come over from the island to buy booze and they'd caught him loading ten cases of beer into the rubber duck, and they arrested him for being in Bots without a passport. We were lucky it didn't cause a major incident.

— **Paul, age 17**

Our job was to patrol the North West province on the border of Botswana, where Madikwe is now, on horseback, riding up and down the border, looking for evidence of the ANC, as that was their main route from Botswana for bringing in guns. When we found spoor, we called the guys in to follow up. The horses took strain, because they were doing between 40 and 60 kilometres a day. That's a lot to do day after day. They lost condition, and by the end of the year were pretty burnt out. Sometimes they got saddle sores and you then had to walk your horse, carrying the saddle, while the others rode. They were very fit and strong, but they had a hard time. — **Martin, age 23**

There was a barge that used to cross between Sesheke in Zambia and Katima in the Caprivi. It broke free and we claimed it and kept it as ours for about nine months. That river, the Zambezi, could be very dangerous. A guy from SACC drowned trying to cross on the cable. We had to go and cut down some trees that were on this island between our observation post and Zambia. We set off in this little rubber duck. The current took us and we got washed past the island and bumped into the side of the barge. The barge floated on big pipes so that it could pass more easily through the current, and the duck got sucked between the pipes, under the barge. We're hanging on the sides of the barge and trying not to get pulled in and under it as well. I thought I was going to die that day. The duck got sucked right through the pipes, and now we had to locate it. We found these scuff marks in the sand on the Zambian side of the river. It looked like a boat had been dragged ashore. We went into the bush and found some fishermen and their dugout. Best approach – be forceful. So we started yelling and pointing our rifles at them, demanding our boat. They are terrified and crying 'fishy fishy fishy'. Some complaint was laid about South Africa invading Zambia – that was me. We spent a lot of time on that river. We had what we called a Swiss, quite a big boat, with twin 85s and a MAG mounted on the front, and we did river patrols to show the Zambians that if they ever crossed the river, they'd be in trouble. It wasn't much fun just sitting in the boat. So we fished and water-skied. We used a metal catering table with fold-up legs. Not quite the same as waterskis, but it worked. We had to watch out for crocs and hippos, though. There were some big ones in that river. It was good fun.

– Paul, age 17

Once on patrol near the Botswana border, we went into this snoepie shop. It was just a little local store run by this Afrikaans tannie for farmworkers. Ten guys arrived, and the first thing they asked this tannie for was pantyhose! Here these fit young army boys arrive and they want pantyhose. You should have seen this lady's face! Boy was she surprised. We bought her entire stock. The pantyhose helped prevent chafing. The guys would get raw between their legs if they didn't know how to ride or weren't riding properly. Some of the guys actually wound up with skin that wouldn't heal, and continuously suppurated. There was no such thing as rest. A favourite thing was to put Prep gel on the chafed area. We always had it because we had to shave every day, even if we were out on patrol for weeks. So we always, thank you God, had Prep.   – **Martin, age 23**

Miss South Africa came up to visit and I was told to take her fishing on the Zambezi. My sister was a model and I'd met a lot of these girls, so it didn't mean a great deal to me, and I had just come back from pass and was really tired. We were always tired. In Basics we used to say that you could fall asleep on the back of a Bedford and in the time from when your head was upright until it hit the top of your rifle barrel, you could fall into a deep sleep. I thought this Miss SA was a bit of an airhead. She was saying all sorts of things because she thought that was what was expected of her – racist comments and such. But I do think she impressed most of the lonely people she met.

                                                        – **Anonymous**

I was based at Rundu, and we used to watch the Canberra bombers make frequent passes when they took off and landed. This was so that no one, neither us nor them, could know for certain how many planes went out and came back, or never came back. I caught a lift on a Dak to go to Mpacha. It had a beautiful bar built around a tree. I know, 'cause I built it in '82. I thought I'd go visit and have a drink just for old time's sake. The flight out was non-eventful, but on the return trip, in a different aircraft and with a different crew, we flew very, very low and fast over the bush, because they'd spotted what may have been a SAM-7 missile on their way in. It was Friday the 13th, and I thought I was going to die just because I'd wanted a dop and a trip down memory lane.   – **Paul, age 22**

Under Attack

On 23 August 1978, out of the blue, a helicopter landed and we were briefed by an officer that there was going to be trouble at Katima Mulilo, which wasn't our base, but we needed to go and give the guys a hand. A lot of the guys from the rest of the battalion were going to be there. Flying into Katima Mulilo and over Ngwezi, the adjacent township, I noticed and commented that Ngwezi was empty. Katima was a town, with civilians, women and children. Each civilian home had a bomb shelter at the bottom of the garden. It was above ground, not below, and consisted of a massive Armco half pipe covered with sandbags, cement, more sandbags, cement, and then even more sandbags. It would absorb most stuff, although a direct hit could cause a few problems. I turned to the officer and asked him why there wasn't a soul about in Ngwezi. He was surprised I'd noticed and remarked on it. Of course I had, it was my job. We landed and went for a briefing with the commandant, who at the time was looking after the intelligence in that area. He said he had received intel that there was a possibility of an attack on the base and the surrounding bases that night, and that we needed to brief the troops. I told my guys to sleep in foxholes and 'stand to' at last light and at first light in case of an attack. It is a military norm up on the Border to 'stand to'. During this, a regimental sergeant major comes around and tells us we are all a bunch of wussies and we don't need to sleep in foxholes that night. We should all be sleeping in our beds, 'cause no one would dare attack us. So we find ourselves beds in the bungalows and move in there.

At 01h05 they started rocketing us from across the Zambezi, from the Sesheke side. The first rocket landed just outside the camp's perimeter. I woke up, started screaming at the guys, grabbed my kit and dived into the nearest foxhole. Then I realised one of my buddies wasn't with me. The second rocket landed just outside the bungalow, in amongst the tents. They were 122-mm rockets, or Red-eyes, as we used to call them. Red-eyes are designed to terrorise and create massive damage to buildings. They are weapons that induce fear. They make a terrifying screaming noise as this red flame races towards you. If they land in an open field, they might kill you because a lot of shrapnel flies around. Inside a bungalow, in such a confined space, they create utter devastation. If you're below ground, you're fine. I realised one of my buddies wasn't with me. I flew back inside the bungalow and grabbed R. Believe it or not, he was sleeping! R slept very deeply. I grabbed him and, as I picked him up, a rocket came through the bungalow in front of me and exploded. It was a long bungalow, over a hundred guys in it, and the rocket hit at the front of it, where all the newcomers, the chefs and engineers were. There were bodies and bits and pieces everywhere. R was knocked out of my arms and I dived for him. I thought he was dead, because I felt a lot of wetness on me which I thought was blood. He was fine; the blast had just knocked him out. I grabbed him and we flew outside and dived into a foxhole, which by this time was full. So we found ourselves another foxhole and we lay there as they bombarded us for a long time. I then started moving around to find my guys and warn them that the ground forces might attack. In conventional warfare, the enemy normally bombarded us to shake us up, then shot the hell out of us with the big stuff, and then the infantry would be sent in. We all got ready, and then I heard the heavy machine guns, the 50-calibre guns, our guys, on the banks of the Zambezi, go off. What went through my mind was that the enemy was now crossing the river in boats and that's why our guys had opened up. Then the mortar camp, which was outside Katima, opened up. The thing that worried me was that the big guns, our artillery, on the western side of Katima near a place called Wenela, hadn't opened up. I heard a little airplane in the sky and I thought, that's it – the guys are spotting. Meanwhile, the bombardment carried on and on and on, and there was a lot of screaming and shouting from the bungalow. So R and I went back there to have a look. There were guys putting out the fire, and bodies everywhere. The rocket attack intensified and pushed us back into the holes. We got out again, started fighting fires and getting men out, and then the big guns opened up and the entire western horizon lit up. Our guys had got going at last. The incoming fire started withering away. It got quieter and quieter, and we knew that either our big guns were being effective, or the enemy was holding back before an infantry attack.

All this was going through my mind as I was getting my troops together. I realised that I had lost a couple of guys. There were ten dead. The one guy's head was lying at my feet. One guy, K, who grew up on a farm very close to where I did, was killed. His father and mother were good friends of my parents. I was holding him and we thought he would hang on even though he'd lost an arm and a leg. But he died after the attack, while I was holding him. It was very emotional when K died.

Early the next morning, we launched a counter-attack with Parabats and guys from other units who had come in. Those of us who could stand and run and shoot, went in. We went in west of Katima, at a little Zambian town on a bend on the river. Some of us crossed the river, while some of the Parabats were dropped behind enemy lines, and we started mopping-up operations. It was intensive fighting, but the fight had gone out of the terrs. What had happened was that the Zambian Defence Force had joined forces with SWAPO to give us a go. I reckon there must have been around 600 of them. They had batteries of Stalin Organs, 120-mm mortars and machine-gun posts. We shot up a truck that was pulling provisions, so it seemed like they were coming in en masse. I was only a corporal so I never got to see all the intel, but they seemed to be pretty well organised. It was thanks to our big guns opening up and flattening them. The next day was also pretty chaotic. We came and went, and went and came, and shot at whatever we could. I remember bringing back 16 bodies myself. We

AN UNPOPULAR WAR

laid the bodies on the parade ground and proceeded to cut off their fingers with bolt cutters, because Intelligence wanted their fingerprints and they were too lazy – well, maybe that's the wrong word – but they didn't want to come out and take fingerprints from bodies that were already affected with rigor mortis. So we had to cut them off and take them packets of fingers. At the time you don't care. You are so angry with these people. You just see K's face and the other guys who'd got blown to pieces and you just didn't care. And that's the bad thing about those sorts of actions and war: you lose your self-respect and you don't feel emotion for or empathy with anyone. The person you fought has a mother and father back home too, and they are only fighting for the freedom of their country. You don't think about that at the time. That comes later. At that time you're quite happy that the son of a bitch is dead, because he tried to kill you. A lot of people are not proud. Not proud of having pulled a trigger. I have friends who saw a lot of action in the seventies and eighties, the really elite guys, like those in 32 Battalion, who were absolutely awesome, awesome soldiers. We talk about things among ourselves, but even then, only superficially. Even now, 30 years on, if you get into the emotional side of things, we'll change the subject or watch rugby or get a beer or something.   – Ric, age 18

I lost respect from my fellow troeps and won it back in Nkongo. It was a small base, as it was only battalion strength, and it was mainly built underground. Above ground there wasn't much more than tents. We were busy constructing improvements on the base. Someone asked me to go up onto the kitchen roof to fetch something. I ran up the ladder and across the newly built roof, and as I reached the peak and looked over the other side, I just froze. It took five okes to bring me down off that roof. Before that I hadn't even known I had a fear of heights. I'd been in helicopters, hanging out the door and it hadn't bothered me, but now? I was so scared I couldn't move. In the army, and especially on the Border, you couldn't show weakness. I had, and now guys avoided me. Okes who before used to walk past and greet me now avoided me altogether and would move away from me if they saw me walking towards them. It was bad enough that I was a Catholic and English, but now I had shown a weakness. I had lost their respect.

Not long after that, the base was attacked at night. I was a number one mortar man and with Base Protection. We had three mortar pits that could fire up to a range of five kilometres, or seven if you threw a cup of diesel down the tube and used maximum loading. You couldn't do that too often or you'd damage the tube, but, man, it gave off an awesome flash, an absolutely stunning and beautiful flash! We were being attacked from three sides, but we were well – very well – equipped. We had snotneuse – 40-mm American grenade launchers – as well as 50-calibre machine guns and 30-mm Browning LMGs from the US. We even had Jeeps with anti-tank recoilless guns on them! We had lots of stuff. We even had napalm before it was banned. That came in a long bomb, shaped like a rocket. If you open it up, it's filled with a green jelly-like substance that smells like petrol. Our white phosphorous grenades were worse than napalm anyway. I was with HQ Platoon, part of Base Protection, and we had a specific fire plan for predetermined areas from where we thought an attack might be launched. Mortars are falling all around, we've got guys all over the place, on the walls, in the pits, but our position is secure. Next thing we hear these guys screaming for help over the radio. It's a platoon that has camped about two kays outside the base. This was common practice, because at night the base was locked down and returning patrols had to camp outside until morning. Coincidentally, SWAPO had located the patrol outside the base and were mortaring them, as well as our base. They were not nearly as well armed as us and only had light weapons, not enough to defend themselves from the terrs who were mortaring them from about a kay and a half away. I lined up my Mills sight. All the while, mortars are going off and I'm listening to the co-ordinates that are being screamed over the radio and I'm calculating. If I'm out by even one degree, it will make a huge difference to where the mortar lands and I could kill our guys stuck out there. The Mills sight is extremely accurate, but you do need to know how to use it and that takes training. It's very mathematical. What was amazing was that I could concentrate on what I had to do and make alterations and calculations as co-ordinates changed, even with all the mortars raining down and all the other weapons firing. From your training, you know which weapon is firing and you can immediately identify it. This thing kicks in and you become like a machine with only two concerns: your buddies and the destruction of the enemy. We got the patrol safely back into base that night and I earned back my respect.   – **Clint, age 18**

I remember a funny incident during one of the battles on the Border. During a rocket attack, a rocket came through the bungalow roof. It knocked over a whole lot of these steel lockers – kaste. One of the chefs leapt up out of bed, but was knocked down by and trapped inside this six-foot locker – the door must have been open as it fell over. It was heavy and pinned him to the ground, but not on top of him: it enveloped him. The rocket must have landed about three metres away from him, and I kid you not, he was unscathed; only his ears took a hammering from the explosion. The kas was buckled and bent and scorched from the fire, but this guy? He was unhurt – just warmed up a little from the flames. The next day he was back to cooking. It was very funny in hindsight.   – **Ric, age 18**

I wasn't that interested in the army or in helping the government; I wanted to study. At that time, you could go to jail if you refused to go to the army. So I had to do my army training, but I was determined not to waste the time. I studied for my Honours in Finance and Marketing at Wits while doing my two years' National Service. My goal was to get transferred from Pretoria, where I was called up to do my Basics in Personnel Services, to Wits Command, as it was close to the university. I'd heard from a friend who was at Wits Command that there was a job going there. I applied, and even though they wanted me because of my computer experience – remember, this was the eighties, so not everyone was familiar with or knowledgeable about computers – it still took months before the transfer was approved. The colonel at Wits Command, who wanted me there, was head of the entire Personnel Services for the Witwatersrand, and even he wasn't able to get the transfer authorised quickly. That's the way the army worked.

Finally the transfer orders came through. I arrived at Wits Command early one morning, during morning parade, which was why I couldn't find out who I was supposed to report to or where I was supposed to go. I was wandering around between the two main buildings being unsuccessfully directed all over the place by various people. I went and asked this guy at an office adjacent to one of the perimeter gates where I should go. The gates were huge reinforced metal sheets that blocked off access to the road that cut through the whole command block. He told me that I should head back into the main building. I walked a short distance and turned into a stairwell. I was on the landing of the stairs, not yet on the first floor, when I felt the ground shudder. Before I could comprehend what was happening, the large cottage windowpanes above and behind me exploded inwards. I suddenly found myself at the top of the stairs, lying on the floor, and, like a good BCom student, still clutching my briefcase.

It was very strange: I couldn't recall hearing any huge noise, any explosion or loud bang whatsoever. I just remember being dazed and bewildered by where I was and why I was lying on the floor. How had I reached the top of the stairs? Had I walked up or been blown up there by the blast? I just couldn't register what had happened. I immediately

AN UNPOPULAR WAR

stood up, feeling very disorientated. I heard a guy shouting from one of the offices, 'Lê laag! Lê laag!' [Lie low! Lie low!] And I immediately dropped back to the ground. There was dust everywhere, and I was covered in it and pieces of glass. A car bomb had gone off outside the gates where I had been standing less than a minute earlier. I couldn't believe how lucky I was. Seconds before, I would have been facing the windows and they would've imploded in my face.

They expected the bomb to be the first of two, and that the second bomb would probably kill more people, as everyone would be confused by the first bomb and would rush to help. When we were given the order to evacuate, I remember, even then, being extremely impressed by the rapid organisation and efficiency of everything after the bomb blast. In less than five minutes of the bomb going off, they had cordoned off roads and had everything under control. There was no panic and not too many injuries. I saw only two people who were wounded. One was a black woman, who I later found out worked at Wits Command. She was lying outside the building, bleeding. I thought that was quite ironic. Only two injuries and one was a black woman. I saw that the gates, which were massive, were completely gone – blown to pieces. There was a hole in the ground and the two cars that had been parked at the gate inside the compound were completely destroyed. The engine of one of the cars had been blown through a wall into the nearby Ster-Kinekor complex, according to later reports. Fortunately, it was early and there was no one in the cinema. It must have made a hang of a noise, but I didn't recall hearing an explosion.

We were quickly evacuated to one end of Joubert Park and sat around, not saying much. I looked around at the civilians milling about in the park, and even though I was very liberal – I'd been involved with political rallies at Wits and been called a kaffirboetie – I felt like I could have taken a gun and shot every person in that park who was not white. These people wanted to blow me up! A guy who knew it was my first day walked past and said, 'Great welcome to Wits Command for you.' Ha ha. I caught the bus home that day, and en route it picked up students from Wits. They were talking about the bomb blast in a really light-hearted fashion, almost joking about it, and I sat in my filthy uniform covered in dust, still clutching my briefcase, thinking that if they had any idea what it was like to actually be there, they wouldn't be so jocular.

Two things stand out after that car bomb. One was when I went to see my doctor and he asked me if I'd been on the beach recently, because I had sand so deep in my ears. The other was alerting the university to the fact that I had been in the bomb blast, and, as I was due to write an exam in three days, I asked them to please keep the option open for me to write the main exam and the sub if necessary. I wasn't sure how I would do, but I wanted to try and write the main exam first to get it over and done with. They said no. I could only write one or the other. I wrote the main exam and passed it, and to this day I couldn't tell you what I wrote or what the course was.

– Michael, age 21

It might have been a terrorist who carried only one mine, as they didn't have the same amount of ordnance that we did at their disposal. He'd laid the mine on an old disused track, so it could have been there for ages before the Buffel went over it. It was a separate patrol from ours, but we were nearby and heard the explosion. When we got to the area, our first concern was that it could be an ambush or some kind of booby trap, although that didn't happen very often. The Buffel had been blown up and there were bits of bodies and clothing in the surrounding trees. A steel door on the Buffel had blown upwards and slammed down across a guy's legs, severing them right off. His legs were shreds of meat hanging in the tree above. He was conscious but there was no conversation. Our medic put him on a drip and I held his hand while he died. The helicopters came and collected the wounded and the bodies to fly them out of Angola and back to South Africa. When we carried on with our patrol, we did all the right things, like wearing our seat belts. There was no feeling really. It just was. — **Chris, age 17**

I had some time off and went up on one of the Bosbok's regular 5 p.m. late-afternoon flights to do a reconnaissance of the jati – the kaplyn. I loved flying and just wanted to spend some time in the air. We had been up for about half an hour when I saw tracers coming up behind the plane. It was terrifying. I thought, should I pray now? I was convinced my time was up and I was about to die. I had my R1 with me, but otherwise was completely defenceless. It's a horrible situation to be in, where you can't fight back. I remember calmly saying to the pilot, 'I think we are being fired upon.' He looked and said, 'Oh my God!' We were flying fairly low, and he went for height straight away. The air was filled with tracers, under us, over us, next to us; just everywhere I looked I saw these glaring arcs glowing in the air around us. Let me tell you, when the terrs used to fire, it wasn't selectively. Their *modus operandi* was to fire off a lot of rounds at once, and tracers were the order of the day. Tracers are selectable, so normally you loaded them by alternating with more regular rounds than tracer rounds, but the terrorists loved them. It was their big thing. If you got hit by a tracer it could cause septicaemia and gangrene if not treated. It burnt like hell. We had unintentionally flown over this contact, and they must have thought we were doing an aerial surveillance for our troops and they had a go at us. It was quite impressive, because the pilot tipped the plane on its wing and then circled in one spot, gaining height. I thought he deserved an Honoris Crux, because he stayed in the area to look down and see what was happening. There was fire and smoke from the mortar explosions, and I would have just wanted to get out of the area immediately. — **John, age 18**

During Ops Mebos we were flying into southern and south-western Angola a lot. We knew which Angolan towns to avoid, as they were marked on our maps with a big red circle. They were the ones that had a protective umbrella over them, as they had very powerful and accurate radar-guided missiles. The terrs would infiltrate south, penetrating as far as Tsumeb sometimes, and then run back north to this protective umbrella. This happened particularly in the wet season, when we had difficulty in tracking them. For three weeks I was Echo, which meant I flew my Puma in position five in the formation. On this one day, 9 August 1982, I was moved from Echo to Golf – seventh position. My Puma was an H-model, which was more powerful than the C-model. My mate, J, took my Echo position, and as he had more troops than I did, I told him to send over a couple of the guys to my helicopter. They ran over and we took off, following a direct track to the drop zone. The Pumas were troop carriers, used for casevac, cargo slinging and re-rats. As far as casevacs go, I must say that only about one in ten was because of enemy action; the rest were stupid things like fights or accidents. The Alouettes were the gunships. The terrs called them *taka-taks*, because of the noise of the cannons. So we flew out in formation behind two Alouettes. Suddenly, as we were flying low level, a battery of anti-aircraft guns opened up on the fifth Puma in the formation. J's helicopter pitched up violently before rolling over and exploding in mid-air; bodies and debris fell to the ground, where all the remaining fuel exploded. It was like watching *Apocalypse Now!* Some of the guys were in the doorway of the helicopter and fell out, but most were burnt to death. The guys who had fallen were later found propped against trees with bullet holes in their heads. I think that was more of a symbolic thing by SWAPO, 'cause the guys couldn't have survived the fall. Hitting the ground at 200 kilometres per hour pretty much smashes every bone in the body. Another Puma was shot to pieces by small arms fire, and some of the troops were also badly wounded. When we got back to the HAG, one of the

Reconnaissance guys responsible for checking out the areas we went into, came and asked me where it had happened. I showed him on the map. With great anger and tears of frustration he said he had told the colonel not to go into that area. There were several hundred Angolans camped on the one side of the ravine and an anti-aircraft battery with eight 14,5-mm cannons on the northern side. We shouldn't have been anywhere near their base. That night I went and lay on J's bed. I didn't cry or anything. I just lay there.   **– Anonymous**

32 Battalion Reconnaissance unit was to determine the position of the SWAPO bases, and two 32 Battalion companies and ourselves were to assault these SWAPO bases once they had been pinpointed and identified. We'd been on a number of lemon operations. These happened when supposed camps had been identified and we would fly in for the assault and the base either wasn't there or the people had abandoned it and moved northwards. On this particular day, two 32 Battalion companies had been dropped by helicopter and they were to sweep in a particular direction and try to determine the base position. I think the pressure was on to deliver results. We were the third company, Alpha Company, and were flown out from the forward Helicopter Administration Area.

We went in, flying in formation, in eight Puma helicopters. There was one stick – that's about 12 people, excluding the three flight crew – in each helicopter. Two choppers transport what we called a *valk*, and the eight choppers made up the company. Unfortunately, we flew right over the SWAPO base position. Until then, we hadn't known exactly where the base was. That's why we had dropped all these companies – to sweep and try to find it. We were sitting in the doorway of the chopper with our feet resting on the step. This was customary practice; when the chopper banked, you were held in place by the centrifugal force – quite an amazing experience. In addition to the anti-aircraft fire there was small arms fire, and our company intelligence officer was shot through the leg (which eventually had to be amputated). It obviously took the SWAPO crew a while to react, because they fired at the fifth chopper and hit the sixth chopper with a SAM-7. They destroyed the section between the rear rotor and the fuselage. Obviously, the pilots lost control and I saw the chopper loop, and next thing there was an explosion and smoke as it hit the ground. We couldn't see if anybody got out. We had banked around to come back, but were told to immediately head straight back to our temporary base, or HAA. That night there were mixed emotions. Up until that point we had felt fairly invincible, but after seeing 12 paratroopers and three flight crew shot down, we were aware that we could also become a statistic. There was a sadness, a truth, but also a need for revenge. We also felt an element of anger because we had been on so many of these lemon operations and it clearly hadn't been part of the big plan to fly over this base. The next morning we flew in again in the choppers, but the enemy had moved north, deeper into the bush. A spotter plane was used to assist with the tracking down of the enemy, and we caught up with them approximately 35 kilometres from the original position where they had shot down our chopper. They moved with their heavy equipment, which slowed them down and afforded us the opportunity to catch up with them and initiate an assault. We even shot a couple of stragglers who were behind the line where we were dropped by the Pumas. The Alouettes, which provided us with air cover, directed us to where some of these individuals were hiding. During the contact we retrieved a couple of web belts, damaged sections of rifle and some dog tags from the bodies of our guys that had been shot. These had obviously been taken as proof that they had shot down the chopper, or maybe just as souvenirs. Revenge was sweet. However, it did not offset the experience we had just lived through or the loss of colleagues. In summary, an incredibly sad experience.   – **Dudley, age 21**

When we stopped for the day we were supposed to dig a loopgraaf, or foxhole, which you were supposed to jump into when you were under attack. To be effective it should be as deep as you are tall. The guys got slack quickly and very few dug loopgrawe, even though they could save your life. The Russians had this amazing aircraft, an Antonov, that used to fly over at about 70–75 000 feet. It had excellent equipment and sophisticated infrared cameras. They had these experts who would interpret the photos taken on reconnaissance, and then they would ID the co-ords where they thought we were and bomb that. If the Russians dropped one of their 1 000-pound bombs on you and you were within the possible kill zone of 1 000 metres, you would die from the shock waves, unless you were under the surface in your loopgraaf. But we would have moved on by the time they had analysed their intelligence and sent the MiGs with their bombs. They often bombed the last place we had stopped. Even though we were about 50 kays away, you felt the earth vibrate, like an earthquake, and then this low boom as the sound waves hit.   – Greg, age 25

There were five of us on a 'look-see' mission in eastern Angola. We walked into an ambush. None of us were killed, but they chased us for three days. It was poor training on their side. Their ambush just wasn't that effective, and it enabled us to get out of the killing zone – and we ran. There were 60 of them. We just ran, as hard as we could. We dumped kit, we dropped all the heavy stuff, we dropped all our food, sleeping bags, blankets, and whatever else we had, we threw away. We kept our ammo, grenades, water and our radio, and we ran for three days. Whenever they caught up with us or when they had the high ground, they shot at us. We'd shoot back and run again. We split up and met at RV points and we didn't have much time for anti-tracking. The guys were good: natural-born trackers. They were baying at us like bloodhounds, and they'd taunt us: 'Boertjie! Boertjie! White man, I'm gonna kill you!' Fortunately they didn't set the bush alight this time, which is something they'd done in the past. They'd burnt thousands of hectares trying to trap us. This time there was thick cloud cover and we couldn't get radio communications to call a helicopter to take them out, so we just kept running for the border. We drank water on the run. We never slept, because we figured they wouldn't chase us at night, so we ran as hard as we could at night and then, in the early hours of the morning, we'd try to catch half an hour's kip. We were tied to one another with a piece of string, and the guy standing guard would pull it. No one had to move or whisper or do a thing other than tug on the string to wake the others up. Our Escape and Evasion training kicked in, but I think it was my fear that kept me alive. I didn't want my arse looking like a tea strainer. We ran about 120 kays. It was terrible. I don't even like to think about it, but I am grateful for being taught endurance. For being taught that little word *vasbyt*. We were taught that when you've had enough, your body can still take seven times more. This situation was proof. After running for five, six hours straight, I said I'd had enough. Everyone looked at one another. We were pitch black, hadn't shaved for two weeks, had cracked lips, we were smelly, thirsty, hungry and scared, and then we started to run again because if we didn't, we'd die.

– Ric, age 18

We were with the 81-mm mortar okes, and we got word that a group was coming down south. We had to provide support for one of our groups that was going to *looi* the enemy group coming down. Now the mortars didn't give us too much buffer space – we had to be within five to seven kays. We moved into place at sunset and we had to get in quite close. We got the co-ords and started *looing* them. *Shoop shoop shoop* with the 81s, and they were *boom boom boom* back at us. Next thing the mortar guys said there was another group of enemy armoured vehicles coming south, moving towards our flank, and they were accompanied by Russian Hind gunships. These were choppers that were armed to the teeth. They were armour-plated, had rockets on either side, heavy machine guns, everything. If you picked up one of those mothers, you were in serious shit. They were evil, evil looking things. They would come at you just over the tree tops. We had to pack up and move out of the area very quickly because obviously they knew our co-ords. So we're moving at night, parking lights on, guys in front of you and guys behind. Rushing to get away from the area. Then, through the bush, I just saw lights. I thought, hey, away you go, thank you very much, this is the end of the story – they've flanked us and now they're going to take us out. It was the most frightening experience. Then I saw that they were our own Ratels, racing to place themselves between us and them. — **Greg, age 25**

Bosbefok

I went to help my buddies in Com Ops load their chopper. They used to do pamphlet drops. I wasn't involved in their work. I just remember this one time I helped them 'cause they wanted to take photographs of these bodies. They had four bodies in the chopper and they wanted to take photographs to put on pamphlets, which they'd drop in Angola. They'd put something like 'We've got your friend', written in Portuguese, underneath it. I used this cardboard beer crate to fan the flies off the dead guys while they took their photos, and I remember we were joking and laughing and all eating chocolate, for goodness' sake. I thought I was such a hero. The more I think about it now, the more I realise it was pure propaganda.   – **Anthony, age 18**

We moved a lot of Recces and 32 Battalion guys. They were mainly Portuguese-speaking former Angolan fighters. They had a great sense of humour and they loved us pilots. We flew food in for them and flew them to hospital when needed. There'd been a big operation, and one of our more unpleasant jobs was to fly the bodies of dead terrs back to Oshakati. There they would be photographed and IDed. The photos and names were printed on A6-size flyers in black and white with accompanying messages like 'Look What Has Happened to Your Friends! Surrender Now!' in Portuguese. An Impala dropped the flyers from a high altitude all over Angola. The flyers were loaded into the speed brake and, at the push of a button, could be released. Before an operation, they would also drop flyers over villages, warning locals to move out of the area if they did not support SWAPO. If they remained, they would be bombed.

We had collected the bodies of the dead terrs, but had run out of daylight and had to remain in the HAG in Angola. The bodies were left in our Pumas overnight. We were sitting under trees for a briefing when we heard loud laughter. A large crowd had formed around one of the choppers, and a 32 guy was pointing with his rifle barrel to something inside. It looked like he was giving a very humorous lecture. We walked over and saw that he was pointing at the body of a SWAPO female. She was naked and her legs were open to the men, and they were clearly getting a very descriptive and humorous lecture on female anatomy.   **– Anonymous**

One afternoon, during a large operation, a radio call came through saying there had been a big contact. None of our guys had been hurt, but the choppers were bringing out enemy dead and wounded. I was ordered down to the helipad to assist in unloading the choppers. While I was waiting for the helicopters to come in, I met the base doctor, newly arrived and freshly qualified. He seemed younger than me, though he couldn't have been. After half an hour the choppers came in, and soon the helipad smelt of hot exhaust gases, and the rotor blades were going *whoosh, whoosh*, rotating above our heads. There was dust everywhere and it was noisy and very hot. The choppers had to be unloaded fast 'cause they were returning, so they didn't even shut down. One helicopter had bodies and the other was carrying wounded terrorists. I was assigned to unload corpses, while the doctor and a medic unloaded the wounded from the other. The flight sergeant had quickly busied himself on something near the engine, leaving me by myself. There was blood and bits of bodies everywhere. I could barely drag each bloody body out of the helicopter. At first I tried to keep the various shot-off body pieces together, but soon the corpses just became things, like bags of potatoes. Just grab a body, pull it out and let it fall to the ground – a drop of about a metre. Grab another, pull it out and let it fall. I remember the sound of the skulls hitting the tarmac. *Thud. Thud.* I worked as fast as possible so the helicopters could leave quickly. The bodies were just things. There was no respect. On the other hand, dead South African soldiers were treated with absolute reverence. The treatment for terrorists and for us was worlds apart. Our dead were carefully lifted out of a chopper and placed gently on a stretcher before being taken to the morgue at Ondangwa. For the bodies of the enemy there was absolutely no respect. The Intelligence guys would go through their clothing, looking for intel, and then the bodies would be put on display outside the base. There were civilians in the area, and displaying the bodies was a message to them. The bodies were also used in posters and photos for propaganda purposes. The more covered in blood I became, the more the bodies became like bags of potatoes, just to be thrown on a pile. In the end I was worried about which head matched which torso. As I pulled the last corpse out, the helicopter flew off, leaving me covered in bloody dust, crouched over this pile of bodies. Meantime the doctor had finished with the wounded. Wounded terrorists were treated, but I think it was only to make them fit enough for interrogation. He came over and saw that one of the corpses I had pulled out was alive. I will never forget him looking at me with complete shock and revulsion. As he frantically began to look for other signs of life, I wondered how many others I might have killed because of the rushed and rough offloading. I wanted a shower to try and cleanse myself of the afternoon, but during the week the showers were off due to water rationing, so I tried to wash from a bucket. That evening I walked out to the perimeter walls and tried to watch the sunset, wondering if I really had become the monster I saw in the doctor's eyes. It was a sad sunset.

– **Chris, age 17**

When you form a battle group, you get an objective, for example to invade the entire southern Angola area. From that main battle group, they split off certain companies and give them specific objectives. It was a stuff-up because the Intelligence we received was wrong. Our objective was a certain SWAPO and FAPLA base. We hit it from the wrong angle, and we had been told it was defended by a platoon, but they had brought in a company in the last 48 hours, so it wasn't a platoon but a whole fucking company we were attacking. The whole fucking thing was a fuck-up. I was near the rear, mortaring the objective as the sun was coming up, and the infantry moved in after we had mortared the shit out of the base and the surrounding trench system. After the attack we all moved up through the objective, and I remember the place was completely fucked and bombed out. There were plenty of burnt enemy corpses lying around and I saw guys pissing on them. I guess it was about dehumanising them. This one FAPLA soldier had been blown in half, and the upper body rested upright on the ground with the arms outstretched. His lower torso was lying elsewhere. Someone stuck a sign in his ear saying 'Stompie', and you could get your photo taken with Stompie.   – **Anonymous**

It was a bit of a strange place for a camp, but it was central to the areas we had to move in and out of. It was about a kay away from the South West African and Angolan border. We were based at an airfield that had been bombed out and there was only this basic concrete structure left. We stayed there for a while, 14 of us and a bunch of terrs that had been shot. There were about five or six of them in Jiffy bags. For reasons that were never made clear to us, we were told to keep them in the Jiffy bags and not bury them yet. I guess they wanted to check the bodies for any ID or documents, and to see what uniforms they were wearing. Intelligence could tell all sorts of stuff. There was this old ammo storage bunker and we kept them in there. After two days, the stink was hectic. Eventually we were told to dig a six-foot trench to bury the bodies in. I remember it was deep, 'cause when I was standing in it, it was higher than my head. This is how we were: we were so excited we ran in there to get the bodies, and the smell was so bad we all gagged, but we grabbed the bags and dragged them to the trench. We had to tip the bodies out, and the Jiffy bags were full of gunk and blood. We poured high-octane airplane fuel over the bodies and set them alight. It smelt just like meat braaing. I mean exactly like a braai. As the flesh burnt, it sort of shrunk off the bones and you could see the skulls. We threw rocks at the skulls trying to see who could smash them in and crush them. It's the most inhumane thing I've ever done in my life. I mean, shooting people when you are under attack is nothing – that doesn't count. Sure, psychologically we were a mess, but you can't keep fighting it, you've got to accept it, the madness, the system, and just go with the flow.   – Andy, age 18

We were on standby in Bloem. This meant we slept with our chutes packed and under the bed. At about two in the morning we got a call that Mpacha, a base not far from Katima Mulilo, had been Red-eyed. We landed at Katima and used helicopters to ferry the troops to Mpacha. I suspect that napalm had been used, because I saw one of the Superfrelons come back stacked high with charred bodies. It was not a pleasant sight. Justice S was standing right next to me and he said, 'Dis mooi, dis fantasties' [This is beautiful, this is fantastic], so they must have been enemy bodies and, ja, at the time I was pleased that they were not our dead. We always believed that we were winning the war.
    – Anonymous

We went out to Fort Doppies, which is a Recce base west of Katima, with some very strange people. I think some of those Recces had a reputation they felt they had to live up to. Some really nice guys, but some … I was talking on the phone and this one guy pulled out this huge knife and pointed it at me saying, 'I want to use the phone.' Ja man, whatever.   – Paul, age 17

I had a photo taken of me drinking a beer while sitting on this dead SWAPO body. He had rands on him, obviously for when he infiltrated south, and we took the money off his body and used it to buy beer from the nearby cuca.   – Anonymous

I almost shot someone unintentionally. He was a little Ovambo boy. He was standing near a water purification plant. We'd just received our new R4s to replace the R1s, and I was sighting the rifle. It was instinctive: I had this black person in my sights, my finger tightened on the trigger and something happened. I dropped the weapon. Everyone asked me what was wrong. I just stared at the weapon on the ground and said I didn't know, but I thought, oh my God, am I that unstable?

– Andy, age 18

Working as a journo for *Uniform*, we could pretty much do what we wanted. Our colonel was preoccupied with many other things. The newspaper fell under him, but he wasn't an editor and wasn't that concerned with what the journalists and photographers were up to. We would pick an area we wanted to visit and tell him that we needed to go there to cover a story. A Cape Town two-day SADF soccer tournament became a five-day one. We would fly up to the Border for a day, which really used to freak the troops out, as they could not believe we had just arrived on the Border and were flying home the next day. I enjoyed flying in the Flossie. There was something special about getting onto that old military aircraft. What I didn't enjoy was the faces of the guys going to the Border. They were so, so frightened. I remember meeting this one very short little guy in the mess at Buffalo, a camp on the Border. He was with a Mechanised Battalion, and he told me about a time he was in his vehicle and drove around a corner, only to come face to face with a long line of Angolan tanks. He said he was so frightened that he jumped out of his vehicle and hid underneath it. Fortunately, the Angolan tanks all just drove off. Even recounting the story, I could see this little guy was still terrified. A little later, another guy came up and asked me if the short guy had told me his tank story. I said he had. He told me it never actually happened. The guy had hallucinated. Without a doubt there were guys up there who were suffering from post-traumatic stress disorder who should not have been on the Border. They should have been sent back, to the old 1 Military Hospital in Voortrekkerhoogte, a low red-brick building where they sent all the loonies. I would have liked to interview the guys there, but I never got permission to do the story. I don't think they wanted anyone to read about people who had lost their minds because of the war.   – David, age 22

We hung around St Mary's Mission, which is right, right on the Border, because we believed SWAPO was getting food and assistance from the European priests and nuns there. So we laid an ambush just south of the mission. We lay there for two days and fuck-all happened. You just lie there for two days, getting very gatvol and bored. Then we heard this singing coming from this little church. B, this mate of mine, stands up and takes this MAG, a light machine gun – y'know, like the M60 with the belt you see in the Rambo movies – and walks towards the church and disappears inside. I thought, fucking hell, B is mal, he's off his rocker and he's pissed off and gatvol and here he is walking into this church with a loaded LMG. I thought, fucking hell, I'd better see what's going on. I walk in there after him, and he's standing at the back of the church with this machine gun and the belt fed into it and the church is packed full of Ovambos, and the choir's there and everything. And this Belgian monk says to him, 'Get out of my church.' B says to him, 'Why?' He says, 'Because you're frightening my people.' And B says to him, 'You are killing my people.' And he adds, 'In any event, I'm also a Christian.' And this Belgian monk says to him, 'You are standing here in my church with a machine gun and you call yourself a Christian?' This argument starts and I thought, fuck, how is this gonna end? It could end with him going bos and shooting the whole congregation. I took him by the arm and said, 'Come with me.' I took him outside and we took the ammo belt out of the MAG and made it safe. We then cleared the ambush we had set up and went back to our fire base about nine kays away.   – John, age 18

One night, while drinking in the bar of one of the many bases we moved through, I met a medic. He was telling tales of 'helicopter safaris'. Flying over the Kaokoveld, they would shoot game from the helicopter. Once they saw an elephant and landed nearby. They chased the elephant and shot it with an RPG-7 rocket launcher. Apparently the elephant stood just looking at them, while the whole ribcage and stomach had been blown away, before collapsing on the ground. They just left the elephant lying there, and flew back to base, to boast in the bar. The Pumas were used more for transportation, but the Alouettes were gunships and heavily armed. I heard stories of how some of the gunship pilots shot game with their .50 Browning machine guns. I don't think they all did it, but I'm sure it happened.   – **Chris, age 18**

32 Battalion wore the same clothing as SWAPO on certain ops. The area in which they operated was frozen, and we didn't patrol in there for obvious reasons. We might mistakenly shoot one another. A group of our people were west of this one particular frozen area, and there was a huge firefight. No report came in from them, but 32 Battalion reported hearing this massive firefight to the west of their frozen area, lasting about two and a half minutes, which is a long time. Our commandant, who was overseeing everything, got very excited and said, 'Skuimballe manne! Ons het weer koppe!' [Scumballs men! We've got heads again!] Meaning we had more dead enemy heads. I said to him, 'Commandant, given the nature of the person leading that patrol, I guarantee that when they make contact they will say, "Stand by for my grid reference."' Meaning simply that they are reporting their physical position and they have nothing further to communicate. So the commandant was waiting for them to radio in to confirm how many enemy they had killed. The transmission came in and it was exactly as I said it would be: 'Stand by for my grid reference.' The commandant called the individual on the radio and asked for an explanation, and the saga unfolded. They had arrived at this kraal

and found a whole lot of terrorist tracks, but couldn't find any terrorists. They assumed that it was utilised as a transit camp for terrorists, so they set up formation and shot the living daylights out of the livestock. They just shot up all the cattle, goats, everything. They shot it all to smithereens. — **Dudley, age 21**

You lose your fear. You become blunted and depressed. You become blasé when you are under constant pressure and guys are trying to kill you 24 hours a day. We weren't supposed to move before dark. There are certain rules you don't disobey – if you do, you get killed. You die. One of those rules is, don't move before sunset. But we were windgat and we were gatvol and we wanted to get moving. It was late afternoon, still light, and we started moving around, removing the cammo nets, and the next thing a couple of MiGs come screaming in low and rocket us. They're supersonic, so they make a helluva noise. We took cover under the Rinkhals. They were blowing up shit all around us, but luckily they were off target. No direct hits and no shrapnel. We were careful about when we moved after that wake-up call. — **Greg, age 25**

On one changeover, we came careening into the base and sat on the runway while we proceeded to get completely motherless so that fuck-all mattered. Within minutes we were being chased out of the base by some still-wet-behind-the-ears major, who actually thought the castles on his shoulders would impress us. To impress us he should rather have given us a warm welcome and a few cold Castles. Instead he told us we were not welcome on his base, and ordered us to sleep in the bush outside the camp walls. In his mind he was sentencing us to a hazardous night, but compared to where we had just been, we hardly cared. Since we knew there was no way the major was going to come out of his base during the night, we shot off all our spare ammunition, rockets and flares into the sky and treated ourselves to a memorable fireworks display. — **Chris, age 18**

AN UNPOPULAR WAR

One drunken night we were playing poker while the guys in the neighbouring house partied to Abba. Now Abba is not very good at the best of times, but after 18 replays on a distorted sound system, it was just too much. What started as a petty argument ended when one of the guys from a neighbouring house picked up his machine gun, calmly walked over to the neighbours, and shot the roof off the house. We rolled around laughing. — **Chris, age 17**

Full Metal Jacket is one of the few war movies I could identify with. The aspects of training were as I remembered them. Our experiences were not like Vietnam, with the ambushes and patrols and such. There was very, very little of that. But in that movie they are coming back from this one battle singing that Mickey Mouse song, and I remember coming back from ops in Angola and we started singing nursery rhymes. — **Paul, age 17**

At War

We went in in June '87 when Intelligence revealed that a battalion of enemy tanks was heading down from northern Angola to annihilate UNITA and the FNLA. Mavinga was Jonas Savimbi's Log Base. That's his logistical base, with all his food supplies, weapons and ammunition. It was way into Angola, about three or four hundred kays in. The brass boys and politicians didn't want the UNITA leader taken out. He and the FNLA were backed by the West – the States – and us, and were fighting against FAPLA and the MPLA, who were backed by Cuba, East Germany and Russia. They were coming down to take them out, and it wasn't just a couple of armoured cars, artillery and a few guys on foot. There were also about 85 tanks heading south. They also had Stalin Orrels, which were excellent killing machines. They could launch 20, 30 rockets within seconds and were very mobile. But our MVLs – multiple rocket launchers – had a greater range and could fire about 22 kays to their 20 kays or so. That made a big difference.

We left Buffalo Base, a beautiful place, on the northern bank of the Kavango River, so it was actually inside Angola, heading overland to Mavinga. We were all ground forces and had no air support whatsoever. There must have been about 1 000 of us. It was the first real push into Angola. 32 Battalion had been in Angola during ops, but this was major conventional warfare. We went in essentially as sub-units and task forces of 32. The commissioned officers and NCOs were made up of SADF, and originally lots of the special ground forces were made up from the FNLA. I, and two ops medics, were in a Rinkhals – 11 tons of armour-plated steel. It's a powerful 4 x 4, with diff lock, low range, everything. Essentially it was a self-equipped medical base unit, a mobile intensive care unit in which you could perform operations. We also had Buffels and troops and officers in Ratels. The Ratels were exceptional. They were troop carriers with a 20-mm cannon. Basically, they were gunships, and they had a lot of firepower. They were also exceptionally mobile and extremely powerful. But although they were armour-plated they were not immune to an RPG, which would go right through them. The troops were transported in Buffels, which were the usual V-shaped landmine-resistant shape. We only moved at night, and even then only using parking lights. To this day, if I smell diesel and dust it takes me straight back to Angola.   – Greg, age 25

I arrived in Rundu with about 40 troops for my first camp in 1985. I'd grown a beard, thinking it would help me manage the much older guys I had to command. The camp was a waste of three months. The OC didn't know what to do with us or why we'd been called up. I immediately got on the phone to SA – the OC of my CF unit – and told them to send us back 'cause we were not expected up there. That didn't work, and so, because they didn't know what to do with us and wanted us out of their hair, they sent us out of the camp lying ambush. We set claymores on this cut line, which was a waste of time, because it was the same place they'd been lying ambush in for the last three years. The best thing was the prawn braais this Portuguese guy made for us. They'd broken him out of prison and he couldn't speak a word of English.

Two years later, my second three-month camp, it was a different story. The situation was very different now: before we had control, but now we didn't even have permanent air superiority. We had some guys from 32 Battalion come and talk to us and tell us what to do if a Russian Hind gunship found us. We were told the best thing to do was to shoot a signal flare at it and hope the pilot thinks it's a Stinger! The commandant was so happy to see us. Not one engineer had been killed since '81, then all of a sudden they'd lost six in the past six months. It was a long time ago and I do recall it was informal info, but apparently one of the engineers was killed by Typhoon – we heard these were SWAPO soldiers that had been brought up in the training camps from when they were kids and were utterly ruthless, determined and crazy. So the commandant appreciated us, which was nice, and we were so busy. As engineers, most of the roads we worked on were dirt, but it was possible to lay a mine under tar. You put a drum down and lit a fire in it. After it melted the tar you cut and lifted it out, laid the mine and then replaced the tar. At 24 I found it a lot more scary than I did when I was 17. We were clearing roads of mines about 100 kays into Angola and saw these MiGs come over. We weren't sure, but knew they weren't Mirages or Buccaneers. We radioed our co-ords in, told them we'd spotted MiGs and asked what we should do. We were told, 'Best you head south.' We said, 'Aren't you sending someone?' and were told, 'We don't have air superiority at this stage.' That was quite a shock. So we headed south. My plan in the event of an air attack was to instruct all the vehicles to turn left and only mine would turn right, increasing my chances of survival!   – Paul, age 24

The night of the actual Lomba Crossing Battle* was unforgettable. When we were moving up, far north of Cuito Cuanavale, we had plenty of time to twiddle our thumbs and pick our noses. And to talk. We spoke about our girlfriends, wives, mothers or whatever. There was this amazing fellow, an artillery commandant – he was 34, a really nice guy, and we talked a lot. He showed me pictures of his daughters, two beautiful little blonde girls who lived back in Potchefstroom. We got to know each other pretty well.

For the actual battle we had brought up our G5s. These were amazingly mobile, extremely accurate and extremely powerful gun-howitzers with a range of about 39 clicks. We couldn't just rely on the MVL, the cannons on the Ratels or the 81-mm mortars – we had a lot of G5s as well. From our intel we knew these guys were coming

---

*   The Lomba River Offensive

down with tanks, artillery and infantry. I don't think they knew as much as we did – that there was a big battle coming. They knew we were in the area but didn't know exactly where we were. If their co-ords were right ... disaster for us.

It started around 11 p.m. We had two batteries of G5s that were *looing* them. The mortars were going too, 60- and 81-mm mortars – big mothers. Night became day. Absolute daylight. If you can imagine the most mind-boggling fireworks show, then it still wouldn't even be one percent of what we experienced that night. I mean that. Our G5s were going all around us. Even though we were right next to one, no one bothered with earplugs. It is the most thunderous experience. The G5 has a huge 155-mm shell that stands almost a metre high. When that is fired, it's absolutely deafening. And it doesn't fire once, hey, it fires in rapid succession. It's not just *boom*. It's *boom boom boom boom*. And of course all down the line the other guys are firing too, so you had this almost staccato machine-gun sound of G5s. When all the batteries open up, it is absolutely deafening. And the ground shakes. Then when the shells hit, anything from 50 seconds to two minutes later, depending on the range, the entire subcontinent would light up. And you would feel the earth vibrate like a grade 7 earthquake on the Richter scale.

They retaliated. They had Stalin Organs, tanks, they had big artillery, big enough artillery. Not the equivalent of the G5s, but big enough. They were firing flat out at us and we were firing flat out at them for at least one and a half hours. We had shells going over us. You reckon your time is up at that stage, and if you get out it's like a lucky break. It looked like the entire country of Angola was lit from the explosions from their shells and ours. It was so light you could see if a guy had something stuck in his teeth! I wasn't shooting, 'cause there was nothing to shoot at, but you were armed and waiting for the guys to come in from the flank. This was more long-range, conventional warfare. Initially you shit yourself, 'cause you don't know where the next shell will fall out of the sky or if they will come at your flank.

But this is the really bad part for me: at about 1 a.m. my persoon-like call sign came over the radio – there's no rank or anything that's mentioned over the air. I was at the edge of a large shona. I was told to be on standby, fully operational – in other words, with all my ammo, my full webbing, the whole toot, plus my medical bag, which had everything, instruments, everything I might need. They would collect me in a chopper while Guy Fawkes was going on overhead. I knew there was big shit, I wasn't quite sure what it was, but you couldn't sit down at a conference table and ask the guys to justify why I should be airborne while all this was going on. I just knew I really didn't feel comfortable jumping into a Puma with this shit going on. I knew something had obviously gone wrong. They were going to drop me and some Recces at the front of these battalions. Luckily we didn't fly and ended up going in on foot.

This little Bosbok, a spotter plane, had passed overhead just before everything opened up. This friend of mine, the artillery commandant, was up with this lieutenant, a 21-year-old pilot. I had seen this unbelievably bright red light rocket up from ground to air. It was a SAM. A SAM-7. The Bosbok carrying the commandant and the lieutenant got whacked by the SAM-7. There was a helluva lot going on and they had gone down in this shona between us and them. There was no explosion – it just went straight down into the shona. So we thought they might be alive. That is what they wanted me for, to go in with the Recces and pull them out. But when we got there, it was just mangled metal. And they were, unfortunately, both dead. As dodos. Okay. It was a stuff-up beyond repair. I hadn't known my mate was in the Bosbok until I got there. I think they died on impact. We had to pull them out, which was not very pleasant. It was a complete mess. It has been years, but I still remember it clearly. It was a nightmare: I had two very dead guys and I couldn't work out which head went into which bag. It really was a mind fuck. The guys were all mangled and limbs were twisted and bent off. We pulled back with the bodies, which had to be taken out of Angola. You couldn't exactly fly them back on SAA.

The day after the battle, myself and two ops medics loaded the two bodies into a Rinkhals and made our way back three, four hundred clicks on our own, with no support whatsoever, and with, unfortunately, the bodies of the commandant and the lieutenant – the pilot – in the body bags, which were starting to stink. Of course, there's no aircon and you can't open the armour-plated windows. It was absolutely terrible. The stench of a dead human is a unique smell and a difficult one to describe. It took us about eight or ten hours to drive back to Mavinga. It was horrendous. There were no roads, you just donnered through the bush, travelling over this black sand. There were MiGs going over, but we were small, just the one unit, and they didn't pick us up. It wasn't pleasant.

The Lomba Crossing Battle was very successful for us, for our forces in general. It was also the biggest sub-Saharan artillery battle in history, and from our Recces, intel and observer posts it was reckoned that there were about 2 500 casualties on their side.   – Greg, age 25

I don't know what the intention was, if it was a final onslaught or what, but there was a massive push in '89 by SWAPO. It was a Sunday, and my wife and I were just about to leave the house. We were already in the car, when this military vehicle pulls up and I was told to pack my stuff – I was going to the Border. We disassembled Alouette III helicopters to take up with us. We only had a few up there at Ondangwa and the attack was quite huge. Later, I found out that this time, 1 April to 9 April, was known as the Nine Days of War. We could load two Alouettes along with a whole lot of ammo into each C-130 going to Ondangwa. The SAAF had come up with some incredible modifications to the exhaust and air filters on the Alouettes.

These were modifications we'd made during the Rhodesian and South West conflicts. The exhaust was called a 'renegade pipe'. It was only fitted when the aircraft was deployed in the bush, in other words to the Border. The main function was to direct the exhaust air through the rotor blades in order to cool it down and disperse it so the enemy could not lock on with heat-seeking missiles. The sand filters were called 'olifant ore' and were a unique invention to keep sand out of the engines. The Operational Area was very dry and dusty and the sand corroded the rotary engine components. These filters protected the engine, but looked funny sticking out of the sides of the helicopter like big ears, hence the name. Another South African invention was 'blade tape'. It was like a thick plastic tape that we stuck to the outer leading edges of the main rotor blades to prevent sand corrosion. All three of these additions helped keep our helicopters operational and were critical up on the Border. We landed at night, but it looked like day 'cause there was so much activity. Everyone was running around and there were a whole lot of casualties on our side. I guess on SWAPO's side too. What I do remember was offloading the two Alouettes and the ammunition and then we started loading body bags. It's difficult to say how many body bags we loaded or how many injured were lying on stretchers waiting to be treated. Body bags are usually black, but I remember these were like a frosted plastic – not transparent, but you could see where the blood had seeped out from the wounds and stained the plastic.   — **Tallies, age 23**

Township Patrols

There was a stoning at Sebokeng railway station. Sebokeng was just one of three townships in the Vaal Triangle. A white woman had gone there to drop off her maid when a large crowd started stoning the car, and the woman's 11-month-old child, who was on the back seat, was killed. Up until then, mid '84, the military had never been in the Transvaal townships. I remember the call coming that we had to get ready, pack all our gear, full kit, rifles and live ammo, 'cause we were going into the townships. I think a guy's moral background and upbringing determined how he reacted and what impact township duty had on him. I mean, if you grew up in a home where you called blacks *kaffirs* and you treated them like they were subhuman, you would handle this, morally, a lot easier. It was all top secret and we weren't to say anything to our families. We were really nervous, as we were led to believe that all hell had broken loose and the cops weren't able to cope so we had to go in to support them. You start thinking, yirra, if the SAP can't handle it, how bad can things be? Then we were told to stand down. Eventually, around 12 at night, we got onto these Buffels. One of the lieutenants thought he was General Custer. He used to stand on the front of his Buffel, haul out his pistol – not the army issue Star but his own Smith & Wesson – raise his arm with the pistol in his hand and shout, 'Voooooooort!' What they then told us was that we were going in there to create a better image of the Defence Force among the township dwellers. Like a goodwill mission. They gave us sheets of paper explaining how to greet the elders or call a young boy in the vernacular, and instructing us to alert the locals that planes would be doing pamphlet drops. These would tell them that the army was their friend. I think the government was starting to realise that things were getting out of hand. They had a whole lot of Noddy Cars (small little armoured cars with big black wheels, a turret from where a guy's head stuck out, and a machine gun) parked behind this sheeting at our camp. Although I never saw them used in the townships, they were obviously there for a reason. The mid-eighties were hectic. But we were told under no circumstances, unless our lives were in danger, were we to shoot. We went in in these Buffels and we heard that some guys had run and lobbed a petrol bomb into the bin of the Buffel and all the guys were burnt alive. I don't know how true it was, but that was what I feared the most – getting trapped inside a burning Buffel. We were to form a cordon around the entire township. Not one resident was to pass out of the township without getting a tjap from the police. It was a Mercurochrome mark on their thumb. On waking up, every resident had to go to points the police had set up with Land Rovers and Nyalas and get this tjap, which they could then present to us and we would allow them out of the cordon. I'll never forget this sight: we were on the freeway, on the actual highway, outside Sebokeng, and there were vehicles with headlights on as far as the eye could see. Every single road around the township had vehicles bumper to bumper on it. Cops, military – guys had come from Potch and Bloemfontein. Every two metres there was a soldier, one of us. At about 4 a.m. we followed a Casspir into the township. The residents had put these big steel rubbish bins in the road, so we always went in behind a Casspir, 'cause it was big and heavy enough to put a wheel on a bin and crush it like a Coke can. The curfew was still in place, and we drove right into the middle of the township, among all these little box houses, and started jumping out of the Buffel. I had a weak knee, so I didn't want to go over the top. I tried to open the flap on the side and it jammed, so I kicked it hard and it flew open and crashed against the vehicle. It was early and it was so quiet, and I thought, oh man, I've woken all these people. But the eerie thing was that not one person appeared, not one house light went on, not a curtain flicked, not a face at a window – nothing. I related this story to my mom and dad, and my mom said she remembered being a little girl in Greece, and when the Germans occupied the town she even recalled pulling the curtains aside to look at them as they came in. Yet in Sebokeng, not one thing moved.

– Nick, age 20

We had to do township patrols. They were so difficult, because you didn't know who your enemy was. They were amongst civilians and you'd been given specific orders not to shoot. If a shot came from a house you couldn't just fire back, because they'd have children in front of the house. Guerrilla tactics were employed. Often patrols would be done in a simple police bakkie with a canopy, because they were very quick. They were much faster than the Casspirs. It was frightening, 'cause you had children throwing stones, and if a petrol bomb came in the back of that bakkie it was a mad rush to get out quickly. The people there were capable of using any tactics to hurt you. I hated township patrols. They were the worst. We were called in this one night to help locate a consignment of R4s that had been stolen from a base near Soweto. It was one thing fighting a guy who doesn't know how to shoot properly and who's using unreliable rounds that might be ten years old. It was another thing to face a well-armed enemy. We went in to try to find these weapons. We were on roofs, in helicopters, zooming around in police bakkies. We ganged up at a door and ran through a house. It was not nice: people were in their dressing gowns tending little fires. We ran right through their homes, invading their privacy. For me, it was far worse doing township duty than Border duty.

– Brett, age 18

It was early morning, about seven, and we were sitting on the pavement, chatting, and there were these two burly cops standing at their police Land Rover. This guy and his son, who must have been about 12 years old, came up and the cop said to him, 'Why isn't your son in school?', and the dad said there was no school. And this one cop grabbed the kid and threw him over the bonnet of the Land Rover and started lashing him with a sjambok – full tilt. This father is standing there pleading with them to stop hitting his son and the cop gets aggro with him and wants to beat the father up. It had such an impact on me. I knew if I was a black guy I would be out there planting bombs left, right and centre.   – Nick, age 20

One of the worst things I saw was in the late eighties, when we were deployed to assist the police and security police with their Cordon and Search operations in the Port Elizabeth townships. They conducted house-to-house searches by knocking on the door, and if it wasn't opened in ten seconds, they kicked it in. They screamed through the houses with total disregard for privacy and with no respect. It was instrumental in making me think: this is not for me.

                                                                 – Anonymous

They caught this one guy in the township with some dagga on him. Some cops and some gung-ho army guys started torturing him by holding his head underwater in a bucket of water and demanding he take them to his supplier! I mean, really, he's an oldish guy who smokes it as part of his culture, and these guys are hoping to get information so they can run off and bring down this massive drug syndicate. Please, man.   – Nick, age 20

I was only 50 metres away when a toyi-toying crowd of a few hundred people passed me. I never realised they were murdering someone. When they moved off down Khumalo Street, I saw this little boy playing right next to the body. The wire around the wrists had cut into the flesh and there was a pool of blood. The boy didn't seem at all bothered. I could not believe I hadn't known what was happening. The boy looked at me and held up a stick for me to play with. I didn't take it. I stepped over the body and walked to the nearest house, where a woman stood in the garden. She frantically waved me away, and I realised that if I spoke to her, she could be the next victim. I walked back to the corpse, where one of the white paratroopers was taking a trophy picture. 'What a fucking waste of time,' I said to a mate of mine. 'This whole place is sick and fucked up, including the doos taking the pictures, like he was on some game drive somewhere.' I was hijacked in February 2000, and when the guy stuck a 9-mm pistol in my temple, he had the same look in his eye as the little boy.

– **John, age 27**

We were camped somewhere near Swartruggens. Our lieutenant, who was as effective as a chocolate fire engine, heard there was a weapon in the nearby township. He'd heard this from the black guy who managed his horses. There were 42 guys – only four were English and there was this one black guy. Even though he was regular army, he was treated very differently because he was black. One day we were the only two in camp, so I invited him to eat with me. When everyone was back on the Monday, I mentioned something about him being in camp eating with me, and I got it in the neck. 'How could you let him eat here?' All that kind of thing. I got punished and had to run and carry sandbags. Some of the guys refused to eat off the table the black guy had eaten at.

Next thing we hear someone has a gun in this local township. Whoop-de-doo. Our lieutenant decides that night we are all going to get on our horses and go out on patrol to find it. He asked for volunteers, and I thought, actually, y'know what? Hold on here, something could happen, and I'm not under orders to do this, so why should I go and do this just for the sake of it? I stood up and said I wasn't going. I wasn't going to volunteer to go and get killed. I thought, what am I going to gain? I could lose the rest of my life for something like this. As it happened, nothing happened. The guys came back. They hadn't found anything, but they all thought they were heroes. I didn't care;

I was sleeping. A snuffel tiffie, quite an attractive girl, arrived shortly after this. We used to send in daily reports, and she'd obviously read those and picked up on this particular event. She was trying to find out if it was a real incident or if the lieutenant was just causing trouble. Tensions were high. Mandela's release was imminent, and there we were, marching up and down past this little township for no reason. Maybe that's why a day later we were shipped out.

– Martin, age 23

Lying in a ditch, I could see a crooked sign on which somebody had hand-painted: 'The Road to Hell'. It hung from a rusted pole on the road between Thokoza and Kathlehong. Very appropriate. I got up and ran past a row of abandoned houses and mountains of rubbish and through sewage to get to the shacks beyond. My flak jacket was so heavy and kept sliding forwards, making it difficult to keep my R4 pointed in the direction of the houses. The officer in charge of the patrol and in front of me kicked a small dog with his boot. The dog howled and rolled away with a broken back leg. A former Angolan soldier behind me didn't even look at the injured dog. He just stepped over it. It was October 1993 and the officers and NCOs in my Citizen Force Unit, 2 Parachute Battalion, were being called up to Katoerus, the collective name for Kathlehong, Thokoza and Vosloosrus on the East Rand. It was expected that the situation would get worse as the fighting between ANC and Inkatha supporters escalated in the period leading up to South Africa's first democratic election. We were to be placed in the field with PF paratroopers from 1 Parachute Battalion, a dress rehearsal if the situation spiralled out of control around election time. When we arrived in Katoerus, our briefing was simple: keep the peace between the warring Inkatha and ANC militia, and learn from the troops who had been there for weeks trying to achieve this. Most of these troops were former members of 32 Battalion, the unit made up of Angolan soldiers who had fought on the side of the SADF.

We were out on patrol once, on foot, when we heard AKs firing and then the rattle of a machine gun. I shouted, 'Fuck! They've got an LMG!' Boutros corrected me: 'RPD.' He and I jokingly called each other Boutros and Boutros after the Secretary General of the UN. But it wasn't funny: we were too lightly armed to take on a Russian 7,62mm RPD light machine gun. I so badly wanted to go home, away from the smoke, the AKs, the rubbish and the shit stuck to my boots. Home wasn't even far ... only 30 kilometres as the crow flies. But no. The next day we were checking vehicles. These two youths looked nervous when I examined their vehicle closely, but I was just impressed by their primitive engineering skills. They'd taken an old car, removed the roof and bodywork, fixed the engine, and were driving around Thokoza on a chassis they'd painted bright pink. I waved them on. Later that night, back at the base, a patrol arrived with the same two youths, their hands tied behind their backs and both bleeding from head wounds. A soldier drove their pink chassis into the base. I asked a corporal what had happened. They had found an RPD hidden on the chassis. I went cold. The vehicle was a gun platform for the light machine gun we had heard the night before. Boutros walked up to me and punched me on the back of the flack jacket. I felt the blow – there was no ceramic bulletproof plate in the jacket. I might as well have been wearing nothing. That night when we set off, I had a ceramic plate in my jacket: my curiosity in township engineering was gone.   – John, age 27

Changes Coming

In the SADF they always had these officers' mess functions, where everyone dons their dress suits and has this big fancy dinner before klaaring out. I think my officer's dinner was the 12th of December '89. We were in full officer's kit, pips, everything, and it was very, very formal, based on those old English traditions. After the starters there was port, which you had to pass with your left hand and pour with your right. You could only have a cigar after the main meal. This was based on the English tradition, where one could only light up after toasting the Queen. It was a very elaborate and formal ceremony – all that traditional stuff, port and cigars, coloured guys serving us – and everyone got very pissed. About half of the 120 officers were PF and the other half NDPs. It was a 'thank you', a 'cheers lieuties, thank you for all you've done' kinda thing. There were lots of elaborate stories: about how many muntus they'd killed and the action they'd seen on the Border. Colonel Ströebel stands up to give his end-of-year speech and address us. He began with '*Manne …*' and then told us that South Africa as we knew it was going to change and we had better prepare ourselves. His speech was met with complete silence. I've never known such silence. PW had just resigned and FW had just been sworn in, and I reckon those colonels had been told, 'Listen okes, you'd better get all your troops and things ready for the change.' To put it in context: some of the senior guys had just got back from the Border, some of the guys would be remaining in the SADF and others would be on civvy street. This was about two months before the ANC was unbanned. No one had an inkling that was gonna happen. I tell you, it was pretty weird. I remember walking out of that room knowing that, ja, there were some major changes about to happen.   – Stof, age 25

After Mandela was released, the role of the navy changed. We embarked on more of a PR campaign, as if to show taxpayers that their money was being put to positive use. We were also fortunate in that the navy did not have any stigma attached to it like the other branches of the Defence Force did. We were racially integrated long before any of them. Sometimes we went on fun trips, like to Knysna, but we knew we had to prove our capabilities to the public, like apprehending gill net fishers, stopping drug smugglers, etc. Once we were asked to help raise a plane from False Bay. The insurers wanted us to lift it from the sea floor without a scratch so they could examine it carefully. I think they had their suspicions that it had been ditched by the owner and pilot, because it had landed in shallow water and both men had waded ashore from the crash site. We had to put all our mattresses out on the deck so that when the plane was lifted and laid on board, there was no additional damage. It was very successful, and they found that there was no fault with the aircraft at all. It was a deliberate ditching. Another time we received a Mayday call from a yacht. This idiot had bought a yacht and decided to sail from Cape Town to Durban with two girls he was trying to impress. He had no Master's Certificate and he thought he could simply motor all the way along the coast. He'd got into difficulty, and the yacht was drifting towards rocks. We couldn't get in too close, because it was shallow, so the divers went over in a DSB to fetch them. The two girls jumped into the DSB immediately, but the owner was arguing with the divers, wanting to know what they were going to do about his boat! We did nothing, and it ran aground on the rocks. People do such stupid things at sea. The girls were absolutely livid, as this guy clearly had no idea what he was doing. They were freezing, 'cause they'd packed inadequate clothing and insufficient food and had been at sea for over a week. They were so angry at this guy. They got the captain's cabin, while the guy moped in a corner and the girls shot him venomous looks for the two days it took to get them back to a harbour. We were very happy to have girls on board! — **Louis, age 17**

I was a lieutenant in 1994 when compulsory National Service ended, and instead of the usual white troops, the intake consisted solely of black volunteers. Trying to instil any remote sense of discipline or make any attempt to discipline them in the manner in which we'd been disciplined was impossible. They'd gang up and say, 'No.' And you could do nothing about it. 'You a racist,' they would say, because most of the instructors were white. They just didn't get it. If you wanted the floor polished – and part of the military training was to make them do it repeatedly until it was 100 percent – tough luck. They'd clean it once, and that was it. They were not going to listen to you and would just ignore you. There was a shortage of beds and trommels, and we had to send these black troops to fetch them. It took them an entire day to go and collect their beds and mattresses. When I did Basics, we had to get everything from the army stores. What we did in a couple of hours took them an entire day! Trying to get them back after mealtimes? Forget it! I felt extremely resentful. We were stuffed around, and now we could do nothing to bring them into line. The annoying part was that they were volunteers, so they could leave at any stage. For us, there was no such luck: it was compulsory, we had to be there and they knew it. They got free housing, free clothing and free food, and got paid, admittedly only about R300. So they'd sign up and they'd get issued with all the military gear – crockery, cutlery, three sets of overalls, browns, cap – and a week later they'd disappear. With all the kit! It was like the guys who came in on the last compulsory intake, July '92. When word got out that this was the last intake, many of them just left! They just ducked. I mean, what was anyone going to do?   – **Paul, age 18**

AN UNPOPULAR WAR

Klaaring Out

When it came time to leave Berede, we had a problem. We were short of our stable kit, which meant we would have to pay a lot of money to replace the missing kit. It's the first and last time I've ever stolen, but we wouldn't have been allowed to leave the army unless we handed in everything. When the new guys came in, they were issued with full kit, so we went into their bungalows and 'borrowed' their kit and handed that in. I felt sorry for the very last intake. Whoever those last kids were … good luck to them.   – Martin, age 23

I will never forget my final parade on the day I klaared out. It was such a great, great day for me! Not for everyone, though. Some guys had extra days to do for going AWOL and things like that, and it must have been so kak for them to stay on. The Unit's 2IC read out their names and the number of extra days that they had to stay in. We were dressed in our step-outs and we received our skietbalkies, which had come very late, and medals. There was no drilling or anything. We assembled on the road just off the parade ground and formed up into battalion formation and marched past the Battalion HQ. The parade ground at Phalaborwa was hot. It was so hot that day, the polish from boning our shoes was melting off. After the final 'dismiss', we threw our berets in the air. Just like in the movies. We were *ou manne*! We had klaared out! Myself and three friends squashed into a tiny Fiat for the long drive back to Joburg. There was hardly room for us because of all the crates of beer we bought. We'd stopped at a bottle store in Nylstroom, where I was kakked on by a staunch Dutchman for wearing my beret backwards. I didn't care and told him I had just klaared out. He said it didn't matter, as I still owed the army 720 days for camps. But neither he, nor getting pulled over by a speed cop in Pietersburg, affected us for long. Now that was a funny incident. It was such a lengthy process when the speed cop asked my friend, who was the driver, for his name. The cop never did get the spelling right, and when he asked us where we were from and we told him, 7 SAI, and he asked us to spell that, we collapsed laughing. He got the moer in and told us, 'You Joburg people must just go back to where yous comes from.' We drove back with reggae music pumping, the sunroof removed, and us hanging out the roof singing Bob Marley songs. It was great. There is a point midway as you come over a rise between Pretoria and Joburg, where you can see the whole of the Joburg city skyline. That was awesome. When I was dropped at my house, my whole family came out when they heard the car door slam. My sisters were there and it is still the one time I can remember being closest to my family. I had my balsak over my left shoulder and I just walked into the swimming pool, down the steps and all the way to the deep end, in my step-outs and with my balsak still on my shoulder.

– Clint, age 18

I don't remember much detail about klaaring out. I remember lying on my balsak at the terminal at Ondangwa airport. But I thought it might be difficult adjusting to life after the military. We came up with an idea, and I'm glad to say it was successful. The plan was for seven of us to meet up on the South Coast and just have a jol for ten days. We would rehab ourselves as a group. I mean, we were scared to even make eye contact with a girl, but as a group it was easier. If we hadn't done that, we would have had inferiority complexes, so I think the plan worked. I am still pissed off that there was no help from the army to move back into civvy life. Such different worlds. Back there we were killing black people. They were the enemy. It was difficult seeing black people and not getting tense. We calmed one another down. 'Chill out, dude, you're not up there any more.' Ja, we were down here now.

– Andy, age 18

The worst thing about getting out of the army was the fashion. There you were – no fashion sense, lekker short hair and a suntan in winter. Everyone was wearing baby pink T-shirts and Instinct pants with a lace-up front, and you'd never seen any of this stuff before!

– Anthony, age 18

I think it was *American Gigolo*. It was some cinema in Norwood, and I was with my mom. This guy – they were all white in those days – says I can't go in: no under-21s! I think I felt more disbelief than anger. I mean, I'd been in Angola, burnt bodies, but I couldn't see this movie! He said he was just doing his job and if he let me in, he could lose it. I said I understood and we just left, which I thought was very civil of me.

– Andy, age 18

I was really pissed off about who got the Pro Patria medal and why. About a month after I had completed my National Service, I got a letter in the post saying I could attend a medal ceremony where they would pin the medal on my chest. Alternatively I could have it posted to me. I went for the postal option, because I was disgusted that some clown who had done nothing on the Border other than spend the minimum amount of days required to be eligible for a medal would be at the parade. The medal was awarded to anyone who had spent 55 days' continuous service on the Border. What a fucking joke. It seemed ridiculous and unjust that someone who had spent the entire time drinking spook en diesel and gathering details about other people's war stories so he could impress his buddies, and just clocking up the days, could qualify for the same medal. These were the type of guys who always went for the parade, so they could have the medal pinned on their self-inflated chests. I spent months in Angola and got the same medal. It didn't seem fair. Was that it? Was that all there was?

– Chris, age 18

I had a massive shiny radio/tape player that I had bought in the SAWI store in Oshakati. It had a recording function and I used those C120 tapes. You know, those long motherfuckers with 60 minutes of recording time on each side. That night I had it in the dugout, in our 'lounge', which had mud and sandbag walls. We were partying and decided to record ourselves. We passed out just before SWAPO attacked. It pissed mortars all around us and we woke to that. You could hear the faraway *whump* as they were launched ... So, many years later, I'm living in a flat in Hillbrow – this was back in the days when whites did live in Hillbrow – corner of Tudhope and O'Reilly Avenue, and I had recorded Pink Floyd's *The Wall* double album onto the same cassette that this piss-up had been recorded on. I set it up and I'm listening to the album and fall asleep. As the album ends, the previous original recording on the cassette comes on. The room fills with the sounds of a mortar attack. I shat myself. Nothing sounds like a mortar attack: it's such a distinctive sound. It's the middle of the night and I wake up to the sounds of this SWAPO mortar attack on the Border, now playing in my Hillbrow flat.   – Andy, age 18

Glossary

101 Battalion: originally consisted primarily of Ovambo troops and white NCOs and officers

1 Mil: 1 Military Hospital in Pretoria

2,4: the 'two comma four' was a distance frequently run and a standard test of fitness

2IC: second in command

32 Battalion: formed in 1975 and originally called Bravo Group, this formidable unit of former FNLA troops was led by Commandant Jan Breytenbach

AFB: Air Force base

afkak: extreme physical exertion; literally 'shit off'

AK-47: Avtomat Kalashnikova Obrazets, an assault rifle designed by Mikhail Timofeyevich Kalashnikov in 1947

Alouette: a French-designed helicopter gunship

Antonov: a Soviet-manufactured transport aircraft used to supply the Cuban and Angolan (FAPLA) forces with weapons and ammunition

Armscor: Armaments Corporation of South Africa

AWOL: absent without leave

babalaas: hangover

balkie: corps colours worn on a beret below the unit headdress badge

ballas bak: lazing around, doing nothing; literally 'ball baking'

balsak: large cylindrical canvas or nylon kitbag

Basics/Basic Training: a conscript's first three months of orientation and physical training

bataljon aantreeparade: forming up of a battalion on a parade ground

befok: mad, fucked

Berede: mounted infantry

bevelvoerder: Officer Commanding

Black Is Beautiful, aka Black Beauty: an oily camouflage paste

Black Widow: type of anti-personnel landmine

Bloem: Bloemfontein

blou: blue

blougat: a troop that was no longer a *roof* but not yet an *ou man*

Boertjie: slang term for an Afrikaner; literally 'little farmer'

boet: usually a friendly or

affectionate term of address;
literally 'brother'

bokkop: the head of a
springbok and the insignia
for the Infantry

boma: a recreational area,
either an enclosed outside
area with no roof or a
thatched outdoor area

bone: method of shining boots
or shoes by applying spit
and polish in small circular
movements

Border, the: South West Africa's
northern border with Angola
and Zambia

Border tour: usually a one- or
three-month spell in northern
South West Africa

bosbefok, bos, bossies: bush crazy

Bosbok: Reconnaissance airplane

bosbus, bossie: (a) 'opfok', in
which troops run after an
instructor who shouts
commands from a vehicle,
telling them where to run;
(b) 'bush bus': tying the enemy
to the bonnet of a vehicle
and driving through thick,
preferably thorny, bush

bos oupa: a soldier who has
completed two Border tours

Bots: Botswana

Buffel: an anti-mine troop carrier

Bungalow Bill: a representative
of a bungalow who liaised
with officers and NCOs on
behalf of National Servicemen
(e.g. communicating their
complaints) and called
troops to attention

buster power: term used by
fighter pilots for full power
or maximum thrust

C-130: a four-engined Lockheed
Martin, commonly known as
a 'Flossie'

C-160: a two-engined Lockheed
Martin, commonly known as
a 'Flossie'

casevac: casualty evacuation

Casspir: armoured personnel
carrier used primarily by the
SAP forces and designed in
conjunction with the Council
for Scientific and Industrial
Research (CSIR). 'Casspir' is
an anagram of these two
organisations' names

CB: confined to barracks,
punishment that lasted
between one and two weeks

CC: Coloured Corps

CF: Citizen Force – men who had
completed National Service,
who were eligible for at least
one camp per year for the
next 12 years

civvies: civilian clothes, or
general public not serving
in the military

civvy street: civilian life

clicks: kilometres

COIN: counter-insurgency

Com Ops: Communication Operations

comms: communications

cuca: a trading store on the Angolan border, usually African-owned; named after Angolan beer first encountered by the SADF in 1975

dagga: marijuana

Dak: Dakota transport aircraft, DC-3

DB: detention barracks

dems: demolitions

diknek: insult implying stupidity; literally 'thick neck'

dixie: metal containers that fitted into one another, used for cooking and/or eating

dof: stupid

doibie: green plastic inner lining of steel helmet. A red doibie signified that the wearer was undergoing punishment. Also known as a *mosdop*

dominee: Dutch Reformed Church minister

donderbuis: thunderflash

donner: strike forcefully; drive fast and recklessly; swine, bastard

doodsakker: killing ground

dooies: dead

doos: derogatory term for female genitalia; stupid person; literally 'box'

dop: drink

doppie: cartridge

DSB: deep sea boat

Dutchman: derogatory term for an Afrikaans-speaking male

ECC: End Conscription Campaign

eenvormigheid: uniformity

eis: own

Eland: an armoured car also known as a Noddy Car

Engelsman: Englishman

Esbit: a paraffin tablet used to heat food or drink

FAPLA: Forças Armadas Populares de Libertação de Angola (People's Armed Forces for the Liberation of Angola)

firing-in: technically means to physically set sights on a weapon by firing it, but the term also applies to a base firing its weapons into the bush at dusk so that the enemy knew the base was alert and armed

Flossie: a C-130 or C-160 transport airplane

fluitjie: whistle

FNLA: Frente Nacional de Libertação de Angola (National Front for the Liberation of Angola)

fok: fuck

FW: FW de Klerk, a National Party cabinet minister, and State President from 1989 to 1994

G1K1: medical term declaring a soldier healthy and fit for active duty (gesondheid 1, kondisie 1)

G4K4: medical term declaring a soldier unfit for active duty. This classification often guaranteed a non-physical position, e.g. as a clerk

G5: medical discharge; South African–manufactured towed gun-howitzer

G6: South African–manufactured self-propelled gun-howitzer

gatvol: fed up

gesondheid: health

gippo guts: runny tummy; diarrhoea

goeiemôre: good morning

gogga: a phase during the SAAF Officer's Course where candidates undergo an extended period of physical exercise and sleep deprivation; literally 'insect'

goolies: balls

grondseil: ground sheet

grootjas(se): great coat(s)

gunship: Alouette helicopter with a floor-mounted gun

gyppo: beat the system; avoidance of duty or unorthodox modification

haak-en-steek: type of thorn bush

HAG/HAA: Helikopter Administrasiegebied/Helicopter Administration Area

HE: high-explosive round

Honoris Crux (diamond): highest medal awarded for valour

hoofhek: main gate

hot area: an area with confirmed enemy activity or presence or where opposing forces engage in combat

houding: character, attitude

Impala: Italian-designed, South African–manufactured medium fighter aircraft

Inkatha: Inkatha Freedom Party

intel: intelligence

intreetoetse: entry tests

jati: a long strip along the Border that was cleared by bulldozer

Jiffy bags: body bags

Jirra: from the Afrikaans *Here*, the Almighty, Jesus or God

JLs: junior leaders; Junior Leadership Course

jol: party; have fun

jollie patrollie: recreational, relaxing, non-dangerous patrol or drive

July intake: there were two intakes of National Servicemen per year, one in July and another in January

jumpers: special heavy boots
worn by Parabats or
jump-qualified troops

jy's niks: you're nothing

kaffir: offensive word for African

kafferboetie: literally 'kaffir lover'

kak: shit

kak houding: bad attitude

kak off: shit off

kakgat: a latrine; literally
'shit hole'

kaplyn: a cleared border area
between two countries or a cut
line cleared specifically for the
purpose of picking up tracks

kaptein: captain

kas(te): steel cupboard(s);
slang for jail

kay: kilometre

kla aan/on: to be charged for
contravening the military
disciplinary code (MDC)

klap: hit

klaar: finish

klaar in: to report for duty

klaar uit/out: to finish National
Service or to clear out of a unit

Koevoet: initially a South African
Police COIN unit, which then
fell under South West African
Territorial Force (SWATF);
literally 'crowbar'

koffiemoffie: slang for a
homosexual flight steward

kondisie: condition

kontak: contact

korporaal: corporal

lag: laugh

langarm: a dance style where
two people clasp one another
around the waist with one arm
with the other arm extended
out – generally considered
conservative; literally 'long arm'

lekker: good, nice

links: left

LMG: light machine gun

loadies: uniformed SAAF load masters

looi: thrash; bomb; get the better of

loopgraaf: trench

luitenant: lieutenant

MAG: a 7,62-mm belt-fed
automatic machine gun

magsnommer: a number allocated
to every person in the SADF;
literally 'force number'

mal: mad

manne: men

Mills sight: an accuracy and
removable sight for firing mortars

min dae: literally 'few days' – either
to complete National Service or
to return to the RSA after a
Border/bush tour

Mirage: fighter jet

MLOS/MAOT: Mobiele
Lugoperasiespan/Mobile Air
Operations Team

moer: hit

moer in: mad, angry

moerse goed: very good, excellent

MP: Military Police

MPLA: Movimento Popular da
    Libertação de Angola (People's
    Movement for the Liberation
    of Angola)

muntus: offensive word for Africans

MVL/MRL: multipel-
    vuurpyllanseerder/
    multiple rocket launcher

NAAFI: no ambition and fuck-all
    interest

nagapie: bush baby, a small nocturnal
    mammal with large eyes

Nasrec: National Recreation Centre

NCO: non-commissioned officer

NDP: Nasionale Dienspligtige
    (National Serviceman)

necklacing: placing a car tyre
    around a person's neck and
    setting it alight

NG Kerk: Dutch Reformed Church

niemand: nobody

Noddy Car: an Eland 90

nogal: what's more

NSM: National Serviceman

Nyala: armoured personnel carrier

OC: Officer's Course or Officer
    Commanding

oke: guy

olifant ore: air filters on a helicopter;
    literally 'elephant ears'

omkeer: about-turn

one-liner: lance corporal

oortjies: little ears

op die looppas: double time

opfok, oppie: fuck up,
    usually through excessive
    physical activity

ops: operations

ops medic: a medic with
    additional training in
    treating trauma and combat
    wounds/injuries

ou manne: varying conscription
    lengths meant the time varied,
    but this was usually a National
    Serviceman with less than three,
    six or twelve months' National
    Service remaining

pa: father

packed out swastikas: ran (arms
    and legs pumping)

pakkie: package or parcel

paraat: prepared; also slang for
    someone who is extremely eager

Parabat: a Parachute Battalion
    member; paratrooper

PE4: plastic explosive

perdeparade: horse parade

Personeeldiens: Personnel Services

persoonlik: personal

PF: Permanent Force

piemp: rat on

pikstel: compact cutlery set with a
    fork and spoon that slid into the
    knife handle

PKM: Russian machine gun

plaaslike bevolking (PBs): local population

plat pote: flat feet

pluk: state of bliss usually induced by drugs

poes: derogatory term for female genitalia; also used as an insulting name

POM-Z: a type of mine

posparade: parade where mail was dispensed

potjiefakkels: trip flares used for perimeter protection

Pro Patria medal: issued to soldiers who saw active service on the Border for 55 consecutive days or 90 cumulative days. It was also known as the ProNutro medal because so many were awarded

PSS/PDK: Personnel Services School/Personeeldienskorps

PT: physical training

PTI: physical training instructor

PTSD: post-traumatic stress disorder

Pukke: University of Potchefstroom

Puma: a medium workhorse helicopter used primarily for troop deployment, extraction and casevacs

PW: PW Botha, a National Party cabinet minister, Prime Minister from 1978 to 1984, and State President from 1984 to 1989 under the new dispensation

R1: 7,62-mm assault rifle

R4: 5,56-mm assault rifle, a smaller replacement for the R1

Ratel: an infantry combat vehicle capable of carrying up to 11 troops. It has a 20-mm cannon and three Browning machine guns. Very quick and lethal, they were named after the honey badger, renowned for its ferociousness

rat pack: ration pack

rats: rations

re-rat: re-rationing: supplying food to troops in the field

Recce: a member of the Reconnaissance Unit

Red-eye: BM-21 missile

regs: right

regsom: right turn

RENAMO: Resistëncia Nacional Moçambicana (Mozambique National Resistance)

revetment: a fortified retaining wall

Rinkhals: armoured, mine-proof ambulance

RLI: Rhodesian Light Infantry

rondfok: to mess a troop around with seemingly pointless activity; literally 'fuck around'

roof(s): new recruit(s), inexperienced soldier(s)

rooi: red

Rooi Gevaar: Communist threat

rooikat: caracal

rooinek: a derogatory term for an Englishman; literally 'red neck'

RPD: Russian machine gun

RPG: rocket-propelled grenade

RSA: Republic of South Africa

RSM: regimental sergeant major

RTU: return to unit

SAAF: South African Air Force

SACC: South African Coloured Corps

SADF: South African Defence Force

SAGDOS: Suid-Afrikaanse Geneeskundige Opleiding-sentrum (South African Medical Services Training Corps)

SAI: South African Infantry (Battalion)

sak: drop (for push-ups)

SAM-7: a portable hand-held surface-to-air missile

Samil: large 4 x 4 general-purpose truck

Santa Marias: voluminous army underpants

sarmies: sandwiches

SAWI/SADFI: Suid-Afrikaanse Weermagindustrie/South African Defence Force Industries

shona or oshona: local name for a dry open area created by a seasonal lake or large pool in Angola

sjambok: whip

skaapdra: carrying a heavy weight during training or carrying one's buddy over one's shoulder

skeef: wrong, crooked or offbeat

skietbalkie: a shooting proficiency badge

skiet piet: infantryman; nickname for a (rural) commando member

skrapnel: nickname for bully beef; literally 'shrapnel'

slang: snake

snoepie: small shop/tuck shop

snotneus: 40-mm grenade launcher (the American M79 grenade launcher)

snuffel tiffie: slang for member of Intelligence Corps

sokkiejol: town dance

soutpiel: derogatory name for an English-speaking man residing in South Africa. He has one foot in England, the other in South Africa and his penis hangs in the ocean; literally 'salty dick'

spook en diesel: brandy and Coke

SSB: Special Services Battalion, Panzer or Armour Corps

S&T: daily allowance for subsistence and transport

staaldak: steel helmet

staan op: stand up

Stalin Organ/Orrel: truck-mounted multiple rocket launcher

stand to: the period at sunrise and sunset when operational units were on full standby against attacks

States, the: Republic of South Africa

steerable: type of parachute

stompie: cigarette butt

stopper group: deployed with an attack group, usually behind the enemy to prevent escape

streef: strive

strek: a way of acknowledging higher rank, involving straightened, stiffened arms to the side when walking or standing, and to the knees when seated. An NCO of higher rank would always be strekked (not saluted), and an officer would be strekked if the lower-ranking soldier was not wearing headgear

stryk: iron

Superfrelon: large French-manufactured helicopter

SWAPO: South West African People's Organisation

Swart Gevaar: threat of black power or rule

Tampax tiffy: medic

tannie: a term of respect for an older woman; literally 'aunty'

taxis: soft, non-abrasive form of protection worn over shoes or socks on a polished floor

TB: temporary base/tydelike basis

terr: terrorist

terrapins: rooms with mosquito netting instead of windows and a tin roof

thunderflash: non-fragmentation explosive device used primarily during training exercises to simulate attacks

tiekiebox: public telephone

tiffies: members of the Technical Services Corps/ Tegniese Dienskorps

tjap: stamp

tokkeltou: a rope approximately 10 millimetres thick and 1,5 metres in length, with an eye at one end and a toggle at the other end

toyi-toyi: a dance that signifies an uprising or rebellion

TRC: Truth and Reconciliation Commission

tree aan: assemble, fall in or form up

troep: troop

trommel: steel trunk

trompoppies: drum majorettes

Tukkies: University of Pretoria

two-liner: a corporal

Typhoon: a SWAPO unit that specialised in deep penetration into South West Africa

uitkak: a telling off; literally 'shit out'

uitpak inspection/inspeksie: a comprehensive inspection during which certain equipment, including a disassembled rifle, must be

displayed neatly, precisely
and spotlessly on the bed
Unimog: two-ton 4 x 4
general-purpose utility truck
UNITA: União Nacional para a
Independência Total de Angola
(National Union for the Total
Independence of Angola)

valk: two helicopters flying in loose
formation; literally 'hawk'
varkpan(ne): metal meal tray(s)
vasbyt: persevere
verkramp: conservative
vetseun: fat boy

vleisbom: nickname for a Parabat;
literally 'meat bomb'
vloek: swear
Volk en Vaderland: the Afrikaner
equivalent of King and Country;
literally 'People and Fatherland'
voort: forward
vrot: bad, rotten

windgat: cheeky, arrogant
WSK: Weermag Sportkompleks
(Army Sports Complex)
wors: sausage
wussies: wimps
wyk: area